My Father's Son

❖ ❖ ❖

Books By Farley Mowat

People of the Deer (1952)
The Regiment (1955)
Lost in the Barrens (1956)
The Dog Who Wouldn't Be (1957)
Grey Seas Under (1958)
Coppermine Journey (1958)
The Desperate People (1959)
Ordeal by Ice (1960)
Owls in the Family (1961)
The Serpent's Coil (1961)
The Black Joke (1962)
Never Cry Wolf (1963)
Westviking (1965)
The Curse of the Viking Grave (1966)
The Polar Passion (1967)
Canada North (1967)
This Rock Within the Sea (1968)
The Boat Who Wouldn't Float (1969)
Sibir (1970)
A Whale for the Killing (1972)
Wake of the Great Sealers (1973)
Tundra (1973)
The Snow Walker (1975)
Canada North Now (1976)
And No Birds Sang (1979)
The World of Farley Mowat (*edited by Peter Davison*)(1980)
Sea of Slaughter (1984)
My Discovery of America (1985)
Virunga (1987)
The New Founde Land (1989)
Rescue the Earth (1990)

Farley Mowat

❖ ❖ ❖

MY FATHER'S SON
Memories of War and Peace

A Peter Davison Book

HOUGHTON MIFFLIN COMPANY

Boston New York London

for Helen and Angus —
I remember

❖ ❖ ❖

For information about permission to reproduce selections from this book,
write to Permissions, Houghton Mifflin Company, 215 Park Avenue South,
New York, New York 10003.

Library of Congress Cataloguing-in-Publication Data
Mowat, Farley.
My father's son : memories of war and peace / Farley Mowat.
p.   cm.
Correspondence between the author and his parents, Helen Anne and
Angus McGill Mowat, during the latter years of the Second World War.
ISBN 0-395-65029-1
1. Mowat, Farley — Correspondence.   2. World War, 1939–1945 —
Personal narratives, Canadian.   3. Soldiers — Canada — Correspondence.
4. Canada. Canadian Army — Biography.   I. Mowat, Helen Anne.
II. Mowat, Angus, 1892–1977.   III. Title.
D811.M684 1992
940.54'8171 — dc20   92-31729
[B]   CIP

Printed in the United States of America
BP 10 9 8 7 6 5 4 3 2 1

Contents

❖ ❖ ❖

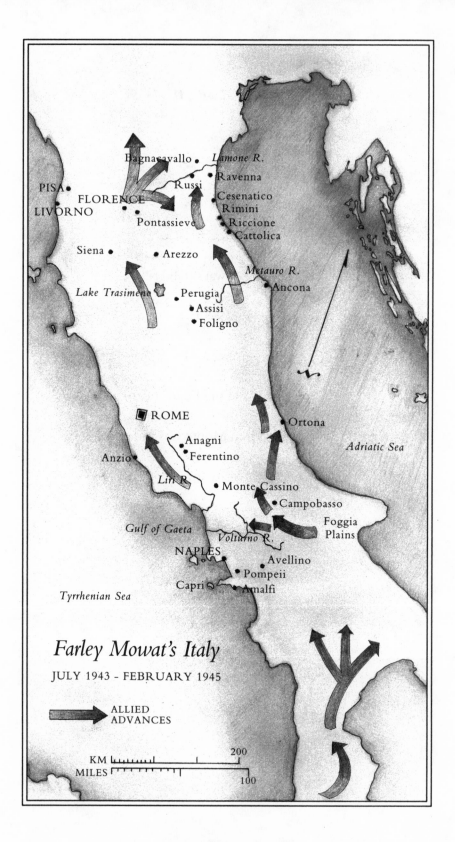

PISA

Bagnacavallo · · Lamone R.
· Russi · Ravenna
FLORENCE · Cesenatico
LIVORNO · Rimini
Pontassieve · Riccione
· Cattolica

Siena · · Arezzo
Metauro R.
Lake Trasimeno · Perugia · Ancona
· Assisi
· Foligno

□ ROME

· Anagni · Ortona
Anzio · · Ferentino Adriatic Sea
Liri R.
· Monte Cassino
· Campobasso
Gulf of Gaeta Foggia
Volturno R. Plains
NAPLES · · Avellino
Capri · · Pompeii
· Amalfi

Tyrrhenian Sea

Farley Mowat's Italy

JULY 1943 – FEBRUARY 1945

ALLIED
ADVANCES

KM
MILES
200

100

P r e f a c e

❖   ❖   ❖

THIS BOOK IS ABOUT COMING OF AGE IN A WORLD GONE MAD.

It is about coming to terms with life in a madhouse.

It is also about the way in which a wise and loving father counselled and sustained his son during a time of trial.

It is largely based on the letters my parents and I exchanged during the latter years of the Second World War when I was in the army overseas, and they were in Canada.

Unhappily, few of my mother's letters survived. I have, however, included some excerpts from those that did in order to convey at least a sense of her vivid and vital presence.

I have edited my father's letters extensively, not because I wished to do so but because to publish them as they originally stood would have required two or three volumes the size of this one; something, my publishers assured me that, in this day and age, neither they nor the book-buying public could afford.

My father was one of the last and by no means the least of the great practitioners of an admirable but vanishing skill. He was a superb letter writer. If the portions of his letters printed here do not do him full justice, they at least bear witness to his excellence at a skill which is rapidly being obliterated by telephones, fax machines and other such dubious devices.

Sewing the contents of our mutual letters together to make one garment has not been easy. Because deliveries were erratic, our letters were frequently delayed for months and were sometimes altogether lost, and they seldom presented a logical sequence when and if received. Consequently, trying to arrange them in proper

chronological order has proved to be impossible. The reader should
bear this in mind and make allowances. It is also to be noted that
official censorship had its effect on what I wrote, as did some
measure of self-imposed censorship designed to spare the feelings
of my parents, and especially of my mother.

Canada was governed throughout the war by the Liberal Party
under the leadership of Prime Minister William Lyon Mackenzie
King, who was a singularly elusive and evasive character, even for a
politician. Kept in power by the support of the French-Canadian
vote, he pandered to the strong aversion evidenced by church and
state in the province of Quebec towards what they called "England's
war." Anti-war resistance was so strong that the mayor of Montreal
was interned for repeatedly advising Quebecers to stay out of the
Armed Forces; although it *was* permissible for them to accept
well-paid work in war plants.

Because of the French-Canadian attitude, Mackenzie King's
government at first refused to impose conscription for military
service and, when pressure to do so from the rest of Canada finally
became intolerable, King introduced conscription for *home service
only*. This meant that volunteers would risk their lives in battle,
but conscripts would not. King's policy was encapsulated in one of
his more infamous evasions: "Conscription if necessary - but not
necessarily conscription."

Although a number of French Canadians *did* volunteer for
active service, most conscripts (including significant numbers from
the English-speaking provinces) refused. These men were held in
contempt by the active-service volunteers, who called them
Zombies – the walking dead of voodoo mythology.

The volunteers held the Prime Minister and his government
in almost equal contempt. As early as 1941 when King visited the
Canadian Army, then in England, he was roundly booed by the
men of the First Division. As will be seen, the Zombie situation and
the conscription policies of the government remained a profound
irritant to the fighting troops until war's end, and after.

A few words about the structure of a Canadian infantry division in the Second World War may be helpful. Essentially it consisted of three infantry brigades supported by artillery and other heavy weapons. A brigade comprised three battalions of infantry. A battalion had four rifle companies, each of which was made up of three platoons of about thirty men, commanded by a lieutenant.

This organization did not differ materially from that of a U.S. division, except that in the U.S. Army a *brigade* was called a *regiment*. This made for a degree of confusion, since a Canadian regiment consisted of two battalions, only *one* of which would be on active service, the other remaining in reserve in Canada. To make matters even more confusing, the term "regiment," as used in the Canadian Army, was virtually synonymous with "battalion." For example: a reinforcement could say with equal accuracy that he was going to join his battalion *or* his regiment, and in fact would be joining both.

The outfit to which I belonged was the Hastings and Prince Edward Regiment, whose active (overseas) battalion belonged to the First Brigade, First Canadian Infantry Division. The Hasty P, as it was affectionately and irreverently called, took its name from the two rural Ontario counties whence it originated. Hastings County stretches northward from a fringe of farms along the shores of the Bay of Quinte into forested, hard-rock mining country. Prince Edward County is an almost-island jutting out into Lake Ontario south of the Bay of Quinte and was, in 1939, almost entirely given over to agriculture.

This book necessarily contains a number of military phrases, terms and references. I have explained most of them by way of footnotes, and I have also included a glossary of military terms at the end of the book.

A word about the name "Squib." This was my father's nickname during the First World War. He acquired it while an engineering student in his freshman year. In mining parlance, a squib was a small tube of black powder used to ignite a large explosive charge – "an insignificant initiator of loud bangs" was how my father explained the term. When this nickname attached itself to me after my enlistment I accepted it without demur. Anything was better than

"Junior," "Shrimp" or "Kid," which had been my lot till then. But there was more to my acceptance of it than that. I thought of it as a kind of talisman which had survived one war and might, with luck, survive another. And bearing it also was testimony to my love and admiration for my father.

Prologue

❖   ❖   ❖

ON SEPTEMBER 9, 1939, CANADA JOINED IN THE WAR AGAINST THE
Axis powers. I was eighteen then and had only just settled with my
parents in a little village thirty miles from Toronto.

Ever since I could remember, we three had lived a peripatetic
life, moving from town to town and province to province, always
roosting in rented quarters. So my father Angus's purchase of an
elderly clapboard house in Richmond Hill seemed to be a signal
that we had finally settled in an enduring anchorage. Helen, my
mother, was gratefully convinced this was the case, but, significantly,
Angus named the white house on Elizabeth Street "Hove To,"
a sailor's phrase which implies no more than a pause in an
ongoing voyage.

The son of a failed hardware merchant, Angus McGill Mowat
was born in 1882 in Trenton, Ontario, on the north shore of Lake
Ontario's Bay of Quinte. He was a freshman at Queen's University
in Kingston when the Great War (as he always called it) broke out.
He enlisted immediately, went overseas in the infantry as a private
soldier, won his commission "in the field" in France, and in 1916
was badly wounded, almost losing his right arm.

Invalided home, he promptly sought out and, not so promptly,
married my mother, whom he had courted unsuccessfully before
going overseas. The couple spent their first year together in the
north woods, where Angus was a fire ranger, and their second year
in Toronto, where he had been persuaded by his adamantine mother
into becoming a clerk in a wholesale grocery business owned by
her side of the family. In 1920 he rebelled against the pursuit of

1

security, quit his job, and became an early hippie. Packing my
mother, who was pregnant with me, into a dilapidated Model T
Ford truck, he drove back to Trenton where, although he knew
nothing about bees, he set himself up as an apiarist. I was born the
following spring.

In later years, Angus used to proudly boast that he had once kept
bees, and this was literally true. The bees never kept us. What with
foul brood and other dread disorders, they barely produced enough
honey to sweeten the soda biscuits which, I am told, constituted our
chief source of sustenance until I was three. Then the good citizens
of Trenton took pity on Helen and me and offered Angus the job of
running the town's tiny library.

He had now found himself – or had been found. Libraries
held him in thrall thereafter. He went on to become chief librarian
in nearby Belleville, then in Windsor, and then in Saskatoon,
Saskatchewan. In 1937 he was wooed back to Ontario to
become inspector of public libraries for that province.

Books, reading and writing had by then become the cardinal
elements in his life, but by no means to the exclusion of other
interests. He was also a skilled carpenter and a devoted sailor. Even
when we found ourselves marooned on the arid prairies during the
drought years, he acquired and rigged a canoe which he then sailed
on the muddy Saskatchewan River and on salty prairie sloughs.
Soon after we returned to Ontario, he found and fell in love with
Scotch Bonnet, a big, black, double-ended ketch into which he sank
the family savings – thereby delaying our eventual purchase of a
house for two more years. A quick, lean and lithe little man who
looked (and knew it) rather like the swashbuckling film hero
Douglas Fairbanks, Angus was dreamer, artisan, romantic and
pragmatist combined, and passionate in all he did. His was an
overwhelming presence.

Helen Anne Thomson was the daughter of the manager of
Molson's Bank in Trenton. Unlike my father, who had only one
sibling (his sister Jean), Helen grew up with four brothers and a sister
in a big and rambling old house imbued with the ante-bellum

atmosphere that marked the end of the Victorian era in Canada. She possessed the graces required of a belle in that now sadly distant time. Convent-educated (though an Anglican), she was well-read, musical and very pretty, with gleaming black hair and rich brown eyes. Although she had known Angus since childhood and liked him well enough, she turned him down when he proposed to her after his return from the war. Then the man she had long loved – an artillery officer – fell fatal victim to an influenza epidemic, and soon thereafter Angus won his suit.

My parents began their married life in poverty and were never affluent. Neither cared. Helen was nothing if not steadfast. Her love for and loyalty to Angus and to me never wavered, yet she made few overt demands upon us in return. I profoundly regret that, during her lifetime, I never comprehended how much she meant to me, and how much I owed her. *C'est la vie.*

Our sojourn as a family at Hove To was all too brief. Being a veteran of the First World War, and a militia reservist, Angus was recalled to service. Abandoning his new home and his civilian job with equal alacrity, he accepted command of Headquarters company of the second (reserve) battalion of the Hastings and Prince Edward Regiment, stationed at Trenton. Despite his forty-seven years, he looked as dashing and as dapper as a stage hussar when he drove off in our Dodge sedan to take up arms again for King and Country.

Helen and I and a newly acquired little spaniel by the name of Elmer were left to hold the fort in Richmond Hill. Although I attended the local high school, I gave it little of my attention. My energies were concentrated on learning about airplanes and flying, for I had decided (despite my father's urgings that I consider the army) to join the Royal Canadian Air Force as soon as I reached enlistment age, which was nineteen.

On May 13, 1940, the day after my birthday, I presented myself at the RCAF recruiting station in Toronto – and was ignominiously rejected. Not only was I too small (I weighed 114 pounds, and the required minimum was 120) but I looked so young that the recruiting staff made mock of me, suggesting that I try again when I grew up.

All through my teens an excessively youthful appearance had been the bane of my existence, and I was infuriated beyond reason by this rejection. I appealed to my father for help. Striking while the iron was hot, he strongly counselled me to enlist in the second battalion of his own beloved regiment, the first battalion of which was by then on active service in England. The second battalion's main attraction for me was that the physical standards it required of recruits were far less stringent than those of the air force and, as Angus was quick to point out, once I had put on a little weight, I could, if I still so desired, transfer to the RCAF.

So it came to pass that I became a private soldier in the Hasty P. The second battalion was scattered through the two counties in platoons and companies, the larger sub-units in towns where armouries existed, and the smaller ones in outlying villages. Baker Company was in Picton, Prince Edward County's seat, and this was where I was first posted.

After a few months in Picton armouries during which I learned some of the fundamentals of soldiering, I was commissioned as a provisional second lieutenant and posted to Trenton, there to serve a much more demanding apprenticeship under my own father. Major Mowat bent over backward to avoid the merest suspicion of treating me with special consideration. Although, come to think on it, he *did* exercise special consideration of a kind.

"You may be my son," he told me one day after I had been especially sloppy on parade, "in fact, I'm fairly confident you are, but in this regiment you're just another snotty-nosed little subaltern who has to be taught to change his diapers and respect his betters."

He was a good teacher but it was with considerable relief that, in February of 1941, I was transferred to Kingston. After qualifying as a first lieutenant, I was posted to Camp Borden, a wilderness of sand and scrubby pines well to the north of Toronto, there to serve as an instructor until such time as the first battalion required reinforcement officers.

The winter of 1941-42 was a time of enormous frustration for me and many other young army officers. We were desperately anxious to "proceed overseas" to join the active battalions of our various regiments, but these were not yet suffering battle casualties and therefore did not need us.

Not until the summer of 1942 did I find myself aboard a troop ship bound for England. In September I finally joined the first battalion and was given the job of Battalion Intelligence Officer mainly, I suspect, because the CO did not believe that one with my singularly youthful appearance and slight build could long survive the rough-and-tumble of a rifle company.

That supposition was put to the test in 1943. Returning giddily to the regiment in June, after a London leave during which I fell in love with an unavailable English army corporal whose husband was in North Africa, I found the unit readying itself for imminent battle. I also found that I had been superseded as Intelligence Officer and relegated to the command of Number 5 Platoon of Able Company.

At the end of the month, the regiment embarked at Greenock, Scotland, with the rest of the First Canadian Infantry Division bound for the Mediterranean theatre to join General Bernard Montgomery's famed 8th Army. Before dawn on July 10, my platoon and I were set ashore by a small landing craft on a remote little beach in southwestern Sicily (the wrong beach, incidentally), as a small part of the assault force which that day began the liberation of western Europe.

In its initial stages, the Sicilian campaign was an exhilarating if exhausting experience for those of us who escaped death or mutilation. But horror at what we were engaged in quickly began to build within us, and fear is horror's close companion. I have dealt with these matters in earlier books* and so shall not dwell on them here. Suffice it to say that, by the time Sicily was liberated, we had been well and truly bloodied and the days of our innocence were over.

Midway through the Sicilian battles, the man who had replaced me as Intelligence Officer was killed and I was ordered back to my old job. I was destined to remain in it for the remainder of 1943 as we crossed the Straits of Messina, stormed ashore at Reggio, and

---

* *The Regiment* (1955); *And No Birds Sang* (1979).

began the long and bitter struggle which was intended to free the Italian mainland from German occupation after the Italian capitulation on September 7.

Throughout October the First Division pursued a slowly retreating enemy – "leaning on him" was the phrase of the time – in the central massif of the Apennines. On November 2 the Hastings and Prince Edward Regiment went into reserve in a village some ten miles from the city of Campobasso, which perches on a high plateau in the centre of Italy's mountain spine. Here, for the first time since leaving England, we went into billets. These stone houses and barns were hardly palaces but they had roofs and walls, and the weather was turning foul as biting rain and sleet squalls began sweeping down from the high surrounding mountains.

The face of Italy became dour and sullen as winter approached. Cold-weather clothing was slow in arriving, and each soldier added to his kit from whatever source he could find. Army blankets were transformed into short coats tailored by local civilians. There was time now to lick our wounds, and the considerable gaps in the unit's rolls that had been opened by disease and battle began to fill with reinforcements.

Soon this alien village in a foreign land had become a familiar place and, as the days lengthened, men came to know it almost as well as they had known their home villages. Matchless scroungers and improvisers by now, we made our rough quarters into sanctuaries of apparent permanence, ignoring the certainty that for us nothing could be permanent.

By the latter part of November 1943 winter was full upon us. New snow built up on the flaring peaks of the Apennines and fell wetly into grey valleys on the Adriatic coastal plains. Everything that was not rock became mud. Lines of olive trees gnarled by a hundred winters stood gaunt upon the shrouded ridges. Vineyards became slimy morasses. In the villages the sad stone houses seemed to draw closer together as freezing rain beat down upon them.

At the end of the month, a great convoy began to roll eastward from the Campobasso mountains bearing First Division to a new battle which had begun a few days earlier when 8th Army assaulted the enemy's winter line along the Sangro River and forced a crossing. The Germans fell back to make a new stand on the line of the Moro River, ten miles northward. Here, on December 5, First Canadian Division replaced an exhausted British division and was told to cross the Moro before the enemy could consolidate his defences.

The Hasty Ps were ordered to mount an immediate attack near the river's mouth – in darkness, without any real reconnaissance, and without even a preparatory artillery barrage.

At heavy cost we succeeded in establishing a small bridgehead where we remained under almost constant counter-attack and never-ending shelling and mortaring until, on December 10, the Germans again withdrew. Those of us who survived that hellish week remembered the Moro as the River of Blood.

There was no respite. In appalling weather, the battle for the approaches to the small coastal city of Ortona now engulfed us. The German defenders were men of the élite First Paratroop Division, and they gave no ground that was not marked by death. The attrition of human flesh, blood and spirit continued unabated as December dragged grimly on.

DURING THE LATTER PART OF 1941, ANGUS HAD BEEN POSTED TO District Military Headquarters in Kingston, Ontario, where Helen and Elmer came to join him in a rented cottage which he tellingly also called Hove To. In 1943 he was again transferred, this time to National Defence Headquarters in Ottawa, whither he had been summoned to establish a book distribution scheme for troops in Canada. Because of the housing shortage, Helen and Elmer could not follow him but had to remain uneasily in Kingston.

Throughout December of 1943, while the regiment slogged and bled in the mud before Ortona, my parents received no news from me and knew only what increasingly gloomy newspaper and radio reports could tell them.

Partially as an anodyne to the apprehension storming through his mind, but mainly to do what he could from a physical distance of several thousands of miles to fortify me and help me to endure what he knew from his own experiences to be nearly unendurable, Angus devoted many of his nights in Ottawa to composing long letters to me. The following passages are indicative of how things stood at the time.

❖   ❖   ❖

Dear Friend Squibb (Mark II). –

It used to be "Squib" when I had it alone but as you insist on adding the redundant "b" I'll follow suit. What do you think you are anyway, a dentifrice?

Last Monday was a big day in Kingston. Helen got two airmails and two airgraphs from you, but the latest dated more than a month ago. There was also a package containing a chapter of Mutt and two pages of verse.* The chapter about old Mutt and the skunks is the best you've done yet but, damn it, didn't I say not to use that story? Didn't I say I had already written it and offered it to a publisher – and had it refused? Is it any wonder nobody makes you a captain when you can't even obey the simplest order?

Although your letters take an age to reach us, you are a good lad about writing. Did you guess that a couple of us do not live for much else? Which puts a rather unfair burden upon your shoulders, but I don't very well see how it can be helped.

My book of the Regiment has reached eighty-six pages. I am not saving all this material just for you, but for the future historian of the Regiment – which might very well be one of the Mowat boys. I feel that this little scrapbook, which consists of newspaper and magazine clippings, letters from people overseas and even bits of army documents, and keeping an accurate record of the casualties, are about my only worthwhile contribution to the war effort. No much, but, by God, many are doing less!

---

* Over the war years, I sent home a number of sketches about Mutt, the dog of my youth, which were eventually incorporated into *The Dog Who Wouldn't Be* (1957).

Funny thing about your picture in the *London Illustrated News*.*
I happened on it and then I looked and looked until, in exasperation,
I muttered, "Turn your face this way, fellow." The resemblance in
stance and figure, and way of holding a cigarette (the Young Squire
attitude), seemed awfully like you. I didn't say anything to Helen since
it seemed pretty far-fetched, but I felt I was right. Now that I know it
was you, I'll pinch a copy from the officers' mess for the scrapbook.
Only next time turn your face, not your backside, to the camera.

You are right. For all its obviousness, "They shall not grow old as
we who are left grow old" is one of the great poems. Len McQuay,
and Gus Quigley and Laurie Lawrence of my old platoon probably
won't even recognize me when I get to Valhalla, because they'll still be
young. Perhaps it's only war that makes you realize the implacability
of the advancing years. My dad never had a war and never knew he
was an old man even at eighty-six. Mutt never knew that the years
were creeping up on him. But you and I, and all the rest who've been
there, can't hide that knowledge from ourselves.

But away vague maunderings. Now I'll tell you about my leave.
The train from Ottawa to Kingston [it takes three hours now] was
crowded, as ever, and it was a bitter winter evening when I got off at
Kingston. But Helen and Elmer had dinner waiting and the cottage
was as warm as three stoves could make it, which wasn't any too
damned hot, so we went to a dance at Fort Frontenac. Everybody had
a lot of drinks but I didn't even begin to feel my six. The whisky's that
weak it's a waste of time. We're rationed to twenty-six ounces a month
now, and that's cut to the strength of barley water.

Next day the streets were quite free of ice so I made an excuse to
get an army motorbike out in solo and did a bit of riding. This makes
the other old fellows at headquarters mad because they can't ride.
Matter of fact, I'm quite good. Unless I go too fast. When I go too fast
I'm too light and my ass gets too far away from the saddle for too long
at a stretch. Elmer, getting his first ride for two months, was a treat.

---

* A photograph of myself with some members of my platoon taken by a British war correspondent as we rested in the market square of a Sicilian village.

He fairly gibbered with joy and challenged everything on four feet to duels as we rode along. And there's a funny thing. Elmer is normally full of the very milk of human kindness, but put him on a bike (standing up on the pillion if you please, with his paws on my shoulders) and all he can think of is yelling canine obscenities and a mad desire to lick his weight in wildcats. Hmmm. Makes one wonder about all of us who ride motorbikes or drive fast cars.

You complain about having had to stand for four hours on parade on the regiment's few days out of the line, waiting to be inspected by a general and told what fine soldiers you are. Well, what do you expect? Was it ever any other way, or will it ever be? I wonder if the Russian generals do that sort of thing. "Spit-and-polish" parades, we used to call them. We used to spend half our time during rest periods at that nonsense. Nine brass buttons, two collar badges, a cap badge, a Canada badge, six more buttons on the greatcoat, AND all the brass end-things and brass buckles on the web equipment. All to be polished to a fare-thee-well.

God, what folly! Only last night I was looking at an aerial photograph of some of us going over the top on a sunny day in 1916. It was shocking. Every man his own heliograph. But we were certainly very pretty! So stop growling about having to clean up for parades. You know a lot of things more than your elders, you young fellows, but you don't know a damn thing about cleaning brass.

You keep whispering "parcels," and we keep sending them. God knows where they get to. Some bastard behind the lines, I suppose. The old, old story. This week we've sent two. One is a tin box which I took to the Service Corps workshops and soldered up myself. It contains Scotch shortbread, Helen's maple cream and a mickey of whisky. The other contains socks and chocolate bars and two of my good pipes, each with a note stating its history. I can't smoke a pipe that has no history. You'll probably never get either parcel.

Too bad you've been disappointed in your promotion. Maybe you'll live to be the senior lieutenant in the Canadian Army, just as I am the senior major. And for the same reasons. As Helen says: "Why, oh why, do you two always have to irritate your betters?" Betters? Hah!

I have never in my life been so ungregarious but I cannot stomach the legions of uniformed rabbits that infest Canada's capital city. I really ought to get out of the army right away and go back to my old library job, but if books are to be got for the troops, then I'm the one to do it; but I just can't sit here for months and months while the brass hats lose the whole thing in their baskets and forget about it.

Looking back over some of your letters – there haven't been any recent ones – I note that you object to being trapped in a hole and shot at by Germans. Furthermore you don't intend to let it go on happening. So what do you intend to do about it? Unless Germans and holes are now a lot different from the ones we used to have, I would advise you to be nice to holes and don't be uppity about keeping your nose in the mud. But if you don't get a Blighty* pretty soon, your mother and I will both be snow white.

There is trouble getting quit of this silly job, but if you make yourself sufficiently objectionable, *They* will eventually let you go. I have. *They* will. *They* do not like it when I stoutly and publicly maintain that all the blasted old blisters from the last war ought to have enough sense and guts to get out of the way. The duffers who inhabit National Defence Headquarters are somewhat short on humour. The first time a fellow disagrees with them they just smile, thinking he be a joker. The second time they give you a cold look. The third time they turn their heads away, and shun you henceforth. They don't even see you when you walk down their damn marble corridors singing *sotto voce*:

> From the town of Napanee
> Came a horse's ass – that's me,
> Where my father shovelled horse balls on the street.
> Till one evening in the fall
> He found me amongst the balls,
> And he picked me up and called me Hasty P.

---

* First World War slang for England; hence a "Blighty" was a wound severe enough to get one evacuated to England.

I'm going to sing it full voiced the day I leave here.

I went to Kingston military hospital the other day and found some wounded Hasties: Privates Rex Shannon of Picton, Len Vancleif of Huycks Point and Albert St. Denis of Belleville amongst them. We had Vancleif and St. Denis for dinner last night, they being the only two who were not bed cases.*

We did not talk about the war. We talked about Vancleif's milk route and farm, and St. Denis' cartage business. Both have been badly wounded in the legs and it looks to me as if both will be permanently crippled, but Van swears he'll run his 250 acres *and* the milk route if he hasn't got a leg at all.

And Helen had a feast for them. A juicy ham which used up all her meat ration coupons for weeks, and one of her famous apple pies, and strong coffee. When they got all that and the beer in them, they really expanded. And I put on an old sweater so they would stop calling me "Major" and saying "sir" all the time.

You send us your verses, and I am grateful and then I don't know what to do about it. You say: "They are just dashed off, you can doctor them up," or words to that effect. So I read them again and again and I sit staring out the window and don't know what to do. I wish dear old Mutt was here – *he'd* know.

In the first place, I am neither a poet nor a qualified critic. In the second place, to tamper with the fruits of another man's meditations is little short of a sin against the Holy Ghost. In the third place, I can't do it objectively, as I might if you were here. But you aren't here. And we can't see you objectively any more because you are too far away, and too much in my thoughts, and the emotional strain of waiting for an official telegram about you is too great.

I must now confess that I sent three of your poems to *The Atlantic.* They haven't come back yet, but they will. And I'll send 'em

---

* When severely wounded men had recovered sufficiently to make the long journey to Canada, they were shipped to military hospitals in their home districts for further treatment. Hasty Ps were sent to Kingston. Angus made a point of visiting them as often as he could.

somewhere else. Nothing like starting at the top. Helen is still somewhat puzzled about them. I try to tell her you are not a Tennyson.
That what you say does not fly up and hit you as the daisies fly up and
hit Ferdinand the Bull. But dear, dear Mum just shakes her head and
mutters: "Morbid, and obscure."

I spent yesterday afternoon between exasperation and mirth. The
damned military council, which is composed mainly of very important civilians, finally met, oh so gravely, to consider my report on
establishing real library services for the troops, and they talked till seven
o'clock, and got nowhere. My exasperation was due to the fact that
they didn't seem to understand a word of the report although it was
written in words of one syllable, just for them. My mirth was caused
by the perfectly obvious fact that they were scared stiff of it and were
squirming in terror lest someone would offer a motion committing
them to agreement. I suspect they believe that soldiers *shouldn't* read
too much. Might give them ideas. Or distract them from the job of
killing or being killed.

What you said in a letter some time ago about taking care not to
lose the important things is a great comfort to me. War does strange
things to some people, and no man can tell how it may affect him until
he has had a good stiff dose of it.

The most unfortunate people after the last war were not those
who were wounded physically, but those who had had their feet
knocked out from under them spiritually and never regained them.
The beer parlours and the gutters are still full of them, poor bastards,
and nobody understands. Or so few understand that it doesn't matter.

I think I should counsel you on one thing, although I suspect you
have thought it through already. Your job, and I mean your duty to
yourself, is to continue keeping that little spark of something or other
that's in you inviolate from war. You say you are managing to do so,
and I say thank God. But the danger of losing it grows as time goes on.
A wearing-down process. I have seen it in half a dozen fellows I knew
intimately. The two most striking cases were Lawrence and Davis,

both of my company in the old Fourth Battalion. Both had had four years of it. Both were simply worn out, spiritually. And both committed suicide. I don't mean that they shot themselves, but they went out and let the Germans do it because there was nothing left alive of the spark within them. They didn't even know what was the matter with them and there wasn't anybody to tell them because we were all too inexperienced to see. If you can guard against that burning out you will be greatly blessed.

❖   ❖   ❖

I WAS IN EVEN GREATER JEOPARDY THAN ANGUS KNEW.

The following epitome of the final pages of *And No Birds Sang* conveys something of the tenuous state of being to which I had been reduced.

When I woke it was morning of the day before Christmas. I was lying on a straw pallet in a corner of a lamp-lit room with vaulted stone ceilings. The place was crowded with sodden and exhausted men. Doc, my batman, was shaking my shoulder.

"Colonel says ya gotta get up, boss," he told me sternly.

I found the C.O. in the next room. The battle had raged all night and was still raging. The rifle companies were only just managing to cling to the mile-long salient we had rammed through the German defence line; and now we were running out of men.

Lt. Col. Kennedy looked up at me from deeply sunken eyes. His voice sounded inexpressibly weary.

"A draft's arrived at San Vito. Supposed to come up tomorrow. I want them here tonight. Go and get them, Squib."

I pulled on my blanket coat and stepped outside. I emerged into a haze of driven sleet sweeping across a blasted landscape whose inhabitants were huddling like dumb and passively enduring beasts in flooded slit trenches or in the gaping ruins of crumbled buildings. The relentless rains and incessant bombardment had turned the whole achromatic wasteland into one enormous wallow through which no mechanical transport could move. Little groups of mules and men laden with food and ammunition sloshed along tracks that were more like running rivers. Tiny, indistinct figures in a void, men and mules plunged half-drowning into the roadside ditches as new storms of shell-fire lashed over them.

A world of shadows, of primordial gloom, of inchoate violence, lay around me and I was staring down a vertiginous tunnel where all was dark and bloody and the great wind of ultimate desolation howled and hungered.

I walked out of the salient like a disembodied spirit. Presumably there was shell-fire, but I do not recall it. I walked in the silence within myself, hearing nothing but an echo of the great wind.

Halfway to San Vito I met our reinforcement draft on its own way forward, led and impelled by my one-time Company Commander, Alex Campbell, returning to us from hospital in North Africa. When he saw me he gave a great, fond shout of recognition and pulled me into a bear hug.

The hundred and forty soldiers following him had arrived in England from Canada only a month earlier. Now they marched behind us in their clean, new uniforms, stared curiously at the debris of war and sang their brave and foolish songs.

The singing faltered as we crossed the Moro and climbed up through the chaos of destruction which was all that remained of San Leonardo. It ceased altogether as we entered the salient and passed thirty or forty of Third Brigade's fatal casualties stacked like cordwood by the shattered road where they had been placed to keep them out of the muck . . . until they could be housed in it permanently. A few minutes later we were enveloped in a brief but murderous bombardment from 15 cm howitzers. Before it ended, seven of these newcomers to our inferno were dead or wounded.

During my absence Battalion Headquarters had moved farther forward and I reported to Kennedy in the ruins of what had once been a large and prosperous farmhouse. Here we spent Christmas Eve while enemy fighting patrols fought to penetrate our salient. The enraged whicker of automatic small arms and the muffled thud of bursting grenades seemed to echo everywhere in a blind confusion of vicious little battles.

Someone passed around a canister of hot tea. Two German prisoners were brought in to be searched. The explosion of a shell in one of the upper rooms set the dust dancing so thickly that for a time the lamp was only a dim, red glow in the grey murk.

Dawn came at last, and it was Christmas Day.

At 0700 hours Kennedy ordered Alex Campbell, once again commanding Able Company, to drive off a force of paratroopers that had infiltrated during the night.

Able's radio set went off the air almost at once so we knew nothing of what was happening until an hour later when the walking wounded began to straggle into our cellar.

One of the first was a sergeant suffering from a deep gash in one thigh. Shakily he accepted a cigarette, then told us what he had seen.

Alex had sent what was left of Five Platoon – my old platoon – to launch the attack, and Five had been caught by enfilading fire from three machine guns. Seizing a tommy-gun Alex levered his great bulk to its full height, gave an inarticulate bellow, and charged straight at the enemy.

He could have gone no more than three or four paces before he was riddled by scores of bullets. . . .

The blanket that screened the shattered cellar door was thrust aside and a party of stretcher-bearers pushed in amongst us. My closest friend, Al Park, lay on one of the stretchers. He was alive, though barely so . . . unconscious, with a bullet in his head.

As I looked down at his faded, empty face under its crown of crimson bandages, I began to weep.

I wonder now . . . were my tears for Alex and Al and all the others who had gone and who were yet to go?

Or was I weeping for myself . . .

Back from
the Edge

❖ ❖ ❖

BY THE TIME THE NEW YEAR BEGAN, I WAS PERILOUSLY CLOSE TO THE
condition Angus called "burn out."

This had become obvious to some of my comrades and to my
CO, Lt. Col. Bert Kennedy. Many years later Kennedy was to tell
me: "I was being pushed to give you a promotion in a rifle company.
But I knew damn well that would be the end of you, and likely of
some other damn good men as a result. So I laid it on the line to
Howard Graham: 'Get Squib out of the line,' I said, 'or write him
off.'"*

The brigadier listened and, not to mince matters, I was saved. In
early January of 1944, I was posted to Brigade HQ for what was
supposed to be a temporary absence.

And so a new kind of war began for me. Although I still found
myself under fire I was no longer a battlefield soldier. From being a
direct participant in the business of killing or being killed, I became
essentially an observer. My inner wounds slowly began to scab over.
Almost imperceptibly the healing process took hold.

After that bloody Christmas, our front became and for some
months remained relatively quiet. Eighth Army's savage struggle to
break through along the Adriatic coast had exhausted itself at the
town of Ortona. But the Germans had been so badly battered that
they had no strength left with which to counter-attack.

Things on the Home Front (a term we used somewhat

---

* Brigadier Howard Graham then commanded First Brigade but had formerly been CO of
the Hasty Ps.

sardonically) did not change much during this period of military stalemate. Angus remained in the service, in Ottawa, but ever more reluctantly as he continued with his bootless struggle to get books for the troops. The capital city had become absolute anathema, and he had all but decided that he would have to quit the army even though it was so much a part – and a beloved part – of him. For a while he eased his anger and solaced his frustration by again taking up work on a novel called *Carrying Place,* which he had put aside when war began.

In Kingston, Helen and Elmer waited patiently for whatever Angus might decide to do next. Like many women of those times, and like dogs in all times, they were used to waiting.

❖   ❖   ❖

[on the Ortona sector of the Adriatic Front]

Jan 1

Dear Folks:

Happy New Year! It's a hell of a war.

Stan Ketcheson, a major now, arrived back at the unit yesterday and got Charley Company. He wants me as his second-in-command, but I'm not delighted. Right about now I feel it's my prerogative to be allowed to scurry off to a job a bit farther from shot and shell – not closer to. I'm now the senior battalion IO as far as the eye can reach and then some and probably the senior subaltern still serving with a front-line outfit in at least one army. It's a distinction I'd happily part with.

At the moment, we are taking it fairly easy, which gives me time to consolidate some of my thoughts, feelings and impressions. I'm afraid they are too grim to talk much about. Alex Campbell was killed Christmas Day, the day after his return to the Regiment, and that was pretty hard to take. Others, too, whom you don't know but who meant a lot to me, have bought it in the last few weeks. We tell ourselves, *"C'est la guerre,"* and try to take comfort in the number of Tedeschi who've bought the biscuit. During one week we took 152 of Hitler's supermen prisoner, and God knows how many we killed.

I guess we've done a good job. The corps commander sent us his congratulations! Probably he'll get a medal out of it.

Celebrated surviving into the New Year with Stan and pals at his company billet, a smashed up Eyetie farmhouse. So help me, he had managed to cart five bottles of Scotch back from England with him! Regret to say that I got saturated, but then we all did.

Glad to hear you are doing things re books for the troops at home, but the need here is so much greater that there is no comparison. We just cannot get reading material. The importance of books to us is something you know about from your own wartime experience. It's a wonder what a couple of paperback novels can do for men who have to sit under shell and mortar fire for days, with nothing else to do but wonder when their number will come up. Sorry, end of airgraph.*

[San Leonardo, Ortona Front]

Jan 11

Dear Ma, and the Other Squib:

Please note the new address: HQ First Canadian Infantry Brigade. After much chin wagging and vacillation, it has finally been decided to give this Mowat a small break. Hence I have a new job, the junior of three LOs – liaison officers – at the Brigade HQ.

It may lead to something if the war lasts long enough – and I can't fail to believe it won't last. Anyway it is a pleasant change and although the posting is only supposed to be for two months, I can dream.

When I left the Regiment last week, I was the sole officer survivor of those who landed in the assault wave at Pachino and took part in every major party thereafter. So I feel I'm entitled to a change of air. The essentials of the new job are not very onerous – basically to act as

---

* A word about wartime mail. An air letter was a single sheet of lightweight paper which folded up in such a way as to become its own envelope. An airgraph also consisted of a single 8 x 10-inch form which was photo-micrographed when it reached England; the film was then flown to Canada where a 3 x 4-inch enlargement was made and sent on to the addressee. The supply of both was strictly rationed, sometimes to as few as two of each per man per month. Ordinary mail went by sea and could take two or more months to reach the intended recipient.

errand boy, office clerk, telephone operator and carrier pigeon for the brigadier and/or the brigade major. All of which tasks are within my capabilities, and I sure aim to please! I may get fed up after a while and go back to the unit, but meantime I am enjoying the luxury of regular meals and a monthly bath. The noises hereabouts are about the same as at the unit, but they don't seem as personal.

I've had a lot of letters from you in the last week or two – latest dated Jan 2. Dispatched another cable today, although I shouldn't think cables would be too good for your nervous systems. Mother, you used to faint every time a telegraph boy came up our steps, "just in case" as you put it.

Got two hundred cigarettes from you but have received no parcels for a long time. But then neither has anyone else. Chapter 7 of *It's a Dog's Life* is now ready for the presses. Gets worse and worse, but I have fun pounding it out between bangs.

[Kingston]

Feb 15

My Dear Son. –

When I woke up in Hove To Saturday morning – having come home for a "short" weekend – I thought it was Christmas Day. For a long time I couldn't figure out what was the matter with me till I woke your mother and asked her. "It's Farley's letter, you old fool," says she. And sure enough, your letter telling how you had been given a job at Brigade Headquarters had arrived Friday morning and I had read it Friday night. Of course I didn't care very much about the news, but Mum was so thrilled she had hysterics. I wasn't there but she said she howled and cried and laughed till poor Elmer lost his nerve and began to howl, too. Then they both went to bed and let the fires go out (it was blowing a winter's gale) and the water pipes froze again, and the little Jennie Wren who is staying with Helen came home and got the flu.* And that was the state of affairs when I blew in off the 6:30 train.

So please don't write any more letters unless you have to.

---

* WRCNS – a member of the Women's Royal Canadian Naval Service.

I started to caution your dear mother that being at brigade is not quite the same thing as being at Canadian Military Headquarters, but as she had already planned for you a brilliant staff career I thought better of it and just let it pass. I guess neither of us quite knew how bad the strain had become while you were still with the unit. Anyway, virtue and ability will have their reward. Reading between the lines, I wonder if you might not even get a motorcycle. This is about as high, I think, as anybody could ever want to go. It is the height of bliss for Elmer and me, anyhow.

What with your blessed letter and two weeks of packing coal in and ashes out, your mum was done in. So was the Wren. So I took a-holt, and ran the fires, and unfroze the taps, and got the food and generally made myself useful, and re-wrote two chapters of *Carrying Place* in my spare time. Coming back here to the soft life has made me feel like a slacker. I forgot to mention that the Wren had a bottle of rye. Had. I hadn't seen one since Christmas. I can't have any beer while in Kingston (unless I go all the way to Fort Frontenac to the mess, which is too far and too cold) on account of we are rationed to twenty-four pints a month, and I save it for Hasties on day leave out of hospital. This being their only chance to have a drink, since the pubs are not allowed to serve them while they are wearing hospital blues. Can you imagine that?

Aren't we the industrious little writers. You with your *Dog's Life* and me with *Carrying Place*. Both of them, probably, to be met with cold disdain by the public. I hope the fishing is still good on the Bay of Quinte when you get home. Won't cost much to live aboard *Scotch Bonnet* on the Black River. Nice harbour there and good duck hunting. And, as ex-Hasties, we could probably get our stuff published in the *Picton Gazette*. Free, of course.

I keep sending you paperback books like Trevor Davies on Russia, and *Madame Bovary* and such like light entertainments. Do let me know if you ever get any. I note with interest and incredulity that you have received two hundred cigarettes. I suppose that runs the score to about 2% of those sent, cigarettes I mean. Our dear Member of Parliament, William Mulock, Postmaster General, publicly continues to insist there are no losses. What do you suppose the trouble is: evaporation?

Did I tell you that Reg Saunders, one of the Toronto publishers, is prepared to publish *Carrying Place*? He'll probably change his mind.

God bless you, pal.

[San Leonardo]

Jan 14

Dear Parents:

This new job has its points. Once every four days, the duty roster gives me the supreme pleasure of being the officer in charge of the brigade (well, contact man at least) during the velvet hours of darkness. This means that I stay up all night and answer the phones and deal with radio messages and call my betters when needs must. But I am often left alone with my thoughts and my typewriter. My thoughts don't amount to much but I am free to bang away at the typewriter as much as I like without being banged away at by Jerry, or at least not very much. So, for the first time in months, I can begin to get caught up on letter writing. And I have a wad of letters from my erstwhile peacetime pals, now seemingly scattered all over the globe. Al Helmsley is back in England after flying thirty ops missions over the Med. He's having a holiday, he says, and God bless him. Doug Reid is in Scotland flying coastal command. God bless him too. Andy Lawrie was recently in Trinidad on convoy duty.* But woe are we of the Poor Bloody Infantry who seem to be stuck here in the Italian mud for ever and ever, amen.

At least things are relatively quiet on our front for the time being, and the fighting troops are getting a bit of a break during the winter "lull." I get down to the unit at least once a week on business or pleasure. Lots of new faces, and not many familiar ones left. Bert Kennedy got the DSO for the last show, and it was damn well earned. He's the best CO I've ever served under, bar none. I'm not working for Howard Graham, as you might have thought. His place has been taken

---

* These were three of my closest pre-war friends. They had volunteered for the air force and the navy rather than the army.

by Dan Spry from the RCR. Howard's old ulcers got too much for him, but he did a grand job as Brig., including, I just learned, plucking me out of the mud. If you see him when he gets home, buy him a double whisky on me.

Did you ask about my moustache? It is still stuck in limbo, as it were. Visible only when the light is right. But I WILL NOT cut it off. I remain horribly healthy and give every appearance of staying that way. Can't even catch jaundice and get a holiday in a North African hospital. Keep the cigarettes and socks flowing.

[San Leonardo]

Jan 18

My second night at Brigade brought with it a story that may or may not amuse you. It has long been an ambition of the brigade major to inveigle a dental detachment to come forward from base and attend to the toothaches which abound in the front lines. But the dental corps has such demanding needs – running water, electricity, refrigeration, heaters and trucks converted into swanky living quarters for the dental docs – and they are loath to expose themselves and their equipment to the uncertain "weather" up where we live.

However, last week the BM succeeded in his machinations and two whopping big trucks full of incisors, molars and dentists rolled into the village square where Bde HQ was laagered. Our camp commandant suggested they might sleep better if they bedded down with us in the nice deep wine cellars of some of the surrounding houses, most of whose upper floors are now in a somewhat dilapidated state. The dentists would have none of that but climbed into their comfy caravan truck parked in the square in the midst of a clutch of ammunition trucks belonging to our supporting tank regiment, and went beddy-byes.

The inevitable happened. Along about 2300 hrs, Jerry did a stonk of the village. One shell fell in the square and set fire to a lorry loaded with 75 mm tank ammo which, as you know, is all of one piece – case *and* shell – and is therefore to be doubly reckoned with if it gets too warm. The dentists heard the shell land all right, and when they peered dazedly out of their daintily curtained windows they saw the flames leaping up from the burning truck. They may also have heard someone shouting that it was an ammo truck aflame.

Well you can say what you will about dentists, they can move as fast as any of us when the mood is on them. And they know what slit trenches are *for*, even if only in an academic sense. They found one handy to their mobile home-away-from-home and popped right into it.

Shortly thereafter the tank shells began to let fly and the square became a pretty lively place. Not that we lingered to enjoy it. Everyone with any sense headed down into the *vino* cellars to wait until the fireworks were over. The two poor sods of dentists were pinned down in their slit trench. No doubt there was considerable squirming and grunting in the narrow confines of their sanctuary, but they had no "better 'ole" to go to, with AP shells, shell-casings and bits of truck ricochetting around the square.

To shorten the story, when the explosions ceased the two harassed trench dwellers were seen to emerge and stagger back to their trucks, which had been well perforated but not immobilized. There was the grind of starters, the clash of gears, then the roar of rapid acceleration as they departed down the road leading to the rear. In the morning, I sauntered over to look at the remains of the ammo lorry and happened to cast a glance into the slit trench that had saved the dental plates. It wasn't a slit trench. It was a latrine trench left behind by Jerry when he skedaddled out of here a few days ago.

Some day I must have my cavity filled. But not just yet.

My kitbag went up in smoke a while back so I'm short of shirts, khaki, Small Officers for the use of. I'd be awfully grateful for a few of same.

Glad to know that you are keeping *Scotch Bonnet* in shape. I moseyed down to a local fishing harbour the other day to look at the Eyetie fish boats. They are broad-beamed, snub-nosed things like you see in old Dutch prints, but carry a gaudily painted eye on their bows. One of my fellow LOs says these are to scare the subs away.

One of the perks of this job is that I have a jeep. I'm in it a lot, and under it sometimes when things get too lively. Couple of days ago I had to take a message to the Hasties and was in time to watch our fighter-bombers working over some of Gerald's positions. The air was so thick with our planes that some of them had to circle for a quarter hour before they could get their chance to dive in and join the fun. I wondered what it must have been like in earlier days when they would have been Stukas, and our lot would *not* have been interested in watching them. I hope Gerald's nerves are good. It scared me just to watch while he got pasted.

[Ottawa]

Feb 22

Dear Mark II. –

Here's a surprise. Reg Saunders insists on seeing what you've sent me of *The Dog*. He is also so anxious to get at *Carrying Place* that he is even going to have his stenographer type a clean manuscript from my much-written-over copy. I read it straight through to my best critic over the weekend. I don't know what I'd do without my best critic. I ask her to criticize. She criticizes. I get mad. And, damn it all, the woman has been right every time so far, and probably always will be right. That's what makes me mad.

Now for your letters, of which there have been three this week. Do not feel guilty about going to Brigade. You did the right thing. It was coming to you and will give you a chance that you would never get by staying with the unit until Jerry plonked you. As far as I can tell by talking with people who have come back, you stand about the same chances of getting plonked in this new job, but a damned sight better chance of promotion. And you are still in close touch with the regiment. So be at ease in your mind.

Your Momma has great hopes for you as a writer. She says you write so much better than I did at your age. Easy, since I didn't write at all then. And besides, she says, you are already more mature than I will ever be. Something in that, joking aside. I'll always be so damned unsophisticated, as a writer I mean. But, oh gosh, if it could only come down to two of us pecking at two typewriters in two cabins at two ends of some little island like Waupoos, or down where the Black River flows into South Bay. . . .

Feb 25

Well, me boy, I guess your old man's on his way this time, and no mistake. I have just come from Defence Headquarters and have succeeded in moving my swan-song letter into, I hope, the last basket.

I find there is only one way to accomplish anything at Defence Headquarters. You first have to locate your letter. This can be accomplished at the cost of a couple of beers bought for a corporal clerk. Then having located the letter, you go to the office it is in and demand to see it. It helps if you are a major or above. After a lot of rummaging in the bottoms of a lot of file baskets it is produced, usually by a lieut. or a capt. who looks young and fit enough that he ought to be up around Ortona somewhere.

You explain carefully and sternly what you want done with the letter. Then – this is really the trick – you get the name of the next officer who will, in the normal channel of communications, be handling the matter. You watch with eagle eye while your first officer makes the correct notation on the file cover in order that it shall continue its journey promptly. Then, next morning, you turn up in the new officer's office a little before nine, and before he is fully awake, and go through the same procedure.

In that way I have now shepherded my poor little letter through nine offices. Now it has come up before a brigadier and his board for final disposal. I was asked to appear before the board, too, but politely declined. I said I was sick of trying to insult military minds, which is all my appearance would have amounted to.

Oh yes and here's another lovely one. As you know, the word "not" when used in military telegrams is always repeated and capitalized. This is a useful precaution in telegrams. But now some nitwit at Defence HQ is insisting that the same procedure be applied in letters. My gentle and long-suffering friend Col. Leary Grant in Kingston was so exasperated by such stupidity that he wrote a letter in reply to the new instruction. The letter contained only one para, and the para only one word. You guessed it. NOT.

Well, *The Dog's Life* and *Carrying Place* are both on their way to Reg Saunders. It's a hell of a state of affairs when a man's son gets to compete with him in the open market like that. But, you damned little plagiarist, I'm not repeat NOT going to re-write *Carrying Place* again in order to take out the dog and skunk story. Damn you, I wrote that in 1938. I wish *The Atlantic* would accept your verses. That might distract you.

About books for the army overseas: as soon as I get back to Toronto, I'll see the publishers' organization and see if something can't be done. When a book is being printed for the trade, they could run off a lot of extra copies on thin paper and bind them in paper covers. This would be just the thing for front-line troops. I'll go to work on it, but you haven't any idea how discouraged I get in Ottawa. The apathy, the red tape, the lack of interest, and the eternal question: "What do I get out of it?" If I hadn't had *Carrying Place* to escape into while here, I'd have taken to drink. If it could be got.

Anyhoo, you just keep on pecking and pecking at the mayor of Assoro's typewriter.* It's practice and practice that does it. And there is likely to be a great writers' market after this war. And with that, and your interest in birds, you can live a pretty ideal kind of life. If you have read much about writers, which I know you have NOT (repeat), you will realize that in a great number of cases it has taken two generations to make the best of them. The old man starts, but remains a plodding minor, and then the son comes along and becomes noted. Now that would suit me very well indeed. I'll go on plodding.

[near Ortona]

Jan 28

Mes Enfants:

The war has become, as they say, static. That means, as Pop well knows, that you don't move around very much, and neither does Jerry.

---

*An Olivetti portable "liberated" from the mayor's office in the Sicilian village of Assoro. It was my constant companion until war's end.

Most of our units are under cover from the rotten weather in what's left of villages or farmhouses, but our Brig is a masochist and so Bde HQ is under canvas in a muddy gulley out in the wide open country-side. I think he's trying to prove that HQ is as tough and rough as the fighting troops.

But who cares? Together with LO II (I'm still numero III) and our indefatigable (how-the-hell-do-you-spell-that) batmen, a pick and shovel and some elementary engineering, we possess a positively sump-tuous dugout, 10 feet x 10 feet x 7 feet, cut into a clay bank in the side of the gulley. It is waterproofed (sort of), floored, wallpapered with sand-bags, and has a stove, bed, writing table and even pictures on the walls.

The stove is made of a large tin can filled with sand into which you pour a cup or two of army petrol, let stand for a few minutes, then ignite. "Dicey," as Doc McConnell, my batman since Scotland, puts it. Fine in the open air, but it'll never catch on for household use. All in all, we are most comfortable, and the envy of all hands from the Brig on down. He, poor chap, has to live in a caravan built onto the back of a 60-cwt lorry. It is comfy, but somewhat flimsy, and I am sure he has vivid memories of the fate of the visiting den-tists I wrote about in a recent letter. After the heavens unleashed a downpour last night (they do it every night), LO II and LO III were the only ones to emerge as recognizable human beings from the con-sequent sea of mud. Drainage is the secret. You talk about Flanders, Pop? Pooey on Flanders.

From our carefully sandbagged door (rain isn't the only stuff that falls from the heavens), I peer out at a desolate foreground of shattered olive trees, which look like the ragged stumps of some ancient and gigantic hag's incisors. But to my right lies the azure sweep of the Adri-atic, very serene and calm, while to my left the powder-blue masses of the Apennines form a magnificent backdrop for the desolate and crumbled heaps of rubble that until recently were little hill-top towns.

I get up to the Hasties often. The lads are reasonably well fixed for shelter, but there is damn all to do most of the time. Fighting patrols, standing patrols and all sorts of other kinds of patrols invented by the Gilded Staff are the order of the day, but the men have nothing else to get their minds off the current scene except letters from home. Why in hell can't the dodos in Ottawa and elsewhere realize that fighting men need more than guns and ammo? Books are one answer. I've seen books up here so worn that guys keep the pages together in home-made little wooden boxes, and still go on reading them.

Do you remember Luke Reid? The young, good-looking chap who used to run a service station near Richmond Hill? A couple of months ago, he and I were on a job with Bert Kennedy. We got cut off and Luke disappeared. I've written twice to his young wife but apparently haven't reached her. Thank God I didn't marry before coming overseas. I don't think I could have faced having to write to women like Luke's wife if I'd had a wife of my own waiting.

So that's me. Still fancy free (who would have me?); solvent (so Ma tells me); in a reasonably safe job and reasonably content. Only I'd like to smack Elmer's little backside once or twice before he forgets me entirely. Tell him from me the Dogs of War aren't what they're cracked up to be.

[Kingston]

Mar 2

Bunje Darling*–

I can just see you sitting in your little dugout, with the family gift for making any place homey. Really, this spot I'm in now in Kingston is hardly more than a dugout, but with the aid of a red checkered table cloth and some red curtains the effect is quite good to the eye, even though the flesh freezes and golly, it's cold tonight.

We got off a box for you including two shirts, hankies, two pairs of socks and things. You'll probably get it in time for your birthday.

My Wren and her husband have gone to a party, leaving Elmer and me all alone. I was so terribly sorry to hear about Luke Reid and to think how close you must have been and in such danger. What helps

---

* This childhood nickname was apparently derived from a character in a novel by H. G. Wells called Bunje. I don't think there was any deep significance in its use by my parents. I think they just liked the sound of it.

me most is the thought of your being so brave. Then, you see, I can't give way, it would be letting you down. Angus has been a different person, so relieved since you went to First Brigade.

Doug Reid is back home on leave and coming to see us this weekend. I hear he has a handlebar moustache and is still single. His lucky mother is bubbling over. I hate to think of you being without books. Angus is busy on that. Good night, God bless and keep you safe.

[Kingston]

Mar 5

Dear Farl. –

How'd you like to be in your old man's shoes? I arrived at the depot yesterday having driven an m/c in combination down to Kingston, leaving That Place behind me for the last time. Had a hell of a ride. It was thawing on the road and freezing six inches above it, and all this was going on for the express purpose of gumming up my brakes and steering forks and chains and front spindles.

Anyway, I reported myself to the adjutant "for disposal," just as you had done on arriving at the depot, nineteen years old and full of beans. I arrived at fifty-one, but still full of beans. Of course the adjutant had not yet received instructions concerning my said disposal. But that's O.K. He'll hear in due time.

Your account of the dugout you are living in takes me back many years. Now hell's bells, if you are going to have that kind of a war for a while, why can't they let some of the more vigorous of us old buggers go over and lend a hand? Believe me, we *can* make good dugouts. Anyway, do give us more details, like the dugout ones. I know that what you do every day, personally I mean, sounds to you like the most boring thing in the world. But that's exactly the kind of detail we long for.

I am sorry to say that *Atlantic*, very politely and with a nice letter in which they asked me to write and thank you, hasn't taken your verse. I'll try somebody else.

Tomorrow I have to turn in my Indian and sidecar as it is now considered obsolete. Just like me.

[near Ortona]

Feb 9

Dear Squib and Mater:

Just finished censoring a batch of outgoing letters. You'd be surprised at the amount of bitching the men do about the mail situation. No, you wouldn't. You *know* all about it. We are told that these air letters will now reach a Canadian destination in ten days! That sounds incredible!*

Hurray, the parcels are coming! I've had two Christmas parcels from you, and several from churches and friends. But Mother, *dear* Mother, please do not send any more tins of stew. It doesn't matter what famous brand, stew is stew, and it is coming out of our ears. I took a hell of a verbal beating as a result of the last can of such you sent me. They call me "Stewie" now and think the whole thing is utterly hilarious.

I still need pipes. Angus's Dunhills haven't arrived, and it is a shame to send good pipes when they haven't a hope in hell of lasting more than a month or so. Buy some half-dollar ones and ship them in successive parcels.

This is not one of my cheerier letters – mostly demands and complaints, but the weather is hellish and I can't be full of joy when the rain has finally got through our roof and is turning our once-snug dugout into a hog wallow. There *is* a rumour that we might be getting into four walls and a solid roof sometime soon. Oh blast and damn, it's started to snow.

Got a letter from WAAF Sergeant Janet Ince and find it hard to envisage my young coz as one of us.** She was only halfway through adolescence when I left, and now she's a big girl with three stripes and a military vocabulary.

We hear via the BBC that "Mr. Prime Minister Mackenzie King and the people of Canada and the troops overseas have decided that, for the good of the war effort, the present government should remain in power until the end of hostilities." So no election. Well, well, well!

---

* It was. This letter took thirty-three days to reach my parents.
** WAAF: Women's Auxiliary Air Force.

Ain't it nice to be fighting for democracy against dictators? Do you suppose anyone actually believes BS like that? Yeah, I know. Lots of people do.

The hell with it. The junior officers of this HQ have by dint of self-denial, perjury, deceit and outright theft accumulated enough alcohol to carry us past the thinking stage for one night. Tonight's the night. . . .

[Kingston]

Mar 13

My Dear Son. –

Oh yes, the mail is very fast indeed – on Parliament Hill! But the air force people tell me they have been allocated just *one* airplane to carry mail to and from Italy, and it has made only two trips in two months! Meanwhile Post Master Billy Mulock and the other bastard politicians shout about how fast the service is.

Last night Helen and I had dinner with the Reids, with rum, and Flying Officer Doug, and all. He seems not to have changed much except for growing a huge handlebar moustache. Is still absent-minded, which is a funny way for a pilot to be, surely. The other day he set out to go by train to Montreal from here, and went the other way to Toronto instead. Probably thinking of something else. He wants to and intends to get back to England where the people know there is a war to be fought. He fully agrees with your Cpl. Shannon, who, as you undoubtedly know, is home with some bullets in his chest, that Canada is a lovely country but, unfortunately, seems to be mostly inhabited by greedy shitheels.

Your message about books is received and understood. But the fact is that the authorities in Ottawa couldn't care less. Nor can the people in general be expected to take much interest. When they have to be coaxed and coaxed to even give blood donations, or buy war bonds, you can imagine how much they care about the likes of you fellows. The only people interested in the needs of the fighting men are the comparatively few who have sons, husbands or other relatives overseas. But that's not entirely true either. The *rural* people do support their soldiers. The *Picton Gazette* is already running a book fund, and boxes have begun to go off.

We will not send you any more stew. Sorry about that. Mum ordered that box of goodies through a commercial firm that specializes in shipping soldiers' "comforts." Talk about sending coal to Newcastle!

And I sent some of your verses to Reg, who replied: "Dear Angus: The poems of Farley's are first class but we need more to make a book. If we can get enough I would not hesitate one moment to publish." But the hell of it is I sent him the best and the others aren't as good but I'll send them anyway. My son, don't let your writing go, no matter what happens.

[near Ortona]

Feb 10

My Good Friends:

This brigade stuff is not bad at all. We three LOs, the IO, the brigade major and the Brig make up the ops staff, supported by the staff captain, Sigs officer, camp commandant and various attached bods from supporting arms. A congenial crowd – most of us fugitives from Moaning Minnies, eighty-eights, and MG 42s or, in other words, from fighting units. Thus all of us have large quantities of suppressed emotions to blow off, resulting in some of the best jamborees I've ever attended. A few nights ago, my dugout was the scene of a Moose Milk revel of epic proportions. We got our attached artillery FOO into such a state that he phoned his battery and, after some false starts, got the guns beating out the rhythm of "Shave-and-a-hair-cut – TWO BITS." Wonder what the Jerries thought of that! Moose Milk, for your ongoing education, consists of issue rum, maple syrup (when available), evaporated milk and/or chicken noodle soup. The last item is optional.

We've still got Jerry's 1st Paratroop Div on our front – a tough lot but they seem to have concluded, like us, that rain, snow, sleet, hail and mud are rotten conditions for battle fighting, and so both sides are limiting their activities to patrolling and "fire harassment." The Paras are good at the latter. They harassed me off the can with mortar fire *twice* in one day.

There seems to be some chance of a relief in the near future and a little peace and quiet. If so I'll spend some of it writing impressions of daily life. I *do* appreciate the fact that my letters of the past few months have been pretty uninformative and taciturn, but you'll understand that the mood hasn't been great for creative writing.

What about the books for the troops?

[Kingston]

Mar 15

Dear Old Boy. –

Howard Graham is now in Ottawa, as a major general and assistant deputy chief of the General Staff. He wrote a note saying he hadn't had time to go home to Belleville yet because there was a job to be done in Ottawa that had to be done in a hurry. Poor Howard! Imagine trying to do a job in a hurry at National Defence Headquarters.

Mar 22

Here is the news about your friend, Al Park, who was hit on Christmas Day. He is in a hospital in Algiers. He was unconscious for a long time but apparently is able to speak a little bit now. But I am afraid he is still a pretty sick boy, and I tremble to think of the probable consequences of that kind of head wound. Poor Tiny Hyatt is pretty permanent, too. His lower bowel is so badly shot up they can't repair it, and he will have to excrete through a hole in his belly for the rest of his days. But he's a game bugger. He says it doesn't matter much because he's trained himself to go only once a day. But he is a steeplejack by trade, and he's afraid it might be embarrassing if he has to change himself while hanging from the top of a spire. Of course he'll never climb again.

I took over your old job of attending to the spring bird migration for a while today. Something kept calling that at first I thought was a hen, then a robin, then a flicker, after which I was at a loss. So I laid down my putty knife – I was working on *Bonnet* – and went looking and finally discovered the thing in a big elm in the yacht club yard. It was one of those little tree-hopper things that flicks and flips around the bole, dark slate in colour on the back, and making a hell of a lot of noise, I thought, for its size. With which description you will no doubt immediately identify it.

Well, by the time you read this I'll be out of the army, or at least on my retirement leave. End of an era? Maybe so.

[Ortona]

Mar 9
Dear Folks:

The mails are in! And what a haul – several from you two, all of fairly recent date. Some things you say leave me puzzled. What the hell's all this about waiting to hear from *Atlantic Monthly*? Have you been peddling my letters to the illiterate populace again? Or are you serializing *Carrying Place*? Explain yourself, Poppa.

Sent a cable yesterday. Seems like it might be a good idea to send a couple every month, if your nerves are equal to the strain. Letters get sunk or crash en route, but cables go so deep the U-boats canna get them!

I'm delighted *Carrying Place* is finally finished. I was afraid its skipper had scuttled it long ago. I'm sure it will do better than *Then I'll Look Up.** It better had: going to be tough for the three of us to live on Pop's First War pension without something coming in on the side. Speaking of which: your comments on the possibility of me earning a pleasant, if scanty, living by birding and writing is prescient. I had decided to do just that some time ago. According to Mum, I've saved something like two thousand from my pay in the past two years, which isn't bad for a Mowat. Together with my little legacy from Aunt Lillian, I should be able to get by on what I've got for a couple of years.

Either Black River or Waupoos sounds pretty good to me.** At the moment, I'm fed up with the wandering life and desperately want to settle down in some quiet, isolated spot. But I wouldn't let these present feelings fool me into getting into an un-scramble-out-of-able rut. I know it won't take many months of inactivity to make me restless again. Dad sounds as if he'd like to rusticate but you won't be able

---

* Angus's first novel, published in 1936.
** These are places on the south shore of Prince Edward County.

to keep me in harbour long, I'm afraid.

And what's this about letting Reg Saunders look at the *Dog's Life*? That is high school stuff! For the Lord's sake, take it away from him. I may *want* him to publish a book some day and don't want him turned off too soon. The stuff I am writing here is purely for my own recreation and I send it along just for your amusement. It ain't possible to write for publication under these circumstances.

You want some more verse? O.K., how about this:

> The carrion crow, I've heard it said,
> Lives on the entrails of the dead.
> It loves to gorge on rotting bowel,
> Which spoils it . . . as a table fowl.

Or in a somewhat lighter vein:

> The double-crested cormorants
> Sport twin cerebral ornaments.
> The female sings in high soprano
> When not engaged in making guano.
> In winter she lies dormorant.

Did I tell you about Prang? Prang is a dog, sort of, that I picked up in a ruined village a few weeks ago. From the rear, he resembles nothing so much as an armadillo with rickets. He puts his back feet in front of his forefeet when trying to climb stairs, with disastrous (and painful) results. Unhappily, he took an antipathy to the brigadier, stole his sheepskin coat which had been hung out to air, and hauled it to the top of a knoll in full view of a Jerry observation post where nobody dared retrieve it until night fell. By then it had been chewed into a kind of rabbit's nest of bits of wool saturated in mud. The brigadier then had an antipathy towards Prang. Alas, or maybe it was just as well, Prang seems to have become pregnant and has been evacuated to the field hospital to undergo tests to determine his/her true sex. And, oh yes, the Brig was so grateful to see him/her depart that he has elevated me to temporary, acting, captaincy. You can now address me as such.

I was called back to Army HQ last week to be interviewed by G-1 Air (a Limey full colonel) for a job as an air liaison officer. You will recall that I qualified as an ALO in England some centuries ago. He listened as I recited my qualifications, then pronounced his verdict: "*Frightfully* sorry, old chap, but you rahlly don't have enough experience for Staff as yet. Goodbye, and good luck." I think our one-time CO, Lord Tweedsmuir, who is now at 8th Army HQ, must have arranged this interview. I had a somewhat oblique note from him later to tell me that the job had gone to an MP's son just arrived out from Britain. But doubtless replete with the right kind of experience. Tweedie also told me that it is 8th Army policy not to take many "colonials" on staff. I expect they think we are more use as cannon fodder.

One more thing, we are out of the mud at last (though not out of action) and comfortably ensconced in the ruins of an Unidentified Italian Town, whose name should be very familiar to you and, I hope, to all Canadians. But I can't tell you what it is. Care to make a guess?*

[Kingston]

Mar 24

Dear Captain Mowat –

How pleased the old folks were with the good news of your promotion you may be able to guess. And you little devil, slipping it in in that casual way just as though it meant nothing to you. Well, we're very proud, and your thrifty mother hopes you'll save even more and so have a nice little nest egg to come home to. You now get more money than your dad, as our income tax is about eight hundred a year. So send me home $100 instead of $50 each month, assigned to me, and you may be sure it will be well looked after.

Your Uncle Jack has a decoration but with customary vagueness neglects to say what it is for. He is in England with the anti-air artillery and I think is still a major.

Angus has just come in after a long day's work on the *Bonnet*. I

---

* This was Ortona.

gave him a good roast beef dinner and now he is going to take his bath, after which he will read to me in bed. We have sent you two boxes of books lately. I hope you are more comfortable now in your little dugout. I hate to picture you sitting there being soaked, with nothing to read.

[Kingston]

Mar 27

Dear Cap. –

Couldn't wait to address a letter to Captain Mowat. We were thrilled with the news, but Mum was very annoyed with the G-1(air) at 8th Army HQ.

So as soon as the clock got within striking distance of 1630 hrs, I headed for the mess where I bought a few celebratory drinks. This is something like "the King is dead, long live the King" because I "proceed" on my thirty-day retirement leave as of tomorrow morning. I expect to sail the *Bonnet* to Oakville in May, where *Mister* and Mrs. Angus Mowat will take up residence in the harbour until September. I'll take a room in Toronto to live in during the week while picking up the threads of my old job. It'll be a bit of a heartburn but, after all, I'm fifty-one, which is too ripe for any man's army, and also I'm fed up being buggered about by the damned nonsensical musical comedy army that this one in Canada has become.

[Kingston]

Mar 31

Dearest Bunje,

It's a good thing you sent that cable in March, though it took eight days, because a mail plane had to get rid of its mail in the Mediterranean and we lost your letters for a while. Hate like the dickens to lose any of them. You know Angus keeps them all and they are a great comfort to us.

I'm expecting him back tonight from Toronto where he went to take over his old job. Wonder how he'll like being a civilian again. Just as well as trying to soldier in Canada, I think.

Now I must get his dinner ready. His favourite dish, bacon and eggs and some soup. He is certainly easy to cook for. Could you have a snap taken? I'd love one.

❖　❖　❖

ON APRIL 1 — AND HE WAS WELL AWARE OF THE SIGNIFICANCE OF THE date — Angus left Kingston and the army for good, returning to his pre-war job in Toronto as inspector of public libraries for Ontario. However, he and Helen could not yet return to our home in Richmond Hill since it was still occupied by tenants.

❖　❖　❖

[Toronto]

April 4
Well. –

I find that my old office has been given away so I am camping in another room at the old Parliament Bldgs. Oddly enough, it doesn't seem a bit strange to be back again. Sir Oliver Mowat* still stands on his marble plinth outside this old red sandstone pile and I think I'll easily slip back into the old ways.

We will quit Kingston on May 1. I'll miss it all, but will miss my army bike more than anything else. They tell me that in my job I can get priority to buy tires for the old Dodge, which has been rusting in her stable in Richmond Hill these many years, but there won't be enough gas for anything except essential driving. All my long library inspection trips and etc. will have to be done by train or bus, and all the trains these days are as crowded as the Camp Borden leave trains used to be on a Sunday night. Terrible, how we civilians are suffering because of this war! I'd like to buy an m'cycle, if one could be found, but Helen won't have it. She says it is time I grew up.

---

* Oliver Mowat was one of the Fathers of Canadian Confederation. He was also for many years premier of Ontario, and my great-great uncle.

Toronto is as dirty and unattractive as ever. There seems to be a hell of a lot of cars running around, and every day the papers have a story about another lot of gas coupons being stolen for the black market. Some people say the Jews are running the gasoline business, and hard words are being spoken against them. But the smug, comfortable and cheating gentiles who buy the stuff are worse than those who sell it.

It is going to be hard for me to live a life in which the war takes second (or thirty-second) place. Although I had no very active role this time in the army, at least the atmosphere was there, and we were involved in the war and with those doing the fighting. Those of us who had been through it once did not feel utterly divorced from you others who are now doing the job. I'll have to learn to talk a different kind of shop too. On my first morning here I ran into a deputation of librarians, six frustrated females and a confused man. They were here to see the director of education so I got dragged in on it. The director is a new man, of a new order, and I was greatly encouraged by his attitudes and even managed to keep my mouth closed, pretty well. Under him I think I might be able to get through the changes in the library system that I was advocating before 1939. So now I look forward to working another four or five years and training up some energetic young man to take my place. A young man with a decent war record. Wouldn't like to go in for library work, would you?

There hasn't been anything from you for quite a while. In choosing your plane, why not select one that does not get engine trouble and have to jettison its mail sacks over the Med.?

[Ortona]

Mar 2

Dear Folks:

An hour ago I returned from an eight-day leave in the southern city of Bari, which is now an 8th Army leave centre and, as any map will tell you, a goodish way from the war. Sort of, as I'll explain in a minute.

This leave came from a clear sky. The Brig gave me three hours' notice that I was off for a week and "Would I like to go to Bari?"

Would I? I damn near ran all the way back to rear HQ there to catch a truck bound south to railhead where I transferred to a stinky little Eyetie train. For the first time in the campaign so far, I then had a chance to see something of Italy as a tourist.

I was impressed by the speed with which nature and man between them were combining to heal the scars of war. Partly demolished farmhouses were regaining walls and roofs; the roads were as good as in old Mussolini's time; new wheat covered many shell-torn fields. If it hadn't been for the endless lines of trucks and tanks and the steady drone of aircraft overhead, it would have been possible to imagine that the last fighting in this region had taken place in Garibaldi's time. Until, that is, the little train came under enemy fire. That's right. We were three-quarters of the way to Bari, trundling along the coast under the shoulder of the mountains when a goddamn U-boat surfaced just offshore and began taking pot-shots at us. Our engineer thereupon crowded on all the steam we could carry and our little whistle began screeching like a stuck pig as we bounced along faster than any train of that vintage had any right to go. It must have been a hilarious sight for the U-boat gun crew. I suspect the reason they didn't hit us was they were laughing that hard. We were *not* laughing. Most of those aboard were soldiers on their first leave in months, and they were madder than hornets. One RCR sergeant knocked out a window and started potting back at the U-boat with his rifle. "You s.o.b.," he was yelling, "try and mess up my leave, will you? Take *that* . . . and *that* . . . and *that!*" Well, I guess it doesn't pay to rile up a sergeant in the RCR.

The appearance of peace was only surface deep anyway. The local people know many bitter things that the general appearance of the countryside conceals. Food is scarce and monotonous. Tobacco must be begged for from our armies. Medicine and doctors are almost non-existent. Curfews send the people running home at the hour when once they were at their liveliest. Of course, these things seem pretty insignificant when one considers what people in the lands occupied by the Huns are suffering. And the Eyeties do seem to be of pretty good cheer. Part of that comes from the fact that they don't seem to have any consciousness of defeat. Their armed forces (now working for us) swagger about as if they'd won. Well, maybe they did – they're still alive, at any rate.

The leave was pretty good. An excellent officers' hotel with *real sheets* on the beds, and entertainment ranging from a pretty good Italian symphony orchestra to an ENSA presentation of "Flare Path." Many and good bars. And Allied *soldati* from the farthest corners of the globe to chat and drink with. I got pally with the captain of a Limey destroyer in the harbour who offered to take me over to Yugoslavia on a run to deliver arms to General Tito. I would have gone had not my military training cooled my ardour. Because he couldn't say when, or if, he might get back to Bari.

Bert Kennedy, who has been CO of the regiment since Lord Tweedsmuir was promoted upstairs, had me down to the unit for dinner just before I went on leave to tell me that 2nd Echelon* wants to post me back to the unit. I am not holding my breath or, I guess, I *am* holding my breath.

And, yes, I had the Mayor's typewriter rebuilt by its manufacturer whilst in Bari. They offered to buy it back for a king's ransom (they can't manufacture any new ones) but I wouldn't play. It is the living symbol of my ongoing existence, you might say, even though I've given up on the *Dog's Life*. The effort of trying to be funny just takes too much out of me these days, and most of what I write isn't funny anyway – just flip. Maybe I'll go back to it sometime. Meanwhile I'm still writing terrible, terrible poetry, just to keep in practice.

[Kingston]

April 8

My lamb–

Easter Sunday tomorrow and we are still wearing furs, but the robins are back. Poor Angus slaves away at *Scotch Bonnet*, and threatened to sell her tonight, he gets so tired trying to get so much done over the weekends.

---

* An administrative cadre.

Probably some of our letters have gone down recently as a plane loaded with mail crashed at Prestwick, Scotland, and five chaps were killed, poor things. But we got a letter from you dated March 2 and were delighted you had a good leave in Bari.

Mr. Walton brought over a funny clipping about "mascot" Bunje Farley Frank William Angus McGill Mowat and his exploits. Since then three other people have sent the same clipping from the *New York Times*.

By the way, there's a new Victory Bond on sale and I have $200 of yours saved, so I'll get you a bond, which will make twelve hundred all told. Can't get rich only saving $50 a month. Increase it to $100. You are only wasting it now and it will be so nice to have after the war.

I'm going to stop now and listen to the opera on the radio. You are so good to write to us so often and you don't know what it means to us, but maybe you do.

[Ortona]

Mar 15

Dear Parents:

As usual I spoke too soon. My promotion has been vetoed by Corps with the comment that "this officer cannot be promoted except while with his unit," to which the Brig, who was really annoyed, said "Balls!" and forthwith returned said recommendation to Div with red ink comments that are certain to ensure my remaining a subaltern for the rest of my natural days.

To ease the pain the Brig, who is a good guy, detailed me to go to a dance that night. Yup. A dance, no less, attended by a posse of nurses from a Canadian hospital and held at the mess of the Saskatchewan Light Infantry – our divisional machine-gun and heavy mortar outfit. Lest you assume from such lurid stories of revels and high celebration that the war is over, let me be the first to disillusion you. We are merely becoming so inured to it (it says here) that we think nothing of having tea dances a couple of miles behind the lines listening the nonce, but with aplomb, for the whistle of incoming eighty-eights over the dulcet tones of the orchestra.

Anyhoo, the dance was a great success though I didn't dance much. Majors and above seemed to have a stranglehold on the supply of nurses. *But*, s'welp me, I found myself in company with most of the Saskatoon of my school days. Do you recall Norm Cramm, Potter Chamney or Bill Shaw? About the only one of my old gang not present was Bruce Billings. An amazing coincidence, and a hell of a party. It sure got me thinking about other times, other places, and much to my surprise I have since written another chapter about Mutt in Saskatoon.

My posting to Bde ends soon, and I wonder what comes next. To be honest, I don't think I could handle being back in combat for very long, so I don't really want to go back to the Regiment, much as I love it. Well, we shall see.

The Tedeschi on our front (which remains "static") are now using Alsatian dogs as anti-patrol patrols. They are trained to wander around behind their own barbed wire and yell like mad if they meet any strangers in the dark. But Tedeschi did not reckon with Canadian ingenuity. We've just received a memo from Div Intelligence which reads, in part, "This HQ has procured Bitches, In Heat, 3 of. Subunits are requested to submit indents for these without delay as the period of maximum efficiency of these animals is only from 3 to 7 days."

At first there was some doubt as to what use these animals were to be put to, and some of the units took it as a downright insult. The situation was clarified by another memo explaining that Bitches, In Heat, were to be tied up in advantageous places for the purpose of persuading enemy dogs to desert. The intention being to take them prisoner, presumably to be interrogated by Div Intelligence. Makes you wonder, don't it? Too bad Prang missed out on this chance to serve his/her liberators.

Have you found the perfect mate for me yet? Apart from Doug Reid and Andy Lawrie (who is at sea and can't help himself), I am about the only batch left in my circle of pre-war pals. It's probably a good thing. The messy marital mix-ups that emerge as one censors the mail of one's men is enough to make marriage look pretty bleak.

Anyway I shouldn't sound so high-and-mighty. I'd probably be married too, if I'd ever been asked.

[Ortona]

March 22

Dear *Major* Mowat:

I presume from your last letter, Pop, that I no longer need call you "sir" and spring stiffly to attention should I meet you on the corner of Yonge and Bloor. I don't think it'll last. Within a month you'll be trying to get into the Home Guard or any other khaki-clad outfit that'll have you. You in civilian garb? While there is a war on? Oh, come off it! Meantime, you remain *Major* Mowat to me.

Have just heard from Luke Reid's wife, and he has written to her from a POW camp in Germany. That makes me feel much better. For months I held out against the official verdict of "missing in action, presumed dead" and wrote to his wife saying I felt sure he was alive. But as time went on I began to worry because his wife believed me, and what if Records was right? But it was a good gamble and I'm glad I took it.

During the present lull, I've got out all my poems and read and worked on them some. All means the last half dozen. The rest were lost in Sicily. Anyway I told you several times they were only rough drafts, and Gawd, how right I was. I've done new versions, but they aren't any better. Stereotyped and inane. But it is good mental discipline working on them, and that's increasingly badly needed. We seem to be stranded between hell and high water. The war is stalled, but people go on getting blown to bloody bits, and more and more the news from Canada makes us wonder whether the people at home, except those with relatives and friends overseas, give a good goddamn about us or what we are doing.

What are you going to do without your m/c, Major? I read that jeeps are now being sold to American civilians and strongly recommend you try and wrangle one across the border. The cost is $900 and I'll pay two-thirds of it. You'll find it worth the money. I am in love with mine, which goes by the name of Lulu Belle and is driven and cosseted by another little squirt of about my own size called Benny

Bennett. A jeep makes being an LO almost tolerable. Absolutely amazing where the things will go. We drive them without windshields, of course, and it's a bit like riding a bucking bronco.

Last night we had some sporadic shelling, and I reacted automatically by rolling into my slit trench, shooting down to the foot of my sleeping bag and pulling the mouth of it in after me. Simultaneously a very large mouse (small rat?) which had been having an orgy on and in the last food parcel you sent me also dived into the slit trench. Finished portrait. Me and mouse/rat huddled together in the bag, jibbering at each other as the shells went "wump – wump – wump." Shelling over, we both emerged. I went back to sleep and he/she went back at his/her orgy. No hard feelings.

Of Mice and Men, Adriatic Version.

The staff captain is getting fed up with the brigadier's attempts to turn me into a captain. So far, my documents have made three trips to Division, four to the unit, two to Corps, and each time back to Brigade for further "emendation and clarification." They are now back at Div and I await their return with a certain cynical resignation. All that paper work must surely be interfering with the war effort.

[Ortona]

March 25

Mes Amis:

Last night was quite the night. My captaincy came back so Doc sewed my third pips back on my shoulder straps and the staff captain (who takes all the credit) insisted I buy drinks for the mess, twice around, once for each new pip. Then I got in a crap game and lost fifty bucks (sorry, Maman). Then I wrote a poem. Then I forgot the password while trying to find the latrine at Hasty P HQ (whither I had gone to continue the celebration) and like to have got shot. I'm not sure if being a captain is worth the wear and tear. But you *do* demand details.

Of more interest was a recent visit with the Desert Air Force, the RAF wing which supported 8th Army in North Africa. It still proudly clings to its old name, still does its old job, still flies the same old planes – namely Kittyhawks and Tomahawks, obsolete U.S. fighters converted for dive bombing and ground strafing in close support of front-line troops. Stripped of their pilot armour and everything else that isn't absolutely essential to flight, they can carry a 250-pound bomb under each wing and a third under the belly, together with a bunch of machine guns or 20 mm cannon.

The pilots (some Limeys, some Anzacs, some Canadians) fly close support, and I mean *close*. An ALO (the job I trained for and didn't get) travelling with the lead infantry companies, or tank squadrons, directs the planes by radio onto targets as close as a hundred yards ahead of our forward troops. Great stuff.

Great guys too, and definitely *our* kind of pigeons. A few weeks ago three of them appeared at Brigade HQ and explained that they wanted to get to know us better, and could they hang around for a couple of days and maybe go out on some patrols? The boss put me in charge of them and we gave them a hell of a good party, hoping they'd forget the patrol-biz. But no, when they sobered up they still wanted to go. So I arranged it with Bert Kennedy who, along with everyone else, figured they were out of their minds. They eventually went out with a Hasty fighting patrol (on a suitably quiet night) and got to fire their borrowed Sten guns and throw a couple of grenades and came back as happy as clams.

That wasn't the end of it. Ten days ago, the BM gets an invite from their squadron leader to send three bods on a reciprocal visit. The BM fingered me and two platoon commanders. I commandeered a 15-cwt truck and off we went.

It turned out that this was one lot of fly boys who weren't living in the lap of luxury. Their "strip" was a length of sandy beach, surfaced with heavy wire mesh, north of Termoli. Everything and everybody was under canvas in an adjacent olive grove, which the endless rains had turned into a worse quagmire than we had at the front. I've seldom seen such a cheerless setting, but inside the tents, with the rain thrumming against them, life was lived to the full. Lots of good stuff to eat and drink and a roistering lot of chappies telling tales, singing and generally raising hell.

The only problem was the weather. There was nothing to be done outside and, of course, no flying. After a couple of days of this, the squadron leader (a twenty-three-year-old veteran of the Battle of Britain) began to get apologetic. What would we *like* to do? he wanted to know. Maybe a trip into Termoli would be the ticket? My two foot-slogger companions thought that would be dandy but I had to be different. *Had* to be? Sure and I'm a Mowat, after all.

I said that I had, with great difficulty and effort, arranged for the visiting pilots to be taken out on patrol. So it seemed only fair that the squadron should arrange to take me out on one. I was only playing games, but it turned out I was playing with the wrong character. The SL gave me a shrewd look, raised his glass and said: "Good enough, Canada. I'll take you up myself tomorrow morning . . . on the Dawn Patrol."

I didn't believe him, but I should have. His ground crew went to work on a Tomahawk, took out the radio and made enough room behind the pilot's seat (these are single-seater aircraft) to squeeze in one small infanteer. I was roused out of a hung-over sleep early next morning, dragged through the mess for a hurried cup of coffee, then to the ready tent where I was accoutred with flying gear. Gradually becoming aware that this was not in jest, I remembered to ask for a parachute. "Sorry, chummy," said the flight sergeant who was dressing me. "No room for you *and* a parachute."

The rest was anti-climax. The ceiling was down to about two hundred feet and, once airborne, there was nothing to be seen. I couldn't have seen it anyway. Tucked away behind the pilot, I was able to look only upward. Nothing to see *there*. Besides I was too busy. Thank God the flight sergeant had remembered to give me a vast brown paper bag. I spent most of the time we were aloft trying to fill it up. That squadron leader was some aerobatic pilot, I can tell you.

There have been times in the past when I regretted not having joined the air force. Not any more.

Things remain quiet around here. Gets now that we three LOs bicker about who's going to be the lucky one to make the runs to the battalions. But my tour at Brigade is almost up and I rather expect to be going back to the regiment since there is no other opening available for me here. HQ jobs are too often filled from behind, which is to say by non-combat officers. As if Poppa didn't know that! For the hell of it I made an informal survey of the origins of the officers at a certain senior HQ. Six out of eighteen had been in action.

[Ortona]

April 1

Dear Squib and Consort:

The Mayor's typewriter is ribbonless tonight so you'll have to put up with my hieroglyphs.

Drafted the last chapter of the Mutt book last week, so now I can be rid of the damn thing. I'll send it back by surface package and if it doesn't make it past the U-boats, no great loss. It has served its purpose by helping me get a grip on myself.

I'm going to lay off writing poetry. The stuff is getting so damned morose that it gives even me the creeps. I enclose an example to show what I mean.

Had dinner with Stan Ketcheson down at the regiment last night. He now has Dog Company. And I found it rather fun being a captain, and senior to all his subalterns in rank and service both, calling their boss by his first name even though he is a major, and drinking his whisky while they swilled *vino*. Must be the latent snob in me! Stan is much subdued since his latest return from hospital and now ducks like a sensible person when he hears that "wheeeeeeee-oooooo . . . CRUMP."

The visit did me little good. I realized that I can't stand up to the fear and wouldn't last long back at the unit. I really wish to God I was to hell and gone out of this war and back t'hame.

Talking of the usual subjects in the mess the other night and, says the padre, outraged by such a dinnertime topic: "Well, *I* never had V.D. and truly hope I never get it again." Slip of the tongue, but it nearly brought down the house, something three months of shelling by both sides has so far failed to do.

We have a genius here who *triple* distils *vino*. The result is known as "steam." Some people drink it. The MO uses it as fuel in his alky sterilizer lamp. We also have an officer who claims to be half Mohawk.

He likes the stuff, so naturally we now call him CNR . . . because he's a steam injun. Yes. Well.

Things remain relatively peaceful except for "vigorous patrol actions." I went out on one a few nights ago, not out of boredom but because I was *ordered* to go. No man's land on a stormy night with lots of mortar fire and tracer whispering overhead is no longer my idea of a cup of tea. If it ever was.

Jerry has not forgotten us. I had been sleeping very soundly these past weeks since we came into town, having found myself a billet in a stone building that is built like a medieval fortress. But yesterday he began sending over 17 cm shells. One came right through the building next door, top-to-bottom, four storeys of it, and exploded in the cellars where it turned Benny's jeep (which was garaged there) into the proverbial colander. Benny doesn't care. Now we have a brand *new* Lulu Belle, Mark II.

No mail for anyone for several weeks. Has Mr. You-know-which-bastard given up on his much-publicized pledge to keep us in touch with home and loved ones? Don't bother to answer that. Kind of blue tonight. And *mad*. I'll have to start sleeping with one ear cocked again.

For Alex Campbell. Killed Christmas Day, 1944, Ortona

Who calls his name across those lonely fields
hears no voice answer for his lips are sealed
against the empty chambers of a mind
where, once, a poet's voice was wont to find
expression for its pangs and fleeting raptures.
Finds nothing now. Nor will again recapture
the beauty seen by eyes or heard by ears,
through the forgotten – and the unlived years.

Who calls to him waits endlessly in vain,
through the chill threnody of wind and rain.
Straining towards the dark, he only hears
the gentle echo of his own heart's tears.

And the shrill, mocking night alone intrudes
on the eternal vastness of his solitude.

April 11

Dear Squib. –

Had a hard week working on the old *Bonnet*, the hardest part being the cabin paint. Burn, rough-scrape, fine-scrape with a cabinet scraper and then sand. All in a cloud of fine carbon. But, by God, she'll be in good condition for you when you want her.

I enclose a clipping about a breach of promise suit against one Elmer Mott. But no, the *Globe and Mail* did not spell the name wrong, and it is not our Elmer. He is really the merriest and lovingest little dog I've ever been shipmates with. He has taught himself to climb the ladder up to *Bonnet*'s deck. She is sitting in her cradle, on a slipway car, and so her deck is pretty high up. The feat is enhanced by the fact that the bottom rung of the ladder is missing and he has to jump for the second one. The fore deck makes a good vantage point from which to survey the dog world. When I am working down in the cabin and hear shouts of amazement from bystanders, I know that Elmer is coming aboard. Getting down is more of a problem. He has solved it by climbing on my back and clinging with his paws around my neck as I descend. This wins him further cheers from the onlookers. It will be a different story when *Bonnet* is afloat. The poor little tyke hates it then because it makes him squeamish.

April 22

Today is the anniversary of the Battle of Ypres, you young veteran, and this is the second letter I've written you this week, and the ninety-fourth since the worst day of my life when you boarded that troop train in Camp Borden headed for Halifax.

People have been sending us a clipping from, of all things, the *New York Times*, written by a Yankee correspondent in Italy. "The mascot of an officers' mess nearby is a youthful Captain who rejoices in the name of Bunje William Frank Farley Oliver Angus McGill Mowat. He is generally known as Squib. Squib, who is exceedingly short" (of grey matter, I may add) "earned local renown during the Sicilian invasion. He stepped off a landing craft leading his troops and shouting 'Follow me!' and promptly disappeared, except for a hand clutching a pistol rippling along the surface."

Now who was drinking "steam" when *that* interview was given? And isn't that going to look swell in the scrapbook of the Hasty P? I'm not as shocked as your mother was. She takes war seriously. But I'll say this to you, and I won't say it again. Remember Laughlin Hughes, and Titus Evans and Harry Boak and Charlie Ackerman and a thousand others I can remember and you never met, and don't drink so damn much, because it can get to be a habit. Try to pattern yourself after your admired great-uncle Frank Farley, whose first name you have apparently now added to your own – along with several others. Frank drinks, and always has, *but only when somebody else pays for it.* Result? At eighty he is still a good figure of a man, and not a pitiable old wreck of a souse. He is also richer. Hope you don't mind me saying this, but drink does grow most insidiously.

It is terribly hard for the lads, still few in number, who are returning now, and will be hard for all those who will, God willing, come home later. They come into an atmosphere of civilian self-interest that they simply cannot understand. Even people who you might think were firmly re-established suffer this dislocation. I had dinner with Alex Bradshaw and family last week. He's been home and out of the army for three months and is now general manager of a big factory, but finds the attitudes of Civvy Street almost impossible to live with, which makes *him* almost impossible to live with. You just can't expect people who have lived for years one-for-all and all-for-one to easily adjust to living in a society based on all-for-me.

The official rehabilitation program is being run by people who have never been through what the veterans have been through. They are earnest and honest and do their best, but they can't bridge the gap in comprehension. They think, for instance (and it is a specific instance), that a man of thirty-six who has been four years overseas and who never got his senior matric because he grew up in the Depression is just crazy because he wants to start in Grade 11 and go through for a civil engineer so he can help reconstruct the wreckage of this war. They try to talk him into grabbing a high-pay job in munitions work so he can start making a fortune like so many of those who have stayed behind have already done. A man who's given four years of his life to a cause he believed (and was told often enough) was just, honest and unselfish doesn't understand that kind of attitude. How could he?

[Kingston]

May 1

Dear William Frank Farley Oliver Angus McGill,–

Since you no longer seem to know exactly who you are, I've been wondering if I could get you brought back here on compassionate grounds. Winston Hyke was brought back from a nice, comfy staff job in England to help his father with the funeral business, so why not you to serve as able seaman on *Scotch Bonnet*?

While taking my evening stroll (yes, dear boy, you may use two "ls" in stroll), I ran into a discussion about bird migration among some of the experts in the yacht club. It was dandy. They got the birds, and the lemmings, and the lost continent of Atlantis so mixed up I didn't know what they were talking about. Neither did they. It would have driven you nuts, but I felt that this was one bird discussion that was being carried out right down at my level. I told them about owls migrating backward in Saskatchewan, but that didn't seem to clear their minds any. They got talking about a bald eagle that got married for life and was widowed and spent the next twenty years mourning his lost wife up on top of a dead pine in Squirrel Lake. I tried to pin them down as to the precise evidence of mourning, and they said it was the way he looked at you. Very sadly. And I said, maybe he had worms, and they got quite indignant.

I've got my Efficiency Decoration. It came the day I left the service, which might tell me something, if I cared to listen. And I ran into your old Camp Borden pal Jerry Austin, sent home with a broken hip that won't heal. He told me a lot about you. Why the hell didn't *you* tell us that you once told General Harry Salmon that a tactical scheme he was commanding in England was all screwy? You didn't know he was a general? Oh, come now. Unless he was mother-naked, you must have been able to see his badges of rank. Or had you simply made up your mind that you wanted to stay a subaltern forever?

I am in Mufti today for the first time in four years. The old brown Harris tweed jacket, grey flannel bags and a jersey-thing with a blue necktie. I don't feel any too happy about it, but ought to be grateful (one "l") to be out of the ossified rump of the army. Denton Massey speaking in Parliament recently took Canadians to task because they are enjoying the greatest economic boom in a century, and making a carnival out of it as if the *war was a good thing*. But he got cut down to size by the rest of the politicians, and by the press.

Dan Spry sounds like a good Brig. Long may he live, to keep you on his staff.

[Ortona]

April 6

Dear Major and Missus:

Strange indeed are the ways of His Majesty's Canadian mail. Nobody here has had airgraphs or airmails from home in more than a month, yet yesterday I got three ordinary letters from you dated March 27, 29 and 30. What the hell goes on, do you suppose? Rocket delivery the last week of every month? That's the fastest any mail has ever come, except my call-up notices to "report yourself immediately for military duty to your nearest recruiting office" which arrive here every couple of months. Some day I'm going to do as instructed, and then won't they be embarrassed?

Bert Kennedy had a stroke of bad luck yesterday and set off an "S" mine but was not seriously wounded. However I doubt if he'll come back to the Regiment from hospital. Stan Ketcheson will now become second-in-command and there is again talk of me returning but, so far, just talk. I hope it stays that way. As a captain, I'd have to go to a company and I don't really think I can hype myself up to it. Dying for King and Country has lost its lustre.

The Boss spent a recent evening reading some of my literary efforts (he ordered me to deliver said, and how could I disobey?) and then firmly telling me what was wrong with them. I did not react as an up-and-coming junior officer should, but as only the mulish Mowats may. He bawled hell out of me but then bought me a drink. Y'never know.

Only the last three inches of the Mayor's ribbon are still serviceable, which means a complicated re-wind job at the end of every second line. For God's sake (and your own) send me some ribbons, any kind, I can rewind them on the spools I have. Also I brew up chicken noodle soup on the coal oil heater in the Iron Pig when I'm on the graveyard watch and can therefore use all the dried version you can send.

Oh yes, the Iron Pig. This is a barn-like vehicle encased entirely in half-inch armoured plate, which houses the main radio and phone sets together with the signals operators and whoever happens to be duty officer at the time. Kind of a communications nerve centre and mobile command post. At the moment, it is parked in the narrow street between two badly battered buildings, and I spend many of my nights in it, and not a few of my daylight hours as well.

At the crack of dawn each day half the population of the town, mostly female, goes past my armoured door (usually left open to prevent asphyxiation) to fetch the day's water in a weird collection of receptacles ranging from ancient *vino* jugs to Jerrycans. They fill these at the sole well still functioning, about half a mile from me, then start homeward with the pots balanced on their heads. Jerry knows all about this routine and seems to take a fiendish pleasure in dropping a shell aimed at the well head about every ten minutes. This sends everyone diving for shelter and the streets get a damn good washing. The other day, one of the ten-minute explosions caught a gnarled old gal with a jug on her head abeam of the Iron Pig. Old lady *and* jug both came through my door. Unlike you, *mon père*, I don't enjoy early morning baths. Or the Tedeschi sense of humour. I watched one little old pappy guy make three attempts to get away from the well with a battered tin pail and end up three times full length in the gutter with an empty bucket and his ears ringing more than somewhat. I don't figure he found it very funny.

❖ ❖ ❖

ONE OF THE PIECES I SHOWED THE BRIGADIER WAS THIS SLIGHTLY fictionalized account of an actual incident in my life as a liaison officer. He seemed to approve of it, but warned me that it would be a military offence to try and have it published, or even to send it home, as long as the war continued. I was sufficiently intimidated to bury it in my kitbag. Here it remained until late in 1944, by which time I had lost most of my remaining respect for army dicta. I resurrected and re-wrote it and sent it home to Angus. Its subsequent fate is described later in this book.

❖ ❖ ❖

Liaison Officer

"Duty off'c'r? Gimme the duty off'c'r."

"Yeah. Speaking."

"Oh, hello, Art. Cal here. Lookit, we're sending an LO down to you right away with the final artillery tie-up. The Brig wants him to stay at your observation post 'n give us a play-back on the show. O.K.?"

"Sure thing, fella. We'll make him right at home."

I was the Liaison Officer chosen for the job. My driver had just come up from a line regiment and had the most extraordinarily fluid ideas about time and space. Reduce both to a minimum as fast as possible. I guess he came by his ideas honestly. Driving a jeep in one of the fighting regiments is no sinecure. He took me over the valley road and down the sloping stretch we called "the shooting gallery" – under enemy observation – so fast that the patient Jerry artillery spotter on the far hill hadn't time to get a single shot away. Or maybe he wasn't looking. We got to battalion headquarters in record time and I told the driver to find an unoccupied slit trench and place himself in it before 0730 hours. That was zero. The assault battalion's commanding officer seemed glad to see me and after I had given him the revised trace of the barrage lines, I explained to him my other mission, that of commentator at his ball game. He didn't exactly snarl at that but he didn't like it.

The observation post was in an isolated, shell-battered, stone farmhouse on a hill overlooking a flat, featureless plain dominated by Tolo Ridge, where the Germans were dug in. Normally nobody used the house any more because it was the most obvious building on our front and Jerry couldn't bear to see it still standing. He was always anxious to do something about that. But it was the only place the battalion CO could find to direct the show from.

"Hallo . . . Hallo, Cal . . . Shorty talkin' . . . Yeah, I made it. I'll call every five minutes after the show starts if the lines don't go out . . . ought to be able to see it all from here. Oh, say, gimme a time-check!"

"O.K., boy . . . Fourteen minutes to go. When you hear the long note on the . . . "

"Nerts!"

In a ravine just back of us, six Sherman tanks began revving their engines and turning their turrets slowly from side to side, as if offering slow dissent to the query, "All set?" We couldn't see the infantry. They were up ahead in a series of gullies, lying doggo till the smoke-screen and the barrage went in.

Things were crowded in the OP. There were three artillery officers and their signalmen to direct the fire of the guns; a couple of reps from the heavy mortars; a couple more on tank wireless sets; and three or four signallers on field phones. Plus the CO and his IO. The CO looked like he might have enjoyed a good fidget. He kept coming and going from the second floor, where the window was, cracking jokes but keeping a close eye on his watch.

"Hi-ya, Shorty here!"

"Yeah, I'm listening."

"Cal, barrage has started. The smoke's coming down right on the line. Tanks moving off now . . . hold it . . . the goddamn smoke's too far over . . . boss thinks it'll blind the tanks . . . gonna cancel it, I think . . . no, wait a sec . . . O.K., wind's shifting."

The lead Sherman made good time up the road. There weren't any mines. A pioneer patrol out last night had swept right up to the forward edge of the Jerry positions. The dust from the barrage was blending with the thick, pillaring wall of smoke. The sound of bursting shells made a blurred, continuous thumping. The tanks seemed to move through it without noise, like toys being pulled on a string. The uneven but continuous curtain of the barrage was beginning to grow ragged now. But it wasn't our guns, it was the SOS – shoot on sight – of the enemy artillery sending shells through the smoke hoping to catch and shatter the attackers.

In the gullies, the two companies of infantry waited. They must have watched that appalling upheaval of ground and sky with horror.

"Hello, Cal. One troop of tanks has reached BLOCO. Another troop's coming up. Smoke's thinned out. Hell of a lot of defensive fire coming back . . . mostly mortar, but heavy as hell! Infantry still lying doggo . . . hang on . . . report from tanks . . . one's gone up on a Teller mine just off the track."

The sergeant hit his head on the turret top and started cursing at the top of his voice. Three mortar bombs crumped savagely in front of the Sherman and they felt her shudder. The sergeant couldn't make the driver answer, and when he bent over him he saw blood. The gunner was snarling like a cat and working frantically at the hand rotating gear. The tank was suddenly very silent, then against its lifeless sides came the thudding of machine-gun bullets. "That was no mine. Musta been a bazooka," the sergeant thought. "Christ . . . only way it coulda got Smitty. The hell with it, we still got shells and the bastard can't hit us twice. We'll stick! We'll stick!" He was yelling into the microphone now and the sound of the troop leader's answer was like a radio turned on loud in a small room, "Roger One – O.K. – out." The concussion as the tank's 75 was fired brought the sergeant round like a whip. "Goddamn! Goddamn!" he screamed at the gunner. "Who the hell told you to fire!"

The loader slapped another shell into the smoking breech.

People were running up and down the stairs of the OP like headless chickens, and the CO was yelling at them to get the hell out of the way. All the sets were crackling steadily and the hubbub was like a busy morning on the stock exchange – only, the words were different.

"Cal . . . only one tank left on the right . . . two on the left . . . they're getting it from some eighty-eights."

In the gulley, the infantry still waited for the word to go. Enemy mortar bombs were bursting all around them now, searching, searching. The company commander was wriggling as if he had suddenly found himself lying on a nest of driver ants . . . thinking . . . "Christ, why don't the tanks get on with it . . . this fire's just bloody awful . . . why *don't* they get on with it!"

The troop commander had the tank hatch open and his head out. Fifty yards ahead, seven Germans were running madly up the slope through the twisted props of a vineyard. A burst from the Browning caught them midway in their rush and they went down. You couldn't tell how many were hit, but they disappeared fast. There was a wet spot here and for a moment the tank bogged, then she pulled out with a deep, stubborn roar and clambered quickly up the slope onto the objective. All the time the gunner was pulling at the lieutenant's leg, trying to get him to draw his head in.

But it was a good thing he had it out. He saw the anti-tank gun as the grey-clad gunners were lifting the tail to swing it, and a round of his HE caught it squarely on the shield. Now the troop leader was shouting and singing like a kid at a ball game. All round him were slit trenches full of Germans desperately anxious to go away, and not daring to try. A low, stone farmhouse a hundred yards to the left of the tank was chattering hysterically as its defenders sent impotent streams of machine-gun bullets bouncing sharply off the armour.

The tank put a round of AP through the wall, then three of HE into the hole. The house shot up and collapsed into dusty silence. There were no shells falling near the tank, and its commander heard the gibbering scream of a man quite plainly over the roar of the motor as the big, rubber-shod tracks crushed his legs.

"Remaining tank on objective and having a field day . . . got one anti-tank gun and God knows how many Jerries . . . running up and down like a street car . . . reports a Jerry tank across the next gulley . . . our tanks on the left all bogged down or knocked out, but two are within a hundred yards of objective and still engaging targets. The CO has just ordered the infantry to get moving but the defensive fire's getting hotter. The artillery reps have been plastering Jerry's gun positions with murder concentrations for half an hour, but it doesn't seem to bother their mortars."

One section of infantry started across an open stretch at the double, all bunched up, and was straddled by four mortar shells . . . ! The rest of the platoon passed through them and only one man looked. "The bastards! The bastards! Those stinking, rotten bastards!" he thought, and a bullet took him just below the left arm, punching up through his neck. The fire grew heavier as the whole enemy front began concentrating on the naked infantry, whom they could now clearly see. Overhead, shells from our twenty-five pounders and mediums kept up a continuous overtone of whines and whistles that blended into one throbbing flight of terrible wings. The attacking infantry could see no enemy. But a corporal let go a burst from his tommy gun into the air. For a moment it made all the men around him feel good. Then suddenly they were going back, running, stumbling, crawling, running.

In the ravine, their company commander clapped on the earphones and spoke to the CO. "We'll try again, sir! We'll try it again, sir!" he said. He was almost crying with rage. The remnants of his company huddled under the lip of the gulley, breathing very fast and shallow, not looking at each other.

Up on the hill the troop commander pulled in his head and banged-to the hatch cover as an AP round from a Mk. IV tank slammed viciously into the ground beside him and spun screaming up into the air again. The Sherman stopped with a jolt that rocked its thirty tons forward on the drive sprockets, and its 75 cracked twice in quick succession. The Mk. IV began to smoke and its turret hung half off. A man got out of it holding his belly and ran zig-zag down into a gulley. The Sherman's loader grabbed the lieutenant's legs and pointed to the ammunition rack. There were three shells left. The commander stuck his head out again and looked quickly back down the slope behind him but could see none of our infantry.

The Brownings started up.

"Cal, 'C' Company's been beaten back . . . can't get through the mortar fire . . . deadly . . . never saw anything as bad as this . . . tank on the objective almost out of ammo . . . claims a Mk. IV destroyed . . . 'D' Company going in on the left but they won't get there . . . maybe they will . . . here's a lull."

One of the Polish privates in the weapon pit looked fleetingly over the parapet towards his German corporal in the next hole. The Nazi's teeth were bared and he was screaming at the two Poles. Their heads down again, they said nothing, just looked at each other dully, and one of them put up a hand to where the MG 34 sat on its fixed mount and pulled the trigger. He fired a good long burst without putting his head out to see if there was any target. He was sick anyway and did not care what they might do to him. He was think-ing, "Tonight I'll desert across the line. Tonight when it is quiet I shall go across the line. When it is quiet." A hundred-pound shell lit with a protesting grunt in the mud behind him. It did not burst and the Polish private did not even notice it. "Tonight, when it is quiet." The next shell was not defective.

The commanding officer stood at the window and there were things in his face that it is not good to see. The smell of phosphorous fumes and of burnt explosives was drifting back so thickly that at times it was hard to breathe. The noise was less, though, and the babble of the wireless sets could be plainly heard downstairs.

Back in the gulley, one or two men were smoking as they sat below the crest, almost oblivious now to the stray mortar bombs that lit near them. Most of the wounded were already on their way to the regimental aid post in the deep ravine. The lieutenant in command of this little group sat by the radio set with his hand held out in front of him. He seemed fascinated by the way it was shaking and he tried all sorts of ways to stop it. Interesting.

"It's over, Cal. Both remaining tanks are back and the CO has called it off. Planes? Thank God! When're they due? No . . . can't give you much on casualties . . . yet . . . but there's four tanks knocked out . . ."

Men looked up quickly when they heard the nasal hum of the planes. Some smiled. One stood up to watch and the lieutenant followed suit. He said quietly, "Give 'em hell! Give 'em bloody hell!"

Like a play that has run overtime, the great noise of battle ceased. It did not fade; it stopped. The fighter-bombers, lazily cruising over the enemy's back areas now, peeled off and came swooping down with the little black shapes of the bombs running parallel to them before falling off in a sharper curve, as if loath to leave their parents.

I honked on the jeep's horn and after a moment my driver came up the slope towards me, munching a piece of pie and stuffing a pocket detective novel into his blouse. "Pretty hot, eh?" he said as we started. "Yeah," I answered, "hot," and we rolled noisily over the bridge.

[Ortona]

April 10

Dear Homebodies:

Frankie Hammond who commands Support Company at the unit came in last night and we sat drinking two bottles of Canadian beer (that's our combined ration for the month, and you can tell anybody in Canada who complains about only getting two *dozen* bottles that they can go suck lemons) and a long-hoarded bottle of rye. He is one of the few surviving buddies I have in this man's army. Lord knows, you make plenty of acquaintances with whom you bandy wisecracks and guzzle *vino* but as time goes on you can't seem to invest the emotions needed to make enduring friendships. You need psychic (sp?) energy to keep an intimacy alive and flourishing, and I don't have much of that left.

We got to discussing the usual thing that we never get anywhere with – namely what the hell are we going to do with ourselves when we get home. We made some pretty futile efforts to assess the changes that have taken place in the way we look at life, and then tried to visualize the adjustments we will inevitably have to make if we are to fit in. And concluded that it couldn't be done. No matter how objective one tries to be about such things, we just can't get distant enough from the storm to see our own "wake," so how the hell can we chart a course to steer? It's like being immersed in a fog so thick you can't see, or feel, or smell anything beyond the here-and-now. "Live, laugh and be merry (if you can) for tomorrow etc." There's no reality either behind you or in front.

We concluded that one thing is certain: any guy who goes home with any expectation of returning to the past is in for the hell of a shock. The ground he used to stand on was in fact a sandbar. It ain't there any more, and the waters over it are deep and cold. We're tough buggers, and we can cope with material changes, but the other side of it looks like being more than we can handle. Truth is, we don't know you any more – you Canadians. And we don't know ourselves. The upshot is that we are so baffled we have little interest in the future. Today is everything.

Even the antidotes to war we cherished so hard and for so long are losing their power to keep us interested in what may come. Drowned, I guess you could say, in a lassitude of spirit. Cruising the world in *Scotch Bonnet*? Building a log cabin on Vancouver Island? All fading out, like dissolving dreams.

Sorry. I shouldn't go on this way. It's likely just the effects of a hangover and will be gone tomorrow. Meantime, don't chew me out for my growing inability to be coherent.

My kitbag, lost for a couple of months and supposedly destroyed, has finally caught up with me again, and I dug out the accumulated letters from the last six months that have been lying crumpled and forgotten in the bottom of it. Read 'em over and decided that some years from now I might get a kick out of them. So they are on their way to you for safe keeping. Read 'em if you want, but Mother may throw a few fits over some of the ones from strange ladies. Threw a few fits over some of them myself.

Spent most of a day and night with a couple of Yank war correspondents a few days back. My job was to show them around etc. Finished with a damn good party at Hasty P HQ. One is the son of the owner of the *New York Times*, and the other a feature writer for United Press. I think I gave them what they wanted, and maybe more. I expect several libellous stories to appear as a result.

Do see, can you find me a bird guide to this heathen country. I am beginning to take note of the odd feathered beast, which is a far cry from a few months back when a bird was just another shell whistling overhead.

Since you are showing appreciation of my shorter verse, I herewith favour you with some more. This stuff is written to amuse the members of the mess . . . who are easily amused.

Nothing Straight About Them

The Earthworm is bisexual.
He's he, but also she.
Though this may *seem* a happy state
It's not quite trouble-free.

For one end is the female end,
The other is the male,
And so the Earthworm seldom knows
Just where to find its tail.

Phlebitus

I think that I shall never see
A poem lively as a Flea.
A Flea who may in winter lair
In my red-flannel underwear.
And who in summertime will bear
Her myriad offspring in my hair.
A Flea whose little claws are pressed
Against my love's sweet swelling breasts
(Which so distracts us from our match
That we, perforce, must stop and scratch).

Poems are made by fools like me.
But who in hell produced the Flea?

The Goose Is a Goose

Some think the goose a wily bird.
Myself, I find this claim absurd.
If it's so clever, tell me why
A goose in hunting time won't fly
To some place far from shot and shell?

I think the goose is dumb as hell!

Unmolested

The shy and self-effacing Mole
Is happiest when in a hole.

Moles seldom to the surface come.
They aren't so dumb!

[Ortona]

April 16

Today, with a smug smirk on my mug, I got two letters addressed to *Captain* F. M. Mowat. It can only be a matter of weeks before Doc is sewing crowns on my epaulets, then crossed batons. The hell of it is that when I get to be a field marshal I'll be in a rut – no place to go.

The war continues its plodding pace. No battles, but the slow and steady attrition of mines, shells, patrols, sickness and etc. However, the weather, thank the Lord, is improving. Almost reminds me of spring. The Brig says he will try and keep me on here although my tour was up a few weeks back. Hope he is successful.

Today I got a bellyful of the *Herrenvolk*. Helped the brigade IO go through a pile of papers taken from Jerry dead, and POWs' pockets. I'm hardly what you'd call a prude, but this was filthy stuff – decadent, degenerate and sadistic. The IO said the owners were animals but I said, no, they were human. I wouldn't link them with any wild beast – it would be libel on the beasts.

I've now had a dozen books from you two, for which thanks a million. But no news of any boxes of books getting through to the regiment. You tried, Pop, but what can one little major do against the blobs in Ottawa?

The View from
Monte Cassino

❖ ❖ ❖

By mid January 1944, the U.S. 5th Army on the west coast
and the 8th Army in the centre and on the east coast were both well
and truly mired. The Germans were tenaciously and successfully
defending a well-prepared line stretching across the Italian peninsula
from just north of Ortona to the Gulf of Gaeta on the Tyrrhenian
Sea. On January 22, in an effort to break the impasse, 5th Army
launched a seaborne assault well behind the enemy defence line
near Anzio. The landings were successful but all subsequent
attempts to break out of the beachhead were contained. Now
indeed the war in Italy was stalemated. It was to remain so until
spring was far advanced.

Spring came late to the Adriatic sector, but during the first
weeks of April the fabled Italian sun began to regain its rightful
place and the seas of saffron mud began to solidify. Olive trees put
out their first silvered leaves, and shell-shattered vineyards began to
cover their scars with new growth.

In the line in front of Ortona, men of First Brigade emerged
from ruined casas to warm themselves in flesh and in spirit. We were
still at battle stations, as we had been almost without respite for close
to five months.

Towards the end of April, First Division was finally pulled out of
the line. Long convoys began to roll south-westward until we found
ourselves back at Canada Town – Campobasso. The individual units
dispersed, found billets in familiar villages and prepared to enjoy what
we believed would be a substantial period of peace and relaxation.

It was not to be. We were already committed to a new battlefield.

The Allied command had devised what it believed to be a sure-fire plan to bring the war in Italy to a rapid conclusion.

After less than a week in the green and quiet valleys about Campobasso, we were loaded back on trucks and driven south to the Foggia plains. Here we rendezvoused with a tank brigade to begin intensive tank/infantry training. It was now obvious that we were to be allowed no proper rest – only time to prepare for a new battle. Although we were not yet privy to what the generals had in store for us, we knew 8th Army had come to regard us as shock troops, so whatever new assault was in the making would find us in the vanguard.

On May 5 we moved again, this time into the western foothills of the Apennines, an hour's drive from Naples, there to spend a frantic week practising river crossings. It was here we learned what lay ahead.

The linchpin in the German defence line was a formidable complex of positions blocking the mouth of the Liri River valley which offered a broad and level passage through the mountain barriers to Rome. The core of these defences was believed by the enemy to be so nearly impregnable that it could safely be named the Adolf Hitler Line. The entire complex was anchored on the east and overlooked by a towering mountain crowned by a Benedictine abbey. This was Monte Cassino.

The plan was for 8th Army to smash the linchpin, unbar the gate and open the road to Rome. The attack would be made in three stages. The Free Polish Corps would first take Monte Cassino. Then 13th British Corps would fight its way through the defences masking the Hitler Line. Finally First Canadian Division would smash a hole in the line itself, through which 5th Canadian Armoured Division could pour its Sherman tanks and rumble on to Rome.

D-Day for this battle, the greatest fought in Italy and one of the greatest of the war in western Europe, was my twenty-third birthday

❖ ❖ ❖

[north of Naples]

May 1

Dear Major and Missus Mowat:

I've been a bit of a heel. In the last week, I've had several letters from you and a box of excellent books – but I haven't written to you in ten days. There were a number of reasons, one being work. I'll detail some of the others.

Firstly, I enjoyed being a captain. Besides it was profitable – my pay shot up from $5 a day to the munificent sum of seven bucks a day. But now I am a lieutenant again. To relieve your mind, the fault was neither mine nor the Brig's, nor Div's. It was the strange and malicious work of a mysterious body which designs the War Establishment. There came a new dictum from Very Far Back Down The Line which decreed that LOs could not be promoted to captain's rank any longer. Presumably the cost in wages was more than Ottawa could bear. However, I am assured the setback is only temporary. To be honest, I am not greatly dispirited. I know everybody in the brigade so well that rank does not make much difference, and I'm still getting staff pay of half-a-dollar per diem, so what the hell?

Secondly, I have just completed an employment as impresario and manager of the Haymarket Club di Campobasso. Conceived and executed by me, the said club had as memorable and as short a life as any nightclub in recent history. We had been pulled out of the line, for the first time since last autumn, and had moved to the peace and quiet of central Italy, and I felt the brigade deserved the opportunity to relax in style. The boss, that decent soul, agreed and gave me *carte blanche*. Acting on the assumption that, after five months of action, we would be at rest for at least a few weeks, I got hold of a luxurious casa in the village of Ripalimosano (which Benny and I had personally liberated in October of 1943). I installed a staff of cooks and waiters in said casa; built the longest bar in Italy; accumulated a cellar full of the rare, not-so-rare, and not-the-least-bit-rare (but potent) vintages; hired a six-piece swing band from Campobasso; and had the place decorated with enormous wall murals painted by an ex-Italian war artist named Vito and which featured bevies of buxom blondes. The whole was furnished in some luxury, including the several bedrooms.

I accomplished all this in three hectic days, at a total cost of five cases of bully beef, sixteen pairs of army boots, about ten thousand cigarettes and sundry other such trifles. A small price to pay in order to provide the Shining First Brigade with a club to do it justice.

When we discovered, on the afternoon of opening night, that the Haymarket Club would exist for only twenty-four hours, after which we would be moving elsewhere, it was like to break my heart. But we opened, and the customers in their unbounded enthusiasm quickly broke everything else, including a leg belonging to an RCR major and an arm belonging to a lowly subaltern from the attached artillery.

It was magnificent while it lasted. The bar never closed for the whole twenty-four hours. The Berkley Grill served more than five hundred *uova* – eggs to you – and numberless tureens of spaget. The bedrooms? Well, in deference to you, *maman*, we will skip that part. The casualty list from amongst the hilarious inebriates nearly equalled that from the Ortona battles. It was, in short, an epic bash.

Next day we folded our tents and crept sadly away, but I was and remain proud of myself. It may have been my greatest single contribution to the war effort. The menus and other memorabilia are being sent to you "under separate cover" as the army would have it.

So what with the move, the demotion and the Haymarket Club, I fell behind in my correspondence. *Scusi.*

To ease your minds (while remaining within the bounds of censorship), I can tell you that for the last week or so we have not been shot at with intent, and a pleasant change it is. We have, however, been engaged in intensive training exercises with tanks, which suggests that there will be exciting events in the near future.

Noted a disconcerting fact the other day. Of my several steady correspondents, only a handful live in Canada. Most are in England, either natural-born residents or Canadian migrants. What with this, and with my acquired passion for afternoon tea, it might seem that I am not caring a whole lot whether I ever see Canada again. When I say that, I of course mean the *people* of Canada, not the land itself. We have been hearing much in the controlled press (is there any other kind?) about how much we all owe to the industrial workers who, with unselfish dedication, have declined to enlist and instead are saving the world by producing so much of the wherewithal for war. When they aren't on strike for higher wages, like the Quebec aluminum workers. We feel for them. Some of us would like to feel for them with the business end of a bayonet.

I'm afraid you may find some of my letters a bit depressing but remember that they are written in the rare moments of meditation. At other times, I am my usual cheerful and carefree self.

[north of Naples]

May 8

For heaven's sake, don't buy any more Victory Bonds with my assigned pay. What with every dollar going into them, I won't have a cent available for immediate needs when I get home. As I think I've said before, I don't want to be greedy and both fight the war and pay for it, too. I'm content to do my part of the fighting. Let the home-based patriots pay for it.

And don't be a couple of silly asses about booze. You should know me well enough to realize that most of my talk about binges and besot-tedness is wishful thinking. Lord knows, I'd love to get tight as an owl for days on end. On good stuff. But you don't dare get tiddled on the local rotgut more than about once a month. You can't do it and still stand the gaff. At my ripe old age I have developed *some* common sense. It is, in fact, a rare week when I get a chance to have more than a couple of belts, and then it is usually issue rum, and I defy anyone to deny me that small pleasure. Also I am NOT repeat NOT smoking myself into an early grave. As for my sex life . . . *what* sex life? I wish to Gawd . . . So please stop worrying about my vices.

You two stinkers provided my component parts and so you ought to know that my capabilities for evil living are not likely to be any greater than either of yours. So I'll stay out of the rough if only because I've presumably inherited too much good sense to do otherwise.

During the current period of relative inaction, I've indulged in some introspection and realize, to my surprise, that I've done a lot of maturing recently. That isn't a very profound discovery, but a bit of a shock to a perennial juvenile. I find I'm a lot more tolerant, because I have to be. And lazier, and less ambitious. And I'm not prepared to submerge the pleasure-giving aspects, if any, of whatever lies ahead in an eternally receding vista of a rosy future that demands incessant labour. I figure now that the whole work ethic is a con man's trick being played on us by the same lot who stand to make a bundle from the war. On the other hand, I don't want to be a lotus eater. I like to work – at what I like to work at; bird studies maybe, or writing, but not for the money in it, or so I can die rich. I've spent much of the best (or at least the best so far) years of my life doing things I hate; living a way of life that I detest; forfeiting all the things that really pleasured me. So I'm going to live the first few years after it's over *my* way; doing what *I* want to do; even if I have to starve ten years from now in consequence. I can't make up for the years of war without some cost, and if I have to mortgage my long-term future, then so be it.

I'm sending a cable tomorrow but in case it doesn't reach you, Happy wedding anniversary, you old hosses! Wish I was there to celebrate it with you. Twenty-five years of good times, and a minimum of bickers. A good foundation for the next twenty-five.

That damn fool reporter from the *New York Times*! I spent a day with him showing him the sights and doing what I could to get us shot at, and the skunk has taken a low revenge. The rat, I ought to sue. Mascot, indeed! However, the bit about stepping off the landing craft into seven feet of water is true enough. Stan Ketcheson spilled the beans on that one, and I could hardly deny it, could I?

I'm honestly touched by the way you two lugs spend so much time and trouble on *Scotch Bonnet*, on my behalf. But, you know, she is *your* boat. Your reward after years of dreams and hard work. I'll be delighted to sail around in her with you for a while, but I am beginning to think my future is going to be in the north. The *Far* North, or, as old Stefansson used to say, "the friendly Arctic." So I want to get away from it all? Yep, that's exactly what I want.

April 22

Darling Lamb.

Two letters from you just arrived and I'm sitting right down to answer them, but Elmer is scratching at the door so I'd better take him for a walk first. Speaking of Elmer, he is the reason we can't get a place to live in Toronto. Rooms are so scarce they can ask any price, and they won't allow pets. Kay Hawley has been looking for rooms for us, but says that Elmer will have to have a stone around his neck, or else be put in a kennel, so I guess I'll stay on alone in the ship with him for a while.

Don't get blue and despondent, my lamb, over your future. Angus went through very much the same thing after his war and was ages trying to recover his health and his cheerfulness. He and I lived on about $60 a month for the first few years, with no one caring or helping. I'm sure after this war, the returned men are going to be looked after much better. Anyway, we are keeping the *Bonnet* up, and when you come on board her you'll get back all your optimism and sense of fun again. It's terribly hard for you now because there seems to be no end in sight, but it must be a tremendous comfort to you to know you've done all that a man would ever be called upon to do for his own people.

I want you to know that when I'm tempted to give way to depression, as so often I am, I think, "I'm Bunje's mother" and I try to be worthy of my son. Sorry, Bunje, forgive me for running on like this, sounds a bit like Horatio Alger stuff, but there it is.

We sent off a box yesterday with some birthday things in it, but I don't suppose it will get to you for months. I saw Louise Reid today; she always wants to know about you so I told her about you becoming a captain. "Something to tell Doug," she said. It isn't always easy to think of new things to say every week.

Angus hopes to sail the *Bonnet* to Toronto in a week or two, weather permitting. I wish we could find some strong and husky youth to help. It's too much for Angus to handle alone. He's getting on but won't admit it, and we both look years older. How about you? Are you still growing the moustache? You should see Doug Reid's handlebar. You can hardly see his face. He has gone back to England again, still flying, I think. The air force men are very lucky. When they have finished a tour of duty, they are sent back home for a long leave before getting into action again. Too bad you didn't join the air force, but then they wouldn't have you, would they?

[Toronto]

May 12

Dear Squibbles. –

I see I haven't written to you since May 1. This continual flitting about the country inspecting libraries that I am now engaged in upsets normal schedules. And I don't carry the old Remington with me. Don't even carry a suitcase because the trains are so crowded and the jams of getting on and getting off so continuous that I find the old army haversack carries enough junk for me and is a lot easier to handle. And being greatly soiled with engine oil, and ripped, and with a strap broken, it is old enough and shabby enough for me to like. On the same principle that my old clothes are my favourites.

Last Saturday I slipped down to Kingston again and rigged the *Bonnet.* Tuesday I went to a regional library meeting in Chatham. I'm getting used to the meetings but at first it was quite a shock to find myself standing up in front of a lot of earnest women, most of them looking on life in retrospect and, poor creatures, not much of a retrospect at that. Born thirty years too soon, alas. However there is always a small coterie who head thirstily for the nearest tavern after the afternoon meetings and have to suck Sen-Sens before the evening ones.

On the weekend, a letter of yours sauntered in, rubber stamped across its face with the brief, interesting statement, "Salvaged from Air Crash." It was the one in which you had concluded you weren't going to get your captaincy after all, and in which the MP's son got the ALO job at Army HQ. Well, you'll find lots of that, my young friend, all the way through the piece. And not only in the army, but in the rest of your life as well. It isn't worth gnashing your teeth about, although I've done a fair bit of gnashing about it myself from time to time.

Hell, that wasn't any veiled comment about the *Atlantic Monthly*. One of my letters must have gone astray. I wonder how many have done that. Anyway, you'll know by now that they didn't want your verse.

[Toronto]

May 15

There was a warm shower at dawn followed by a warm sun, and the soft maples and elms are positively creaking in their haste to get all their leaves unfurled. Even in Toronto, the morning walk to work is a delight, and what must it be like down the lanes around Black Crick, or Prinyer's Cove, or out on Waupoos? But I shouldn't talk like this to you.

The car is back in commission and despite the fact that even for official purposes my driving is strictly limited, I'm dying to get out on the road and be able to take Helen and Elmer with me. I've applied for enough gasoline for five thousand miles, about half my yearly peacetime working travel. I still must get the damned door fixed, where you opened it with an axe, presumably, after locking the keys inside on your embarkation leave.

I see you have been promoted to lieutenant. That's a mean break, feller. In spite of pretending that you don't care, it can't be pleasant. I had thought the army in action was run with a little more intelligence and with more fairness.

[Toronto]

May 26

I remember well one dark night, Ney and Bonaparte and I sitting around a fire discussing a bottle of *vin rouge* and spitting sausages over the coals, and Bony said, apropos of nothing, that in his opinion "the best possible defence is a vigorous offensive." So I'll begin my offensive, as a counter to the severe wigging you give me in your letter of May 8, by asking politely what the hell you mean by continuing to call me Major and addressing your letters to me by that title? Didn't I tell you that I've not only reverted to reserve status, but am listed as "retired"? Do you take me for some kind of Yankee "Colonel"?

I am "Mister" Mowat now, so get it right!

And, all right then, you *aren't* drinking too much. Or smoking too much. Or sleeping with local girls of dubious virtue. And you aren't getting your feet wet. Or telling divisional staff officers what you think of them.

I've already answered your snarl about Victory Bonds. You don't see why you should finance the war as well as fight it? Because it pays, is why. They bring in 3% as a lasting record of Canadian patriotism, as opposed to the 1% paid by the banks. However, we won't buy any more if you say so.

Now about your "component parts," as you call them. Anyone would think by that phrase you had been begotten in a garage, gestated in a machine shop and brought forth in an armourer's tent. You say they are in good shape and I'm not to worry about them. Swell, I knew you'd take my friendly warning as intended, but remember this. Your maternal grandad, Harry Thomson, drank too much. So did his old man. So did mine. And my Uncle Jack and Uncle Herbie drank the hell of a lot too much. And the only reason I haven't done so too (or have I?) is because I never had enough money. Or I didn't have enough when I was bringing you up on soda biscuits and honey from our hives. We do, you see, have an inherited weakness for strong drink.

Bless the stuff!

As for taking a good long holiday doing what you want when you come home. Well, what you *ought* to do is enrol in one of those Houses of Refuge called universities and start hard studying, the day after having your last drink at Fort Frontenac. But will you? I don't think.

And I know all about it, brother. I had several such "holiday" months after my war, but Helen was saying she didn't love me and couldn't marry me, and my arm was in a cast and hurting like hell, and Dad had got everything at home into a hopeless financial mess, so those months weren't much good to me. So then I went to work in an office, adding up accounts all day for $40 a month. And, oh God, what a hopeless adder I turned out to be.

Conrad has Marlow say somewhere: "Woe betide you, lad, if you cannot learn to give yourself to life." Well, that's what your mother and I did instead of "trying to get ahead," and people called us (especially me) irresponsible. The only thing we set out to do with determination and intention was to beget you and try to beget some brothers and sisters for you while we gave ourselves to the life around us. The snares caught us in the end, but we had a damned good run for our money – or our lack of money.

So you get yourself through the war with not too many vital "components" missing, and I'll aid and abet whatever adventures with life you want to undertake. You'll end up writing, or I'll miss my guess and eat this typewriter. But you will, for a time, be homesick for the army. Oh yes, you will. It gets to be like a distant green field because of the male companionship and camaraderie, which you lose when you become "Mister" and can never regain in any other walk of life. That's a warning, too. Or a pre-view.

[Toronto]

June 3

I got on the late night train to Kingston last Friday, got Shine O'Hara out of bed (he'd agreed to come along as crew), and we let go *Bonnet*'s lines and set sail for Oakville. Dear Shine, as I fully expected, turned out to be the laziest, dirtiest, most useless shipmate I have ever had.

Listen. We had both agreed to buy a twenty-six-ouncer of rum (then representing one month's rations, now cut to thirteen oz) and to keep same for the passage. I did, but Shine had ate all his up. He arrived aboard in the dark in a yachting cap. He lay and watched me get the vessel under weigh and then, between naps, watched me sail her to Picton.

That took us twenty-four hours and I was beginning to feel the need of sleep. So at Picton I called Vic Bongard, my boyhood sailing companion, and he jumped at the chance for a sail again. But Vic has lapsed a lot physically. He couldn't stay at the tiller without drifting off to sleep.

I took her through Nigger Narrows in the blackout (yes, there is a blackout, to confuse German U-boats no doubt) and never touched a thing. At daybreak I woke my crew, cooked their breakfast and washed the dishes in a calm and then sailed on through the canal and out of the Bay of Quinte while the crew had some more rest.

We lay off Presqu'ile in the open lake from three in the morning till seven at night, during which time the crew felt bored and drank up all the rum. At dawn on Tuesday, we arrived in Whitby harbour where I left the ship in the hands of Little Cap, at the yacht club there. Which is as near as I know to leaving something in the hands of God (in a loud-shouting mood). My crew? I don't really know. They must have just quietly faded away.

But I went on to Toronto by bus, got the car and picked up Helen and Elmer and set out for London, to Inspect. We enjoyed ourselves. In dealing with lady librarians I am not having to deal with men who ought to be in Italy so I am being surprisingly happy in the old job. Also, as I've probably told you, I am in the happy position of being able to organize a revolution, if only in libraries – but then nothing needs a revolution more than Ontario's libraries. I have hopes of getting things in such a state that we can get ex-service men and women interested in the work and pay them decent wages. No Zombies, or others who happily sat out the war, need apply.

We sighed many times that you were not with us. All through the Niagara peninsula and Norfolk County, the world looked at its best. One would never have known that good men were getting shot down over Germany, or shot up in Italy, or drowned in the cold North Atlantic. That is, until you talked to a gas pump guy and learned that one son had been killed and another wounded. For the majority of the people one met, however, the conversation was about how much they were making, and what the hell did the government mean by cutting the liquor ration.

Huh! The *Globe and Mail* has just telephoned to ask if they can publish my report on the need for service libraries. Yes, I am still trying to get books for you fellers. But don't count on it.

Now I'm going to pick up Helen and drive out to Whitby to

spend the weekend on *Scotch Bonnet*. I'll tell all the red-winged black-birds in the marsh that you were asking after them.

❖ ❖ ❖

THE FOLLOWING LETTER WAS WRITTEN ON THE DAY THE BATTLE FOR the Liri Valley began. We were in a concentration area behind the lines waiting until we would be needed for the assault on the Hitler Line itself. We had already been waiting for a week, during which those of us who were in a position to do so had taken advantage of this lull before the storm.

❖ ❖ ❖

[the approaches to Monte Cassino]

May 12

My Fond Progenitors:

On this, my natal day, I am indeed as one reborn. I have just finished three days celebrating having survived for twenty-three years, and because I know it will make you happy to hear that this little holiday has occasioned me more pleasure than anything that has happened to me since leaving England, I shall give with some of the details.

Do you remember me writing to you about a Hasty P party in Sicily just after the conclusion of the campaign there? I must have mentioned the fact that Frank Hammond and I had an incredibly swell time at that party with two darn nice nurses from 5th Canadian General Hospital. Well, the fates decreed that three days ago I was given an unexpected three-day leave from the uninhabited Italian wilderness where we have been incarcerated and discovered that Frankie had also been so lucky. So we joined forces and set out in my jeep for Napoli.

On the way, we passed a sign indicating that 5th General was somewhere in the vicinity. We stared at each other with a wild surmise. I spun Lulu into an Immelman turn and we went searching for the joint. The hospital was set up in a big resort hotel . . . and the first people we saw when we entered the lobby were the two ladies of Sicily, and *both were carrying haversacks!* S'welp me, Gawd, they were setting out on a three-day leave to Naples! Mother, dear Mother, from now on I am going to be a practising Christian. No mere coincidence could have possibly brought this about. And remember, we had not seen nor heard from these angels of mercy since Sicily. High Command away up there in the sky just must have arranged it.

It took maybe thirty seconds to effect a reunion, load girls and haversacks into Lulu and take off for the city of Volcanoes and Vermin. It was the first time any of us had been on the west side of Italy, and what a change it was, especially since this was spring. The lush fertility and the magnificent rolling plains backed by the now distant Apennines, and the absence of any of the debris and destruction of war, were as catnip to us four. Ortona seemed to lie a million years away.

But Napoli, that storied Baghdad of the Med, was so damn lousy with Yankee *soldati* that we could hardly see Naples between the GI caps. We figured that if the Yanks have a quarter as many soldiers at the front as they have here in the rear, the Germans will simply be trampled to death. In any case it was Yankeeville, and no room for *Canadesi*. Eventually we prevailed on the Colonel-suh! in charge of a U.S. hostel (*We* prevailed? The ladies did) to find room for our nightingales, leaving Frankie and me to find spartan shelter in a transit centre. None of us, however, spent much time in "quarters."

Our first stop was the Orange Grove, beloved in song and story throughout the Med. This den of happy iniquity is Naples' Allied Officers Club. It clings to the cliffs high above Napoli itself and originally served the high-ranking Fascisti in a decadence of which Nero would have approved whole-heartedly. The place was built for Bacchus. Although in army hands it may have lost something of its virtuosity, it is still the hell of a place to watch the moon set over Naples harbour while the grim shapes of naval vessels are transformed by some spectral alchemy into the shadowy forms of Tyrrhenian galleys; off to the south Vesuvius, mumbling sleepily, is still aglow from her recent eruption.

And, yes, there *is* an orange grove at the Orange Grove; and flagstone paths through the gardens, polished to such a glass-like surface that one can dance (two is better) anywhere along them; and the heady smell of jasmine (vaguely underlain by the odour of bourbon whisky since this is, after all, a Yankee-run establishment); coloured fountains filled with goldfish who must all be alcoholics, considering the amount of booze that gets spilled over them; and shrubbery everywhere, sufficient to provide all the privacy anyone could ever need.

After a shower at the transit camp and a liberal dusting of AL 69* ("It kills the lice, and makes you nice"), Frankie and I put on our best shirts (we own one each), picked up the ladies and gunned Lulu up to the club. The place was like an international military bazaar. There were statuesque Sikhs in their turbans; Soviet sailors; Moroccan Goums; Polish parachutists; French Spahis; a couple of Tito's boys; South African pilots; Norwegian frogmen (they do underwater demolitions); and many others-such, together with countless Limey and Yankee sailors, airmen, *soldati* and etc. The one thing they all had in common was they were turned out like parade-ground soldiers. Spiffy! All except me and Frankie who, in that glittering array, could have passed for street sweepers.

Not to care. We dined on filet mignon (which may well have been horse, but *good* horse), artichokes, octopuses and sundry other delicacies whose names I have forgot. Dessert was chocolate ice cream smothered in green chartreuse. The whole washed down with good Vesuvian *vino rosso*, and a sweet bubbly called Lacryma Christi. Over coffee Frankie stared dreamily out over Naples and murmured: "Gee, I wonder what the poor folks back home are eating tonight." Marie Antoinette would have applauded.

But what the hell, we deserved it. And then we danced, and talked, and dallied a bit while the moon rose and sank and the dawn began to shimmer through the definitely sultry air. And then, since nobody seemed tired, we climbed into Lulu and let her carry us up old man Vesuvius's dusty slopes until we could feel him rumbling underfoot. The recent eruption was evidently a calculated gesture on the old

---

* Pure DDT! It quickly killed lice, flies and any other small creatures. Its effect upon us soldiers, and on Italian civilians, was never investigated – which is doubtless just as well.

boy's part. The war was getting too big a press; Man was making too much brag about the destruction he could wreak. The sunken ships in Naples harbour and the waterfront battered by German bombs were a challenge not to be ignored, and so he blew his stack. In a minor way, mind you, but sufficient to get the message across: "You bifurcated worms think *you* can be destructive? Small-time stuff! When *I* turn on, I just annihilate." Fanciful? Well, I guess, but that bloody great pile of slag with a heart of fire helped me put myself and my kind into some kind of perspective again.

The morning being well started by then, we descended and explored Pompeii and Herculaneum. It was pretty strange. Instead of the colourful mobs of peacetime tourists, there was only a sprinkle of people, all in drab uniforms of every kind from Free Italians to Popski's Private Army.* But one thing hadn't changed, I guess. Scores of ragged and dirty vendors, mostly kids, peddling "feelthy pictures" or their sisters, "very nice, very clean."

Not interested, thank you. I was, and am, kind of interested in one Ellen Brown, automatically known as Betty. She's from Winnipeg, where she trained before serving a year in the north at Churchill, nursing Eskimos and Indians, the year before I went there in 1935 studying birds with Uncle Frank, so we had that common ground to yarn about and ended making us both yearn for the north again. She came overseas in '39 and was herself hospitalized at Taplow with a broken leg (got bombed during a London leave) when I was also there in '43. We missed meeting then. She tells me she led an uneventful existence until we did meet in Sicily, and the same until we met again yesterday. I'll believe it even if thousands wouldn't. She's very pretty and has a whimsical way with her even if she is (Mother, keep your shirt on now) twenty-nine.

The morning was getting hot and dry and we couldn't find a drink in Pompeii, so we got a Jerrycan of good *vino* out of Lulu, and a bunch of issue mugs. The four of us then set out our wares in a little

---

* A special service unit of the 8th Army commanded by a Russo-Belgian officer famous for his unorthodox methods.

wine shop which had not served anything over its clay counter for a couple of thousand years. We did a land-office business! The charge for a mug of *vino* was a promise to meet again sometime . . . in Serbia . . . Greece . . . Ohio . . . Glasgow, well you name it. And just for a little while Pompeii seemed to come back to life.

I don't intend to describe Pompeii. Any tourist guide will do that. The most fascinating thing I saw was a one-room house on the outskirts, possibly twenty centuries old, that had braved the earthquakes, the lesser eruptions, been buried under a final inferno of lava, remained entombed into our times, and then been brought back into the sun a few decades ago by archaeologists . . . only to be blown to smithereens by an unaimed bomb that probably was made in a factory ten thousand miles away in Canada or the U.S. The bomb succeeded where the vast rage of nature and the erosion of time had failed. Is there a moral here?

That afternoon we let Lulu have her head and found ourselves in a mountain village that neither Jerry nor our side had thought worth pulverizing. It seemed untouched by war until we bounded up the twisty little main street, paved with lava blocks, and were greeted by happy cries of "'Allo, Joe! You gotta ceegarettes? Choon goom? Mars Bars?" A universal song in Italy these days.

So we drove on and picnicked by a mountain stream (mostly dry) in company with a posse of curious goats and ate – wait for it – Spam sandwiches. But drank good *vino bianco* out of straw-covered bottles.

But I have to get some sleep, not having had much for three glorious days, and now I am twenty-three. And even though we can again smell powder smoke in the offing, I feel great. And I've got a date at the Orange Grove two weeks from now, God willing. Who with? Well, a Canadian nurse . . . or had you guessed?

❖ ❖ ❖

NAPLES WAS THE MAIN SUPPLY PORT FOR THE ALLIED FORCES IN ITALY. In the spring of 1944 the German high command, all too well aware that the Allies were preparing a new offensive, ordered the Luftwaffe to destroy Naples' harbour facilities. There followed a series of daring raids, one of which we watched from the eyrie of the Orange Grove Club. Censorship did not allow me to mention the incident in my letters of that period, but I later sent home this overwritten and slightly fictionalized account of it.

❖ ❖ ❖

"See Naples – and Die"

We sat on the terrace of the "Orange Grove Club" and looked out over the ethereal blue of the Tyrrhenian Sea towards the ill-omened Island of Die. Beneath our feet the bay lay quiescent. Along the curve of the shoreline, towards Sorrento, glaring white buildings with red and garish roofs clustered on the foreshore close to the brilliant sea as if in terror-stricken flight from the gargantuan threat of Vesuvius smoking thinly above the grey line of mountains behind them.

It was very hot, but up on the crest of the ridge, suspended over the teeming, stinking cesspool of the city, we were touched by gusty little breezes that came, high-flying, from the snow-capped peaks beyond Cassino.

Frank slumped in an ornate wicker chair, a glass in his hand full of a sticky concoction composed of equal parts of gin and ice cream. He looked out towards the purple loom of the island called Die and said, "My mother used to tell me that joke – 'See Naples – and Die!'"

"Hell!" I said. "I'd sooner Siena and suffer."

He turned his head lazily, eyed me for a moment and replied, "Mowat, it's too goddamn bad Jerry didn't put a Teller mine under your jeep. You don't deserve to live."

The afternoon was passing very pleasantly. The drinks were lousy but they were at least cool. The conversation was sparse and aimless. Best of all, the war was five hundred miles away.

I sprawled back in my chair and peered up into the blue dome, thinking how much it resembled summer skies over the prairies. I thought that if I looked hard enough, I might even see a red-tailed hawk soaring ponderously in great lazy circles. Suddenly I did see something. In the shining expanse of emptiness, there had appeared a tiny cloud, a puffball of a cloud, a foolish little white cotton dab that seemed ridiculous in that majestic cone of space.

At the same moment, my ears caught the dull "woof" of a shell-burst and I was instantly flat on my belly on the marble terrace. I got quickly up and sat in the chair again, wiping the dust from my knees and feeling foolish. "It's those goddamn reflexes," I said. "They double-cross me every bloody time. . . ."

Frank was leaning forward, his head cocked sideways like a terrier. Then I too heard the faint irregular beat of engines, muted but menacing, penetrating the dull moan of the city's noise as the whine of a fly penetrates the sultry murmur of a crowded school room.

Next moment there was bedlam beneath us. Sirens on ships, hooters on destroyers, sirens on buildings, cluster after cluster of ack-ack guns all joined their angry and indignant voices in a shattering cacophony. The sky became speckled with the little cotton dabs and the wump, wump, wump of the bursts came back to us as something felt rather than heard.

"My God, my God!" Frank yelled. "Caught our silly buggers napping for sure! Oh Jerry, you smart sneaking bastard!"

Right out of the eye of the sun, an evenly spaced string of twelve tiny silver beads appeared and began to sink gently towards the sea. A destroyer had slipped her cable and was dashing across the fairway in the bay below, belching greasy black billows from her twin funnels as she laid a smoke-screen. Along the docks and from every high point around the harbour, other massive pillars of smoke began to rise.

The heavy whack of the 3.7 flak guns became a thunderous tattoo that came to us through the solid rock under our feet and set the glasses on the table tinkling. Interspersed amongst their basses was the slow regular hiccup of Bofors guns, "Bup – bup – bup – bup

– bup," and I could follow the red globes of their tracer rising effort-
lessly into the sky as if by some act of levitation.

Then, clear and evil through the vast bellowing of the guns,
came a new sound. A high-pitched, unnatural whine that sent every
nerve in my body into a twitching effort to flee. This time I denied
my reflexes.

Over the mouth of the harbour, the glittering beads had miraculously expanded into the smooth and efficient forms of aircraft
hurtling seaward. The bellowing of the big guns was now almost
drowned in a crackling roar as hundreds of smaller cannon and
machine guns joined in.

The leading aircraft began to flatten out over a rift in the artificial cloud that now cloaked the bay, and I saw plainly the bulbous
shape of a single big bomb as it sank away from the plane's belly and
slid gracefully downward in a slowly lengthening curve.

Before the crunch of the explosion reached us, the plane had
crossed the harbour and was climbing steeply under the cliff on
which we stood. We stared down at it and saw the simple black cross
against the greenish drab of the fuselage.

"He's smoking!" Frank yelled, but I too had already seen
the fine spume of white vapour that bled outward from behind
the cockpit.

What followed is hard to describe for it happened in an instant.
The wounded machine flung itself convulsively away from the cliffs,
sideslipped and then swung back towards the granite wall. Time
seemed to freeze and fragile wings to hang suspended in a passing
caress with earth, and so close below us that we could see the round
brown head of the pilot clearly under the dome of the cockpit.

I remember thinking, "Why doesn't he fall?" and then there was
a livid flash of orange flame and a slow rain of fire sinking down
towards the foot of the cliff.

A few minutes later, the sirens began to sound the all-clear and
a waiter came casually into view in the centre of the terrace.
I raised my glass of gin to my lips and drank it down at a gulp, shud-
dering slightly at the oily, rancid flavour.

And the words flashed unbidden through my head. "See Naples, and die!"

❖ ❖ ❖

[Anagni, south of Rome]

May 24

Ma Famille!:

Haven't written in two weeks, for which I apologize, but seldom in my young life have I been so all-fired busy. You may have read the newspapers. If so, Monte Cassino and the Adolf Hitler Line will be familiar to you – but not as familiar as they are to me. Not by a damn sight!

We've just finished the best job done by Canadians in this war, and maybe in any war. In thirty-six hours First Division smashed, over-ran and passed through a defence line which the Germans assured the world was the most impregnable defence ever built.

I've just finished examining the remains of the enemy fortifications on the brigade front. That flesh and blood could get through them smacks of a miracle. Amongst the things I saw were the turrets of Mk. V Panther tanks set at ground level in concrete emplacements three feet thick, with a cleared 360-degree killing ground around them; scores of MG 42s set in three-inch thick, steel turret emplacements; fields of mixed anti-tank and anti-personnel mines a hundred yards deep, themselves protected by wire entanglements thirty yards wide; scores of dug-in tanks and self-propelled guns; uncrossable anti-tank ditches; networks of dugouts and infantry emplacements equipped with concrete and steel underground bunkers; and the whole sited in some of the most defensible terrain any army could wish to have to hold.

Our lads fought their way through the works! The regiment did a magnificent job and our losses were less than was to be expected. Can't go into details, but I can tell you that hundreds of the Nazis' best streamed into our POW cage and many hundreds more have been dug in for good.

This day I am proud to be a Canadian, and I am prouder still to belong to the "band of brothers" who volunteered for overseas service. Today I don't despise the Zombies who refuse overseas duty – I pity them, for they will never know what it is to be a man among men. Men! Not supermen, just men, who have learned to act together from no selfish motives but as comrades willing to risk death for one another. After the busting of the Hitler Line, the squirmings of the politicians and the war profiteers and the other gutless wonders at home won't bother us as much. By God, we *know* who *we* are, and what *we* amount to.

This may read like stuff from a pulp novel, but some day I may be able to put how I feel this day in better words. Meantime, you can be proud of us.

No time now for more but I'll try to fill you in later.

[Ferentino]

May 26

I might be home in Saskatchewan at the moment. A dry, very bright day in a broad valley filled with green fields and bluffs of poplar trees. Just below me flows a smaller version of the South Saskatchewan River in spate, all muddy-brown swirls and ripples and raw, crumbling cut-banks sliding off onto shifting mud flats. The scenery is a little too green for the prairies, however, and a background of wooded mountains rather spoils the illusion. Just the same, the more of this world I see, the more I suspect that there are only a dozen really different kinds of country in it and that, with slight variations, you can probably find most of them in Canada. A few of our lads are wading naked in the current, looking moodily at the muddy swirl about their knees just as we used to look at the uninviting waters of Beaver Creek, wondering whether to risk the current for some coolth, or just sprawl out under a diamond willow and gently sweat the afternoon away. I think I'll try the river shortly.

You will no doubt have gathered from the noisy and often inaccurate war correspondents that the battle was one of some complexity. Because of General Alexander's meticulous preparations, it was a hell of a lot easier than many of our other shows have been, although casualties were about the same. The weather made a lot of difference. It really seems easier to risk death under blue skies and a balmy breeze, than in a winter gale and mud and snow. With fine weather, marvellous support from arty, tanks, the air force, and the Polish Corps in the overlooking mountains, First Div has done a job that defied our predecessors in 8th and 5th armies for months.

There is an astounding change in the enemy. He is still a good fighter – still wants and hopes to win, but now he is becoming a mole, a dweller under the earth and a hider from the light. The faces of most of our recent prisoners were as white and pasty as cutworms just turned up from under the sod. These men have become so hole-conscious that even when miles behind the lines they dig and dwell in noisome pits lit by kerosene lamps or candle-light. I don't blame them. At the start of this show I watched, and heard, a thousand of our guns go hog-wild, hurling ton after ton of shells into the Hitler Line and keeping it up for hours on end. I can well understand Jerry's subterranean urge. Behind the lines, he is bombed by an enormous Allied air force by day and by night. Almost unbroken shelling and mortaring are his lot anywhere near the front. And the deeper he digs, the more he hates to emerge into the open air. Even in reinforced concrete and steel crypts far underground and safe from anything we've got, he wants to dig ever deeper.

His weapons, the famous blitzkrieg weapons, have changed their spots. He no longer builds fast cruiser tanks for use in the attack, but immense, almost immobile steel fortresses like the Royal Tiger. His MGs have been given a greatly increased rate of fire that is fine if you are in a defence position with lots of ammo stored for ready use – but in the attack, they use up all the ammo a team can carry in a matter of seconds. Jerry artillery is now generally protected with thick armoured walls and mounted on tank chassis for ease of retreat. Immense quantities of steel are going into prefabricated defences like the armoured pillbox known as the Crab, and armour-steel cylinders buried underground as shelters for a mere four men.

The irony of all this is that Jerry has become infected with the Maginot Line disease – the very thing he scorned in the French. Had the Jerry troops in the Hitler Line been in slit trenches, in exposed fighting positions, we would have had to fight a different and much costlier battle. Put a soldier in a bomb-proof hole and he'll tend to hunker down and hope that hell will pass him by. But put him in a slit trench and he'll fight back, because he knows he *has* to fight or be obliterated.

The German high command knows all this, of course. So why the Maginot ploy? Not because it conserves manpower – it doesn't. You may lose fewer soldiers killed or wounded, but you lose a hell of a lot more as POWs. The only reason I can see is sagging morale. Soldiers on the defensive against an aggressive attacker with fire superiority in the air and on the ground can do only one of three things. Surrender. Flee. Or cover up. No one of these responses will win a war, but the cover-up response may hold off defeat a little longer. Obvious? Sure. But what it means to us is that, for the first time, we can envisage Germany being beaten on the basis of the evidence at hand. In 1942 we had no such evidence. We just believed blindly, or blindly hoped we'd win. Now we know we will.

It probably won't be soon, though. Jerry's morale is still surprisingly high, at least in the first-line units. A good many of the POWs we have taken admitted that they have no hope of victory, but their fear of what they expect will happen when the Allies, and especially the Russkies, finally conquer Germany stiffens their spines. It is *easier* to keep on fighting than to be flung into the chaos of defeat by armies and nations who have every reason to hate their Nazi guts. Our demands for unconditional surrender may be a hell of an attractive political goal, but it is going to cost a hell of a lot more blood, and not all of it German blood by any means.

The results of our own battles become more and more predestined as the weight of our fire-power grows. No one enters a battle now with even the remotest thought of failure – it's just a question of how long it will take to crack this bunch before moving on to the next. That may not be too healthy an attitude since we could still see a pretty good spurt of Jerry nastiness before the end, but most of us have at least come to believe the legend of 8th Army's invincibility, and that's damned good for morale.

The one thing that worries us is the attitude of the people back home who smell victory before it is born and welcome the slightest excuse to slack off and slide back to a "normal" way of life. If they do that, a lot more of us are going to die. We are crumbling the German wall, but if support from behind us drops off, the wall will take that much longer to overthrow.

Well, after all that I guess I'll go for a swim, before someone remembers I'm supposed to be on duty this P.M. Keep gunnin' her!

❖ ❖ ❖

EIGHTH ARMY'S DESTRUCTION OF THE HITLER LINE FORCED A RAPID withdrawal of German forces south of Rome. Those Allied troops which had for so long been penned into the Anzio beachhead now broke out, and on June 4 entered the undefended Eternal City.

This was both a real and a symbolic victory of enormous proportions, especially to those of us in Italy. But two days later it was completely overshadowed by the launching of the greatest seaborne invasion in history: Operation Overlord. The long-awaited invasion of France had begun.

❖ ❖ ❖

[Toronto]

June 6
Dear Old Boy. –

I am sitting at a desk littered with unanswered letters, and the contents of a parcel from you – three shawls from Bari for Helen and a Fascist officer's cap for me – and the radio going full blast. At the moment, the Grenadier Guards band is playing "Colonel Bogey," and I wish these stinking civilian clothes I'm wearing were burning in hell. I'm supposed to be getting up a speech for the annual meeting of all the librarians tomorrow, but the hell with that – the invasion is on!

Of course there hasn't been any real news except Churchill's brief statement. The radio announcers assure us that all is going according to schedule, but there is nothing else they could say, or probably know.

Darn it, if a fellow could even get on an m'cycle and go tearing down the highway to see why the Brockville Rifles' strength return is late, or something equally futile, I wouldn't feel so utterly and abysmally *out*.

Ho! Mackenzie King has just come on the air. So I've turned off the radio. No time, this, for platitudes from that old woman.

Your letter of May 24 arrived yesterday, in just twelve days, a record for speed. How amazed we are when the wheel turns full circle again. I suppose there are things in our physical blood, or in our sub-conscious, which render it inescapable that we see things in the same kind of light as our parents saw them. Because it was on the evening of the ninth of April, twenty-seven years ago, that I came up over the last crest of Vimy Ridge* with the small remnant of my platoon remaining after an arduous twelve hours of battle, and looked down over the first open German-held country that I had seen in my nearly two years of trench-slogging. And what *you* felt – and expressed – after the Hitler Line was exactly, thought for thought and eye for eye, what I felt then, but didn't express.

And I can say this to you, my brother, that the moment of elation, which goes deeper than any man could express, and that feeling of oneness with the finest of mankind will live with you forever – to your death and, I have some hope, beyond. Of course, life being what it is, some let-down will follow and there will be moments of bitterness, and disillusion, and resentment but beneath it all nothing can ever take that moment of insight and understanding from you. And this is a gift reserved in its fullness for the infantryman. The sailor, and the airman, and the tanker and the gunner, all of whom run machines, can never know that utterly complete experience because it derives from some-thing so much greater than the strength and power of the machine – from total unity with one's fellow men (not just with individuals) – at their absolute best.

No man who has ever felt that emotion can be delivered into the emptiness of cynicism about the war experience. Anger with people,

---

* Vimy Ridge was perhaps the fiercest and bloodiest of all the battles fought by Canadian soldiers in the First World War.

yes, but not cynicism which, in my interpretation, is a synonym for hell.

You have a gift for expressing these things more simply and clearly than I. It may be one of the gifts of youth which, as you once said, is a better time to look back on than to be in. Anyhow, your last two letters have brought you closer than I have any means of saying. I guess we have memorized them. To your mother they still mean, more than anything, the small boy in a black romper suit turning his porridge bowl upside down on his head as an initial episode in his inquiry into life. To me they mean, more than anything, the days at Trenton Armouries in 1941 when I watched you breaking out of the happy dream of birds and facing up to the hard realities, and overcoming the natural misgivings at what then lay ahead. That's where I am chiefly carried in reading those two letters. And if I say that the pride I felt in those now far-off days has greatly deepened, who can blame me – and what the hell do I care if they do?

[Richmond Hill]

June 16

I am just back, this bright Friday afternoon, having been out on the road since Monday. I took a woman and a dog with me. We wandered (I almost said "idly") round the counties back of Whitby and Oshawa and had a very pleasant few days, thank you. Because of my new synthetic tires I drive at thirty-five m.p.h. which, combined with being in a closed car, is a very different matter from tootling down the highway on an Indian m'cycle at sixty. But I am seeing more of the countryside than I ever saw before and arriving rested at my destinations. Not to say somnolent.

Ontario has never been lovelier than in this moist spring. If only you had been along to check the various marshes and help the ducks attend to their brood raising, along with the other mysterious denizens whose breeding habits elude my knowledge, but not yours.

In Peterborough I had a long chat with Al Park's father. As you know, Al survived the bullet in the head, but he is going to be left in a bad way. He seems able to think clearly, but his eyesight is shot and the "executive" side of his brain is not functioning fully. He can dictate a letter, but when he tries to write it himself he goes haywire. It is very much too bad.

Reg Saunders is trying to do something with *Carrying Place* in the U.S. market. He says we now make a better book, physically, than they do in the States, so he is going to manufacture it here then try to get a good firm, say Scribners, to act as an agent for it south of the border. That would be reversing the usual and age-old state of affairs with a vengeance! Just imagine, Canadian books and writers swamping the U.S.A. – instead of vice versa.

So last night we finally came home to the real Hove To in Richmond Hill. The woman and three small children we had rented it to had smeared butter over everything, turned everything inside out, and plucked out the English violet bed, the pride of your mama's heart. There goes my summer's sailing a-glimmer in the mist. It will take us all summer to even get the grounds in presentable condition. I have to cut the lawns with a scythe. Why not you instead of me? It's because you never seem to come home.

I got such a thrill out of your leave in Naples. I'd like to meet Betty. Winnipeg *and* Churchill sound O.K. to me. How'd she be on a long portage? The six-years' age difference wouldn't make any odds now. But it would at forty. And life isn't over at forty – not by a long shot, as your young mother and I found out, despite the assurances you once gave us that it was. But this is not advice – it is merely thinking aloud. I rejoice with all my heart in the three days' fun you had.

[Richmond Hill]

June 20

Dearest Bunje –

Home in Richmond Hill at last, and about time as everything was in pretty bad shape – Angus sees years of work looming ahead, but he always wants to do everything at once and nearly kills himself. He misses your help sadly. Can't get either a char woman or a gardener, but we'll do the best we can to have the place in shape for your homecoming.

The gardens in R.H. are perfectly lovely. Everyone works hard and takes so much pride in keeping their places up, and there are a number of new houses. One would hardly know that there is a war on, as they say.

Why are your girlfriends all years too old for you? I'll be seeing Ev soon. Her husband has been decorated and is a major now, so there is surely no hope for you in that direction.

[Ferentino]

About June 3
Dear Parents:

Eighth and 5th armies are now playing follow-the-rat. If you can catch him, he fights. But not unless. And he is a remarkable sprinter. I don't know if POW figures from our recent shows have been published (God knows why, but we are not supposed to disclose them) but they are incredible. Also the number of Germans fertilizing the countryside is very heartening. And, Lordie, the equipment that man Adolf has lost, you wouldn't believe. I even had a hand in that myself.

I was duty officer in the command post at Tac HQ the night after the Hitler Line breakthrough and had the graveyard shift, 0400 to 0800 hours. Just after dawn I got a radio message from the Free French Corps, which was in the mountains on our left flank overlooking the whole Liri Valley. One of their advance patrols of Goums (Moroccan hill fighters who slice off German ears for souvenirs) reported a column of Jerry tanks, SP guns, and trucks filled with troops heading towards us along the south bank of the Liri River. The French thought it might be a counter-attack in the making.

Well, the Hitler Line battle was already *over* and most Germans in the region were in frantic retreat. The bunch the Goums reported must have got out of touch with reality. Maybe they thought they were re-staging the Charge of the Light Brigade, or just got lost. In any case, I had to decide what to do about it. The Brig was sound asleep after being on deck for two days and nights and I sure and hell wasn't going to wake him without damn good reason. The BM was back at main HQ and I couldn't reach him. That left me nominally in charge, so I rose to the occasion.

We had a French LO attached to us so I got him rousted out of bed and we put him in direct touch by radio with the *sous-officier* heading the Goum patrol. I also called in our artillery rep – a captain from the 2nd Field Regiment who is as crazy as the rest of us. I told him what was up and we looked at each other for a moment, then both of us said: "Let's get 'em!" And we did.

He got on his radio link to Corps Arty HQ and reported a Jerry counter-attack developing and asked for a mighty stonk to be set up on call. Using the Goums as arty spotters, he then registered a crossroads a couple of miles ahead of the Jerry column. Then we waited. And when the Goums reported that the lead vehicles had passed that crossroads, my pal called down the stonk.

For a minute we figured the Third Front had opened! At least a hundred guns let loose behind us. The air overhead was suddenly full of passing objects sounding like everything from screaming jeeps to railroad trains. In about a minute, the Brig comes bounding into the Iron Pig in his pyjamas, looking like a wild man from Borneo.

"What in hell is going on!" he screams.

I tried to explain, but it wasn't easy, what with the whine and whistle of passing shells, and the roar of guns, some of which were in a field about two hundred yards away. That, and hysterical messages coming in from all sides wanting answers to the same question. A couple of the infantry units even stood-to to repel attack.

Ten minutes after the first bang, the stonk ended as suddenly as it had started. Then all I had to do was try to avoid a second, verbal stonk, obliterating me.

But just then a message came in from the Goum guys. It went something like this: "Allah be praised! There's going to be enough German ears available to sink a ship! Thank you, Canadians!"

It took until next day to get things sorted out, during which time your son was under something of a cloud. But it was finally discovered that somebody senior at Corps HQ who really liked fireworks, or thought we all deserved a truly memorable victory salute, or was a practical joker on quite a scale, had put *all* the field guns and mediums from 1 Corps into the stonk, plus a couple of batteries of 7.5-inch army heavies, and even a regiment of 3.7-inch anti-aircraft guns cranked down to fire air bursts over ground targets. Our arty rep figured that this little episode must have cost the Canadian taxpayer several hundred thousand bucks. But it was more than worth it. Armoured cars of one of our recce squadrons reached the crossroads about noon and reported thirty or more burned-out or still-burning trucks; a dozen smashed or abandoned Mk. IV tanks; a bunch of SP guns, and a goodly scattering of dead Tedeschi. So all was forgiven, and I am not being sent to dig latrine trenches in the rear.

[Richmond Hill]

June 21

Dear McGill, –

I guess, pardner, I'm actually getting house-broken at last, and so is Elmer who has got a feud going with the dog catcher, who can't catch him (Elmer) and is going crazy trying to. Do you remember the dog catcher in Saskatoon who arrested Mutt and charged him with "being large" after nine P.M.? Mutt never really did get wise to what that arrest was all about. There were such delicious odours around the dog pound that after we ransomed him, he spent most of his time hanging around the pound begging to be let in, until the dog catcher took to pleading with us to keep him home. Poor old Mutt. I came across his collar in the drawer of a chest in your room the other day. And what else didn't I come across – rotten birds' eggs, stuffed snakes, a mummified bat (did you put it in there, or did it crawl in by itself to die?) and boxes and boxes of junk unmentionable. We are leaving everything in your room intact so you can have the fun of sorting it out, although it may get us in trouble with the health authorities.

No recent letters from you but, through the papers, we follow your travels the length of Italy with breathless interest. At least I get breathless just trying to keep up. What a swell show you lads are putting on.

June 10

Dear People:

I've just finished reading a current (sort of) issue of the Canadian version of *Liberty* magazine. It has a Soldier's Page. A marvellous idea. I'll bet the five contributors to this particular page (all of whom are fighting the war in Canada) are absolutely delighted that a real, live magazine has given them space to bellyache that they can't get by with only two weeks' leave every six months; can't afford the current rail fares; and are being "pressured" by their officers and by returned veterans to sign up for overseas service. One does feel so sorry for the whining bastards. The perils home service soldiers have to face! Makes me want to puke up everything I've eaten for a week.

The good news of course is the exploits of the *real* soldiers who are chasing Jerry out of France. But the treatment of this *new* invasion of continental Europe (we don't forget that we were the first to do it) by the Canadian press and radio broadcasts is contaminated by the most nauseous bull ever to come out of the slimy political dung heap, as our revered politicos gush about how grateful the country is to "its soldier sons and heroes" and how richly they will be rewarded for their gallantry and sacrifices, and how they will be remembered for centuries as the saviours of democracy!

Sorry if I am frothing at the mouth but a guy I know just got turned down for a compassionate leave to Canada to help his mother and sisters deal with a dying father and a family business that will also die without a man around. This soldier hero has been overseas a full three years, has been wounded but has survived eight months in action. Maybe when, and if, we do go home, it should be with fixed bayonets.

C'est la guerre, n'est-ce pas?

We are also more than a little brassed off at our reward for busting through the Hitler Line and chasing Tedeschi north at a dead (no pun intended) run. As you may by now have guessed, 8th Army, with the Canadians in the lead, was set to enter Rome well before anyone else. But we were reined in and ordered to halt so that the Yanks could get there first. *Rome Liberated by Americans* may be good politics, but it is bullshit. And we pariahs who did most of the dirty work are forbidden to enter Rome *at all*. Instead we are parked in another blasted olive grove thirty km from the Eternal City where, Mum will be happy to know, we are safe from the temptations of the flesh.

Actually, it isn't so bad. We are high on the side of a broad valley with a terrific view of the early Italian summer, and it's amazing how fast the evidence of the recent, late unpleasantries is vanishing from view under the succulent growth of grain fields, vineyards, fruit trees and the like. All is not entirely peaceful, however. Jerry sowed his own crop before he left – Schu mines. These are little wooden boxes (so they can't be detected by magnetic mine detectors) full of explosive scattered about just under the surface of the ground. They seldom kill, but almost invariably blow off the foot that steps on them, whether it is a donkey's foot, some old Eyetie farmer, or one of us. I thought to go on a ramble today and spot some birds, but thought better of it when I heard a bang not far away and Benny told me some poor bugger of a signaller got one while laying telephone line.

Last night we had a bit of a do in the mess, which consists of several fly nets slung from the branches of olive trees, over a collection of busted furniture originally looted from the Eyeties by Tedeschi, and liberated by us from the wreckage of one of his retreating columns that got strafed by the RAF. The Brig had evidently forgiven my recent trespasses with Corps artillery, because he suggested I nip down the line to 5th General and bring Betty and any friends of hers who might be free back for a party. No sooner said than done. What I did not know was that I was being set up.

Ever since Naples, it's been a standing joke amongst Betty's and my mutual pals that we two would celebrate a marriage if and when Rome fell. Well, cuss me, I had forgotten all about it. Halfway through the party (which was a noble effort attended by a goodly number of Hasty Ps), the Brig calls everybody to attention. Then he singles me out, recites my life history in a censored version and proposes a toast, saying that it was time I got my just reward. This was most gratifying and I could almost smell a majority, let alone a captaincy in the offing.

But as I sat there trying to conceal my self-satisfied smirk, the horrible strains of Mendelssohn's "Wedding March" rendered by two pipers, a harmonica and a two-toned Italian trumpet split the night air. Then Betty (who had earlier disappeared, and I never ask ladies why they disappear) reappeared on the arm of Lt. Col. Don Cameron, the Hasty's new CO, complete with a mosquito-net bridal veil, war brides for the use of, followed by several beaming nursing sisters laden with calla lilies.

Oh my God, did my memory ever get a jolt. But it was too late to do a bolt, and anyway a posse of fellow officers closed in to cut off any attempt at escape. So, while my feet shuffled wistfully towards the woods but got nowhere, Betty and I were married. By the Brig. He claimed that being Captain of His Ship, he had the authority to do so, and as Guardian of Morals for the Brigade it was his bounden duty to do so.

It was all quite touching. We were then escorted to a distant grove where a nuptial hammock had been stretched between two fig trees and sternly ordered not to reappear before breakfast time. Well, you know what an obedient servant of the King am I!

But not to worry, Mother, it was all in fun. The Brig's service was definitely unorthodox, although about as close to the real thing as I ever hope to come. His closing words were, I think (I was busy wrestling with a flea at the time), "I now pronounce you man and woman, and if you ain't married now, you damn well ought to be!"

Enclosed is a snap of my famous dugout, taken last winter on the day the sun shone. Briefly.

❖ ❖ ❖

ONE OF THE DIFFICULTIES ABOUT WRITING LETTERS TO MY PARENTS jointly was that I had to exercise censorship with regard to my love life. This was made easier in Italy by the fact that opportunities for love-making were all too rare. Having carefully attended to the messages about venereal disease dinned into my ears by the army, I was afraid to lay a hand on any Italian woman of doubtful virtue, and the virtuous ones would not tolerate the laying on of hands by such as I.

In consequence of these difficulties, I became much enamoured of Betty and, in the manner of young men in need, fancied myself in love with her. She was a kindly and understanding woman who, while certainly not in love with me, generously gave me what solace she could. I suspected even then (and am sure now) that her affection was of a somewhat maternal nature but that didn't deter me. We made somewhat awkward love in the hammock, and elsewhere – for which benison I shall be forever grateful to her.

❖ ❖ ❖

[Richmond Hill]

July 3

Dear Squibbie. –

I've discovered what makes Elmer such a gentle soul and why he is always on the outer fringes of the mobs of dogs that hang round bitches in heat looking worried and a bit puzzled. I mean Elmer. Well, I was romping with him on the lawn last night and inadvertently grabbed him by the knockers. He didn't even yelp. And why? Because there was practically nothing there to yelp about. I was so surprised that I made a more detailed examination and can say I have never seen anything more diminutive since the night your mother was having a dinner party in Saskatoon and you burst in upon the second course with a couple of dots on a bread-and-butter plate and excitedly announced to all that these were the testes of a yellow-bellied sap-sucker you had just dissected.

But that house of yours, and that boat of yours. I'm getting sick of hearing about "Farley's house" and "Farley's boat." So help me, I'll burn the one and sink the other if something isn't done about it. If I sit down under the cherry tree with a bottle of beer for five minutes, or if I try to slip away from Little Cap's wharf long enough to discover whether the Whitby beer house is still open, I am greeted inevitably with, "Now remember, you're digging out those weeds from Farley's garden," or "Do come and polish Farley's dining-room table," or

"Farley wouldn't like it if his deckhouse wasn't scraped and painted."

I'll take the canoe and leave home. I've always had a hankering to make the voyageur's trip up the Ottawa to Georgian Bay. So there I'll sit in my old canoe, nothing to think of and nothing to do. No burdocks to battle, no grass to pitch. Just sit there and paddle the sonovabitch.

I think the best thing you can do is come home and start looking after your property yourself. And by the way, the front wheels of your car are out of line. Shall I straighten them with a garden fork or a marlin spike?

Your indignant father.

[Anagni]

June 22

Revered Parents:

My week-long "annual leave" came through unexpectedly on the fifteenth and I was away in about ten minutes. Benny, Lulu Belle's regular driver, was sick so couldn't come but Doc McConnell, my indomitable batman, was in fine fettle for a jaunt and became Lulu's nominal driver. He can't drive but what the hell? This is the army.

Rome was still *verboten* to any but U.S. troops, so we headed for Napoli and late that evening Lulu was nuzzling the gates of one of our general hospitals. Betty could only get the evening off, but we whipped into Naples and spent most of the night staggering from nightclub to nightclub. I returned the wench to her duties in the cold grey dawn, and Doc and I unrolled our sleeping bags in a big quarry about a quarter of a mile away.

It seemed only minutes later I wakened from an uneasy dream of being beset by a mob of Valkyries to find myself surrounded by a hundred or so large, tough-looking women, all of whom seemed to think I was guilty of attempting to rape their daughters. Such a wailing and caterwauling has seldom been heard except at feeding time at the zoo. I took one unbelieving look at this irate female mob and hurriedly pulled my head into the bag. It did no good. The howling grew in decibels and I had to emerge and face the music (?). It was actually pretty scary. I found myself backed up against a thirty-foot cliff and hemmed in by arm-waving female behemoths who were clearly angry as all get-out. I got panicky and whooped for Doc (who had bedded down some distance away) to come running with his tommy-gun. But, poor guy, he couldn't. Another contingent of furies had backed him into a cave – and Doc can be scared into conniptions by just *one* woman acting peaceable. We were rescued by an old geezer on a donkey who rode up and blistered the ladies to such effect that they scuttled off down the road towards the nearest village. The old number gazed after them with some disdain and volunteered this strange remark: "Justa lika in Peets-burg! Wimmin, dey alla da same! Lika da president, he say!" I tried to find out what president said what, but got nowhere so I gave him some cigs, but we did learn our contretemps with the ladies was all a misun-derstanding, and kind of a sad one. The women had been hired for a few lira a day to crush road stone, by hand, for the Limey army. The Limey officer in charge had since departed, and the women had not been paid. They simply wanted their back wages and couldn't tell the difference between their former boss and me.

I restored my shattered nerves somewhat by driving Betty (who managed to get the day off) down to Salerno and then around the Sor-rento peninsula which, according to the guide books, is one of the most beautiful regions in Italy. It is, but Gad, what roads! In twenty miles along the coast, which is mostly vertical mountain face, there are at least five hundred curves requiring more than a ninety-degree change in direction. Obviously it was originally made by mountain goats a couple of thousand years ago and ain't been much improved on since. But it truly was gorgeous. Gleaming white villas clung to the cliffs and ancient maritime villages hung like barn swallows' nests. The few level ledges were covered with lemon trees in bloom. Below the road, the cliffs plunged three or four hundred shaggy feet to end in a blaze of glory in golden sands and the iridescent sapphire of the Tyrrhenian Sea. The sun blazed over all, and far out to sea the Isle of Capri lurked like a gigantic dreadnought. A few old fishing boats lay becalmed below us.

And nowhere was there any sign of war!

We moseyed along, stopping frequently at little trattoria perched like alpine chalets for a glass of Marsala and, near Positano, for lunch served to us two alone on a patio overhanging the whole incredible scene. The whole thing seemed to be out of time and in a sense it was. When the Jerries were here, they reserved this stretch of coast for the delectation of high-ranking officers only and, since it was its own defence against invasion, as it has been since Homer's time, did not deface it with fortifications. When the Yanks took it over, they too reserved it as a rest area for especially favoured troops, but now that Rome was theirs it was practically deserted by the military.

When I finally got Bett home that night (after a round trip of a couple of hundred craggy miles), it was so close to dawn that I stumbled into the first vacant tent in the hospital compound and flaked right out. No more rock quarries for me! But, you guessed it, lots more women! Of all the tents I might have picked, I chose the anteroom tent to the nursing sisters' mess marquee! And they eat breakfast early. Lord, the fuss they made! Now I guess I'll really have to marry Bett.

Unfortunately the hospital was moving up the line that day, so Bett and I said our adieus and then I drove back to the magic peninsula. I bluffed my way into the "reserved" village of Amalfi and established myself in a villa/hotel overlooking the whole Bay of Salerno. In peacetime, my spacious suite would have set me back about ten bucks a week. In wartime, it set me back ten bucks a day. But what the hell. The food was marvellous; the wines good; the local people good-looking (especially the *signorinas*) and friendly; and the company was certainly varied and interesting.

The *soldati* who (unlike me) were there legally were all officers and included some British Commandos; U.S. Rangers; some Special Service people recuperating after being dropped into Yugoslavia and Greece to help the guerrilla forces; and a couple of Desert Air Force jockeys, one of whom had had three Spits shot out from under him. It so happened that I was the only guy with independent transportation so I got included in all kinds of events, some of which were a little hairy.

There was, for instance, the night we entertained the King of Italy.

One of the Commando captains had heard that H.M. Vittorio Emanuele was ensconced in a palatial (why not?) villa not far away, under "Allied protection," which we figured meant house arrest. One night a bunch of us got talking about the Little King as we sat in a bar testing the *vino* and listening to a four-piece Eyetie band playing U.S. hit songs. We got to wondering if he was lonely and began to feel sorry for his nibs, and the upshot was we decided to go and pay a call and cheer him up. "We" being the aforesaid Commando captain (call him Mack), the Spit pilot and a lanky Yankee (aren't they all?) who never would tell us what his specialty was. And me.

When we all piled into Lulu, she was like to bust her corset, mainly because we took the band with us so we could entertain His Majesty with a midnight serenade in what the Yank assured us would be royal style. He was a fluent Eyetie speaker, so while I wheeled the Old Girl up a mountain road, he was busy instructing the band as to their duties. I didn't know what he was telling them, but was to find out soon enough.

And let me say right here that our (mine, anyway) intentions were of the best. A quiet little serenade outside the *palazzo*, then home to bed with the glow of a deed well done to warm our vitals. If H.M. liked the music and invited us in for a nightcap, well and good. If not, we could rest content with a good deed. But that Yank . . .

The King's casa was guarded by a couple of platoons of Eyetie San Marco marines, tough-looking guys and fully armed. They did not greet us with delight, but Mack and the Yank undertook to explain the peaceful nature of our mission to their guard commander, having first instructed me to unload the band, form 'em up, march 'em into position outside the big front gate and be ready to lead 'em in a stirring rendition of "Funiculi, Funicula."

The band wasn't easy to line up. Wasn't easy to *keep* up. The pilot and the Yank had been feeding them swigs of issue rum on the way, and they weren't used to it. But they were enthusiastic, and without even waiting for the maestro to lead the way, they bust out playing. Burst, bust, blatted . . . allee samee. It was awful. And it wasn't "Funiculi." Mack and that Yankee fiend had bribed, brow-beaten or boozed them into striking up the "Internationale."

The first three bars confused me. The next three bewildered me. And then, oh Mother mine, I took a horrified glance at the guards and they were all hunched over their machine pistols looking puzzled and suspicious. Then I saw Mack, the Yank and the Pilot hiking for the jeep, and it seemed a useful thing to be doing, so I did it too. The Pilot took the controls and flew us back down that mountain path at a speed a Messerschmidt couldn't have matched. The band? Well, I'm not sure. I hope they've returned to duty at the pub (I haven't been back to see) but, if not, their names will at least be inscribed in the honour rolls when the Communist Party takes over the government. Shouldn't wonder if they all get Stalin medals. And, Poppa, do NOT repeat NOT send *this* story to the *Picton Gazette*, unless you want to start an international incident.

When I got back from leave I didn't recognize this HQ. Everybody from the Brig down seemed to have been promoted, sent home to staff college, posted to a Higher Headquarters, or RTUed.* Naturally I wondered if I alone was to remain but no, I was told to report to Div HQ "for disposal." In my case, the disposal looked like being permanent, into outer space. When I got to Div nobody knew what to do with me or, officially, even who I was. When I queried this evil state of affairs, I was parried on all sides by that first requisite of all good staff officers, evasiveness. At last by dint of great perseverance, I finally discovered that my file, containing my army records, had been misplaced. This meant I could neither be promoted nor posted since officially I no longer existed. In the army, as the revered Major will know, your only *real* existence is on paper. So there I was, not even a blip, or a cipher, but totally non est. And since the Powers who had lost me were not going to admit to error, I was in limbo. I might have stayed there forever had I not bribed a records sergeant to dig out the missing me. In due course, he disinterred me from some paper graveyard and I am now back in the land of the living.

And I escaped from Div HQ, which was too full of stooges, red

---

* Returned to unit.

tape, red tabs and general imbecilities to be endured. I am back with the Shiny First Brigade! More than that, I am wearing my third pip again and, this time, one hopes, more or less for good. Even more. I am now Brigade Intelligence Officer with an office truck of my own and surrounded by minions to do the work. So all is well, even though it took six months from the time I was first nominated for this job until it finally came along.

To make things even rosier, today I got my 39/43 Star, the only medal to come my way that I am proud to wear. Only those Canadians who landed in Sicily on D-Day are eligible, and there are very few of these remaining with the fighting units.

Heard another pleasing thing today. Alex Campbell is to be posthumously awarded the DSO and bar.* Too late to mean anything to Alex, but to those of us who knew him it restores at least some respect for the so-called "Valour" awards. That the bravest, fighting-est, best-loved soldier the Hasty Ps have so far known in this war should have been written off as just another guy gone west** had rankled with those of us who knew him, particularly as we watched decorations "coming up with the rations" for people who had hardly heard a shot fired in anger, but had the right connections.

Mother, please note. Starting next month I'll be assigning $100 instead of $50. With your shrewd assistance, I'll be financially independent in ten more years.

[Alife, in the Volturno Valley, fifty miles north of Naples]
June 25

For the past couple of weeks we've been languishing under canvas in another wasteland of the sort 8th Army delights in selecting for the likes of us colonials – an arid, scorching stretch of rocky foothills inhabited mainly by lizards and goats. Those of us with access to transport can escape occasionally to the coast and swim in the sea but most of the troops are doomed to stay here and broil until the powers-that-

---

* It was not, in fact, awarded.
** First World War slang for being killed.

be have another job-of-work for us rough soldiers to attend to. I'm cooking up a swindle that might get me out of here for a few days heading Rome-wards. I'll let you know what transpires.

Picked up a copy of the *Maple Leaf* this morning and note that reinforcements have arrived for the Canadian Forces in Italy. A contingent of CWACs,* no less! God bless the ladies. They clearly have more guts than the neutered Zombies wearing the same uniforms as ourselves who refuse overseas service. Well, bad cess to the lot of them, at least we've got the CWACs, and the WRENs and the WRAFs to back us up. You can send this bit to the *Gazette* if you want to. But I'll bet they won't print it.

Having given vent to my usual burst of bile, I'll have a lemonade and relax. The lads in Normandy are doing *bueno, bueno* and what with the state of Tedeschi in Italy at the moment, I think I begin to see a gleam of light at the end of the tunnel. The Brenner tunnel. But it may not mean much to us unmarried *soldati*. We hear that we will be retained in Europe after the war to help put the place back in order, or else get shipped to the Pacific theatre to take on the Japs. Married men will go home first. I guess that is O.K., but when the hell do *we* get a crack at starting our own families? Well, there I go, still bitching. . . .

So now I shall have a bath, and you can keep your derogatory comments to yourselves.

[Alife]

July 2

Our concentration camp in the hills has become hot as hell, and a lot more boring. High Command says we were sent here to train and has deluged us with exercise after useless exercise. Last week Ed Phillips, the senior signals officer, and I put our leetle heads together having decided if you can't beat 'em, jine 'em. So we dreamed up our very own training scheme – a "joint signals/intelligence communications scheme" which calls for a lot of radio signalling from trucks travelling to distant places, and damn little intelligence. The training staff

---

* Canadian Women's Army Corps.

O.K.'d it without a quibble and, wadda ya know . . . Ed and I found ourselves in Rome for a few days. Even more amazing was that Bett and another nursing sister also happened to get to Rome for part of the time. Pop, I may have been a slow starter at this army racket, but I'm learning fast.

The trip north was a revelation of how much we owe the RAF. On average every twenty yards along the highway running west from Cassino was a burned-out Jerry tank or truck or gun. Hundreds and hundreds of them, strafed by the fly-guys. Being a truck driver in Kesselring's Army these days must be the most suicidal job in the world.

But Rome. Ah, yes. My first impressions were . . . of the women. Oh heavenly day! After a year of seeing almost no female forms except dowdy mama-mia types, the sight of well-made and well-dressed girls galore was almost too much. The streets were overflowing with gorgeous gals. However, we had other business to attend to, so apart from some low growls and suppressed yips of wolfishness, we made no moves towards cementing international friendships.

Instead, we picked our own ladies up at a leave hostel and spent the rest of the day driving around at a hell of a clip, in ever decreasing circles, rubber-necking. The Yanks have taken over the town and own all the good hotels, night spots and restaurants. This is not their fault. In fact, their High Command is to be congratulated on being smart enough to make things pleasant for their troops when they aren't in action. Would that the Brits and Canadians would do likewise. But, God bless your Old School Tie, it is not to be thought of. "When the blighters aren't fighting, put them in the back pasture" seems to be *our modus operandi*. There was just one hotel Ed and I could get into – a Canadian Officers Transit Hotel with no bar, no hot water, army issue rations and, would you believe this, a twelve o'clock curfew!

We solved the problem by the simple expedient of making friends with a couple of Yank *capitanos*. The presence of Bett and friend made this a cinch. The Yanks fixed us up in their swanky apartment, then took us to Broadway Bill's, a humdinger of a huge, rambling cellar club with a first-class orchestra, food like manna and whatever the little heart desired to drink. Heaven was here and now!

Things got a little unclear later on, but well after midnight I found myself deep in the bowels of Rome, viewing the catacombs by the light of cigarette lighters and rolled up U.S. Army newspapers serving as torches. I don't know *how* I get into these situations. There were bones everywhere. I'm still a-shiver.

Our ladies had to go back to work next day, leaving Ed and me to entertain ourselves, which we did to such effect that the following morning I rose with the noon sun and dragged myself into a little sidewalk café in a blinding array of bright tresses (amazing how many recent blondes there are in Rome) and bright dresses, and slurped at an eye-opener, feeling sorry for myself. After a while, an eye opened and roved to the next table where sits a very sweet young thing and her all-too-clearly-maiden auntie.

This young thing is acting very full of beans and is executing a hop-skip-jump routine while sitting in her chair. I am watching this character with some surprise and wondering how long the chair is going to last, when she turns towards me very quick and lets fly like a burst from a Sten gun: "Allo please-I-mus-tell-someone-next-wik-I-go-to-U.S.A.-very-excitement-is-not-it?" Well, I am hardly in the mood for gay repartee but I manage to croak: "Is not indeed." Which sends her into a Schmeisser-like burst of laughter, whereat the auntie gives us both a very disapproving stare. This has no effect upon the bubbly one, who proceeds to tell me that she has her U.S. passport in her pocket, is eighteen years old, and if she never sees Europe again it will be too soon.

Now there are many American *soldati* in this joint, all with only two ideas in their heads. One of these they are drinking, and the other they are looking for. And since this sweet young thing has opened her trap so loud, they are all looking at her. It is clear to me that my bouncy little friend has stirred up considerably more interest than she is capable of handling. It soon becomes clear to her, too. The sound of chairs being pushed back and army boots shuffling across the marble floor is like the sound of a twister approaching a corn field. The young thing is now wishing she had said she was going to Siberia or, better yet, had kept her mouth shut. The old auntie has produced a rolled umbrella and is brandishing it and has a wild look in her eye. As for me, I get painfully to my feet and, making shameless use of my rank, proceed to extricate these two females from their predicament.

The upshot is that I find myself in my jeep with the two ladies and with a distinct feeling that I ought to get moving before the tidal wave of irate GIs emerging from the bar catches up to me. The young thing has begun bubbling again and is bouncing all over the jeep. As I wheel down the street, keeping a wary eye peeled for MPs who take a dim view of civilians riding in army vehicles, I learn from her chatter that she is a Hungarian Romany, a gypsy, who has been on the dodge from Himmler's SS police since she was thirteen, and is quite overcome with the idea of going to the U.S.A. where all she will have to dodge is GIs.

All this effervescence is making me feel somewhat alive again, so I invite both individuals to have lunch with me, which we do at a *ristorante* that serves black-market steaks (horse) smothered in fried eggs (duck). During this repast, both ladies drink a glass or three of Marsala, which they are evidently not used to drinking. The bubbly one gets bubblier and the old auntie friendlier and begins to tell me how good she can minuet, and how she used to hobnob with the Hapsburgs, and why doesn't she teach me the mazurka right here and now? She is a very odd old duck indeed, but before the dance begins she slips off into dreamland, for which I am more than somewhat grateful.

Ever the gentleman, I proceed to drive the ladies to wherever they call home, so Auntie can rest in comfort. But when I weave my way through the maze of military traffic to what turns out to be a Red Cross refugee centre, the little gypsy does not wish to be decanted. She is now bouncing with such vigour that I fear for the jeep's springs, so I agree to take her for a drive and look at Rome while Auntie has a nap.

The afternoon turns out to be very good fun indeed, since this young thing has considerable whimsy. She insists that the tickets which Hadrian gave her for the show at the Coliseum are for the first tier and not the gallery, so that is where we sit while fourteen Gestapo creeps are thrown to four black Nubian lions. While this event is in progress, Susi (did I tell you her name before?) is reading ahead in the program (which is an oldish-looking brick with some scratches on it) and tells me the next event will be a gladiatorial combat and, since her pal Hadrian has promised her to the victor as his reward, maybe we should go?

We go. Outside the Royal Palace I am happy to tell her that King Vittorio is an acquaintance of mine, in a manner of speaking, and would doubtless be happy to give her an audience if he is at home, but she declines in favour of tripping off to the Vatican in search of a papal blessing from one of the Borgia popes. She does not care which one, but says that they were *all* such *interesting* men.

Did I tell you that this young thing is also very easy to look at, having copper-coloured hair and wide green eyes? But alas and alack, I had to return her to the refugee centre before the dinner hour or her auntie would have had conniptions. Also she was due to be moved to another camp, at Aversa, in the morning. I said goodbye to her with considerable reluctance. The parting also seemed to make her a little bit unhappy until she remembered that she would write to me from the U.S.A. and maybe come and visit me in Canada.

Now I want to tell you about this kid. Susi was thirteen, and living in Vienna where her father was a Hungarian diplomat, when the Anschluss arrived. Susi's mother was a popular gypsy singer, so one night the Gestapo came for her because Hitler had decided to eliminate the gypsies. When her husband made too much fuss about her disappearance, he vanished too. Susi and her two brothers were then smuggled out to France, but after the Germans took over France, somebody peached and they had to separate and go into hiding again. Susi finished up in Switzerland after sundry adventures which she did not talk about. Then the Swiss threatened to deport her to Austria, so she was smuggled into Italy. By then she was seventeen and had run out of relatives and friends except for an old auntie who lived in Florence. When Italy got out of the war and the Germans took over the country, the two women fled to Rome, finding sanctuary in a convent where they stayed until Rome was liberated. Meanwhile, both her brothers had been turned over to the Gestapo by the French.

Getting this much of her story out of her was a bit like pulling hen's teeth. But I really don't think I'd have wanted to hear the details anyway. Something I'd have to live with when listening to people back home grousing about how the war had disrupted their lives. This kid had certainly taken more than most of us will ever have to take and yet had come up smiling . . . asking for nothing except maybe some affection and someone to share her love of life. I sort of wish it could be me.

Ed and I spent part of that last evening in Rome viewing the Coliseum by moonlight along with a lot of other gawkers in uniform. It wasn't the same. Everybody saying "ooooh" and "aaaaah" and nobody but me seeing the big naval battle between triremes and biremes, or the African camelopards chasing the Christian martyrs. Later we drove out to Ostia and the Lido, both ghost towns except for some loud and tawdry bars. It was anti-climax, and I came away from Rome at dawn next day feeling pretty low. I have given Susi your address so she will have someone to write to on your side of the water, from the U.S. refugee camp where she is being sent. Let me know if you hear from her.

[Richmond Hill]

July 10

Dear Captain (what, again?)

Your airmail of June 22 and July 2 arrived with a loud, double "whump" this morning. Boy, *eight days* for the letter that you slipped through the Yank postal system. One has to hand it to them for the moral support they give their troops. I've been sitting here chuckling my head off at your brief sojourn at Div HQ and about the Rome leave.

Our letter files, by the way, are becoming enormous. Perhaps some day you'll put them in a book, or perhaps in the waste basket. Sister Jean sent me a few letters that Dad had been keeping of mine. Mostly from France. Gosh, I hope mine to you aren't quite that dull. Apart from patrols and the odd raid, which we weren't allowed to write about, our life was dull as dishwater till one of the big, "over the top" shows came along, and the vast majority of us never got to see more than one of those because the rest of the time we were in hospital, or pushing up daisies.

I ought to get back to writing now, and hard, and I'm not turning a hand to it. But what the hell does it matter whether I write or not. It should be young voices being heard. All the older generation does is get in the way of the younger generation, until the younger generation gets old enough to get in the way of the next lot. Something ought to be done about that. War might be an excellent answer if we could only arrange to have it attended only by older men. Boy, wouldn't that be some war? It'd be fairly harmless because it would all bog down in paper at the rear.

Hell's bells, if here isn't another letter! About the trip to Naples with Betty and getting attacked by nurses and Italian women in a stone quarry. Or have I got it wrong? And about playing the "Internationale." Well, why not? If we had listened to the people who *did* listen to it long ago, a good many tens of thousands of young men wouldn't be where they are today. You wouldn't, any of you, be where you are today. There would have been no Hitler or, if there had been, he would have been as impotent as little Elmer. I wonder for how long we will remember that, but for the Russians and the "Internationale," we would most likely have already lost this war.

You're a dear old feller, Squib, to write so interestingly and so often to your friends. We wait for your letters like old Mutt used to wait for the gopher to come out of its hole. By jingo, if you had a dull time of it during the winter you've certainly been going to town in all senses of the word recently, and seeing people and places that make my eyes pop just to read about.

I'm wondering if your gypsy friend Susi will write, and what I'll say if she does. Helen, with feminine intuition, has already got you married to her and she has turned out to be a fifth columnist who has done a lot of sabotage in New York, and you have been court-martialled, and it's all the damnedest mess you ever heard about. I think you and Helen ought to be the full-time writers in the family. I'm simply running along behind, panting, and wondering what the next chapter will be about.

I've cooled down about the house and boat problem. It is going to work out all right, and all your future possessions will be in order when you return. And certainly there is going to be, God willing, a proper home for you to come back to with books, work bench, "quiet room," stuffed and moth-eaten birds and a dog wanting in or out most of the time.

[Alife]

July 9

Mes Enfants:

I celebrate the arrival of a parcel from you containing the bar of maple sugar, upon which I got sick as a hog, and the pound of chocolates which did nothing to settle an already queasy stomach which is afflicted with a return match of Sicilian dysentery – otherwise known as the Italian trots.

Reference the boat and house dilemma. Just stop trying to do so bloody much! Relax. Better to find the house and boat both in ruins when I return, than both of you in wheelchairs. Or why not sell the house and buy another on the Bay where you can take your ease? Natch, this would require that Pop quit wrangling librarians and settle down to writing books. Though you wouldn't be affluent, you could chuck the present life and be happy. And *I'd* be much happier about it all. Don't repeat DO NOT drive yourselves over the wall looking after "my house" and "my boat." They *aren't* mine. They are yours and will always remain yours. And who knows, maybe I'll go off and live with the Indians when I get back. I certainly like the Indians I've known in this man's army. Stout fellas, every one of them.

At the moment we are on another effing scheme consisting of practising how to drive convoys of trucks from point A to point B and back again, thereby uselessly consuming oceans of petrol while grinding the already lousy Eyetie roads into such obstacle courses that even the local goats eschew them, thereby demonstrating the utter imbecility of the red-tabbed gents who think they are running this war while creating monumental balls-ups. Did I tell you about the cartoon drawn by my I-Sgt here? He's a cracking good artist. The picture is a back view of a bull elephant, well endowed, and the legend under it reads: "The higher the formation – the bigger the balls!" *C'est la vérité!*

In case you are wondering what my new job entails, the Brigade Intelligence Orifice is set up in a 60-cwt covered truck housing me, an I-Sgt, an I-Cpl and three ORs. One of our tasks is to receive mountains of bumph from Higher Formations about the German army's order of battle, disposition of troops, equipment, tactics and etc. *ad nauseam*, then filter out what might be of use to the battalions. The concentrated residue is then sent to the unit IOs. Don't ask what they do with it. Use your imagination. For their part, the unit IOs gather gen about the enemy on their front and send it back to me. My guys then transcribe it into the prescribed form of military gobbledygook and start it on its way back to the Brains in the distant rear. (Like the dinosaurs, the army keeps *its* Brains in the rear.) Our other duties include keeping the battle maps up to date; keeping the official war diary; and writing reports of every action the brigade engages in. I am also responsible for security and for hoodwinking the enemy whenever possible. This is somewhat more difficult than hoodwinking the blithering idiots in the rear, a skill which I am beginning to acquire under the tutelage of our BM who was once a dairy farmer from Napanee and is, as he proudly says, expert at spreading manure where it will do the most good.

Another batch of old letters is on its way to you. Store 'em away amongst my birds' nests somewhere.

Some casual figuring leads me to conclude that I now must have about $3000 salted away in one place or another. This means I won't have to take a job for a good four years. I just might spend a little time at university – if they let me do it my way. But I don't intend to waste any more of my life doing "brain exercises." If I can take the subjects I want, and only those, with or without getting a degree, I might take a crack at it.

One thing about being IO. When the BS gets too much to bear, I can "disappear" on a Secret Intelligence Mission. I'm going off on one right now – to spend a couple hours under a fig tree reading *Adam Bede*. Why *Bede*? Because we still ain't got no books, and he is all I can find.

❖ ❖ ❖

DURING THE LATTER HALF OF JULY AND INTO EARLY AUGUST, my parents were cruising in *Scotch Bonnet*, in and around the Bay of Quinte – home waters to both of them since childhood. Although they continued to write to me weekly, none of their letters during this period have survived.

❖ ❖ ❖

[Alife]

July 16

Dear Folks:

Our incarceration in the Eyetie Desert continues. Hotter than the hobs of hell, and the local wells and river are all drying up. Even the little green lizards are sitting in the shade of the rocks, panting. Cold beer is a daydream in a nightmare. But we still have *vino*. Speaking of which, some genius stuffed shirt decided we are drinking too much of the stuff. So the other day we get a stern warning from High Above that there is as much alky in a quart of *vino rosso* as in a bottle of rye whisky. The word spread like wildfire and is considered the best news to have come out of the rear end of the army for many a moon.

There's been a lot of changes recently. We've got a new boss, and Dan Spry has a new job, alas. He took with him a bunch of the staff from our HQ, most of them pals of mine. So we've got a flock of new bods, and life ain't the same. But we had one dandy Hail and Farewell party for the old lot, and again the Brig singled me out. Not to get married this time, because, I regret to say, my bride has been sent back to England to take charge of a nursing establishment there. Maybe just as well. Anyhoo, the Brig in his farewell speech predicted I would some day write a book. He claims he likes my poetry, especially the one about the ptarmigan:

The Ptarmigan (a kind of grouse)
Lives in the Arctic with his spouse.
Though Ptarmigan are smart and perky
They don't taste near as good as pturkey.

Personally I think this was why he didn't take me with him to his new job.

The regiment is now almost unrecognizable. Everybody you knew, and most of the ones I knew, are gone. But we had a Regimental Bash in Naples a while ago that will long live in memory. I somehow ended up aboard a U.S. cruiser in Naples Harbour, fending off the attentions of a Hindu guy who said he was a maharajah. The details of the whole affair are somewhat unclear, but the family virtue remains unmarred. I recall being set ashore by a Yank naval officer wearing enough braid to be an admiral, and being packed into Lulu Belle Mk. III by the ever-faithful Benny Bennett and carted back to camp. So here we remain and, from the look of things, may remain forever. I enclose another entry for Mowat's Bestiary. Writing such things helps preserve my sanity.

Well, Hardly Ever

A poet named E. Allan Poe
Kept a raven that talked like a crow.
It quoth, "Nevermore,
You mad son-of-a-whore!"
Which, for Poe, was *le mot à propos*.

[Alife]

July 30

Breaking in a new boss and all the new bods around here is keeping me so busy I barely have time to eat or, pardon the word, crap. Lord, Lord, why do all new brooms feel they have to sweep a clean swathe ten miles wide? The new boss's name is Calder, from the Saskatchewan Light Infantry. Seems a good type, or will be when he slows down a bit.

A bunch of the fellows left for the Heartland yesterday, but obviously I wasn't among them. I still go on looking about nineteen, and as if I had a good ten years of battle-fighting left in me. If I could only look properly ancient and decrepit I might get sent home. Why in hell did you produce a cherub for an offspring? Cherubic looking, anyway.

This damn war looks like becoming an Einsteinian exercise in infinity. The news has been getting "better" for about three years now. Its "betterness" seems to have the power to accelerate in the minds of news commentators and reporters until it runs away with them. If this mess isn't over with in another year, the "better" headlines won't leave any *room* for the news of peace. Never *finito*. Just getting "better" and "better" and "better" until I want to howl with frustration.

Tonight I may howl for other reasons. I have to participate in a Golden Gloves fistic encounter with that notorious slugger from the Hasty Ps, Wensley the Battling Banker (otherwise the unit's paymaster). We will fight for possession of the Brigade Mighty Midget Belt which, I hear, is a ten-foot length of tank track. I fight under the nom-de-plume of "Muscles Mowat" and I guarantee da bum won't lay a glove on me. . . . How in hell I get myself into these things I'll never know.

Mail has again become very slow and erratic after the much publicized reorganization of the post office in Canada. What happened? Did the postmaster general get re-elected in a by-election and so can now relax?

There is a new damn fool regulation limiting us to nine hundred cigs a month. Seems we've been accused of using cigs as money in dealing with the Eyeties for eggs, *vino* and . . . whatever. Or is it that the Zombies back home are running short? Not to worry. Nine hundred cigs a month never got through to us anyway, even when you were sending a couple of thou a month. But the crackdown may be hard on the poor fellows in the rear areas. As for us, well, business must go on, but the quartermaster will have to indent for a lot more boots and blankets, bags of flour and sugar, and such like so we can continue to pay our way.

Frankie Hammond just came in to tell me he is posted home. Yep, back to Canada. With his majority, and an MC, he is now in clover. But I'm a little disappointed to see him so obviously glad to go. Maybe that's just jealousy. But God only knows, the guy has earned the trip. Hasn't seen his wife in over three years, and him just married a week before he left for overseas. He will bring you some stuff from me. If you two aren't using the boat, you might let him have it, just to live aboard for a few days with his wife. He needs to go off somewhere and find out what she's like – get to know the stranger in his family, so to speak. I know he'd be tickled if you made the offer.

Again I holler, "Why doesn't Pop *retire*?" Forget the BS about how much the libraries need him. Go write some more books, like a sensible man, and desist from harassing those poor lady librarians.* As for finding a young and worthy male successor – the worthy ones are all over here, and by the time they get back they'll be grizzled and impotent. So why not get some nice young female type to do the job? Don't plan on holding it open for me. I don't intend to go to work for anyone once I leave the employ of King George. Not going to waste time sitting at a desk in some dirty stinking office making money for some dirty stinking boss. Maybe I'll keep bees. It's been done before, I hear, and I like bees, which are honest little critters. But to be truthful, I don't have a clue what I will do. All I can think of are the things I won't.

[Richmond Hill]

Aug 20

My Dear Young Feller. –

Yes, we were "advised" in the daily "news" about Brigadier Spry's promotion and supposed he would take you with him. Which we see he didn't. I'll look forward to seeing Hammond, and he can have the boat as much as he wants. We are going down to Whitby tomorrow to sail her to Toronto, or Oakville, or wherever the wind blows.

Are you beginning to take my kidding about what you'll do after the war seriously? If so I'll quit. And do stop talking about the old man retiring. I will. Sure I will. But try to get it through your head that the whole new libraries act and provincial library organization has got to be revolutionized, and that's my job. And when I speak of a worthy young man to succeed me, of course I know where they are, but some are trickling home more or less bust up in the body as I was

---

* Far from harassing the lady librarians, Angus had, as I learned some years later, been doing his best to alleviate the loneliness of as many of them as would let him into their beds. And that was quite a number. Perhaps this extra-curricular activity throws light on his bland indifference to my suggestions that he retire and go live quietly in the country.

when I got back, but with the determination and maturity to tackle this kind of job.

We feel the way you do about the official war news. Actually we get more genuine news out of a good small paper like the *Picton Gazette* than we do out of the city papers, which have to out-shock each other with headlines every twenty-four hours and are completely sick-making.

Coming back out of the army this time after four years of utter frustration, I find I'm just as much upset as the last time I came back after being a real (well, fairly real) soldier. I don't know what the hell I want to be. And that is the way you'll be, so you are quite sensible in standing out for a period of sitting on your fanny till you see which way you want to jump – or whether you want to jump at all. But you won't sit still long. You've got too much of your Poppa's restlessness and curiosity about life and things. What you'll do is write. You won't be able to help it. But for that you have to have perspective, which can't possibly be achieved in your present position. That's why, for instance, there are no really good war books until quite a time after a war. Things have to sift themselves out in a fellow's subconscious, which they can't do with Moaning Minnies and such things crumping around.

I now think *Carrying Place* is miles ahead of *Then I'll Look Up* but I don't see how it could possibly be a best-selling book. It would have to be strident and screaming and packed with libidinous suggestions. I'm busting to get at the next, which will be called *Living in a Snug Cove Afloat Without Paying Rent and Not Having Distressing Adventures at Sea*. I still haven't thought up any chapters except the one about what guests do to bugger up the toilet. Sorry. I oughtn't to mention toilets to one with your affliction. But I picture the *Bonnet* in some lovely cove with wings folded and the two of us wrangling as to who's to have the typewriter for an important chapter. Make it soon, son.

A Pauper Army

❖ ❖ ❖

First Division spent more than a month incarcerated in the dusty Volturno Valley. Meantime the pursuit of the German armies north from Rome slowed to a crawl, giving the enemy time to regroup and to establish a new defence line (to be called the Gothic Line) across the wide part of the Italian leg from Pisa on the west to Pesaro on the eastern coast. Here the Allied advance was brought to a halt.

The overwhelming victory that Allied military planners had confidently predicted had eluded us; now the strategists began losing interest in the Italian Theatre. By the end of July, most of the U.S. 5th Army, together with the Free French Corps, had been withdrawn from action to prepare for a seaborne invasion of southern France. Eighth Army was seriously weakened by the dispatch of several of its divisions to northern France. Patched up with scratch formations, including some reconstituted Italian divisions, the 8th was now given the task of preventing the enemy from withdrawing any significant portion of the twenty-five German divisions defending northern Italy, for had those divisions been free to move to France, they might well have turned the tide of battle there against the Allies.

The only way Hitler and his High Command could be persuaded that the Allied troops remaining in Italy constituted a real threat to Austria and southern Germany was for the 8th to attack, attack again, and yet again. There was only one sector which could offer any hope of success to a new offensive. This was on the east coast, where a narrow plain, less than ten miles wide, opened between the shoulders of the Apennines and the Adriatic Sea.

On July 25 First Division left the Volturno on a long, slow journey northward. Our initial moves were designed to hoodwink the enemy into believing that an attack would be launched from the vicinity of Florence, whereas 8th Army's real intention was to thrust northward on the Adriatic coastal plain.

Like a gigantic tourist caravan, the convoys rolled through central Italy, seeing Rome (from the back of moving trucks), Assisi, Perugia, Lake Trasimeno, Siena and finally Florence. Security was supposedly very tight but in fact we made certain that the Germans would hear about this peregrination. Then, having demonstrated our presence in the Florence area for a few days, we moved swiftly eastward, this time in *utmost* secrecy. On August 22, as our convoys descended from the interior mountains, we began to hear the roar of gunfire from the coastal plains below us. The attack on the Gothic Line had already begun.

It was a vastly different First Division that prepared to engage in its second trial of arms on the Adriatic coast. Although we had been much praised for winning a great victory at the Hitler Line, we had received small reward. Reinforcements needed to bring the units back up to strength were few in number and consisted mostly of soldiers wounded once, and even twice, who were now being returned to face the guns once more. The flow of volunteers from Canada had been withering, and what was left of it was now mostly being diverted to reinforce the Canadian divisions in north-west Europe. We were short of men but we were also starved of equipment. Although our war-worn vehicles were in a state of near collapse, they were not replaced. Even our guns were wearing out. Soon we would find ourselves short of ammunition. While great battles raged in France and Russia, we were becoming a pauper army.

Nevertheless we were of good heart. Although we no longer placed much trust in our senior military leaders (and none in our political leaders), our faith in our own community grew ever stronger. Our world shrank until it encompassed only the few thousands of comrades with whom we were committed to battle. We had no illusions as to what that battle might portend. Fear of death and dismemberment grew like a worm within, but we had become a tight-knit tribe, sustained by the knowledge that, whether we lived or died, we would do so in good company.

Most of us were also sustained by those who cared for us at home. Because they willed it so, and strained every effort of mind and spirit to make it so, my parents kept alive for me another, inner world of sanity, of trust, of love. This they made manifest through their letters – which had never before been of such vital consequence.

[Florence]

Aug 7

Dear Folks:

Getting somewhat lax in letter writing, but things are a bit difficult at the moment, so excuse.

A letter from you, written aboard *Bonnet*, has just arrived and it makes me drool. Why they couldn't post me to the defence of the Belleville Bridge or the Murray Canal I can't understand. It would free up a Zombie and I might even be more use there than I am here since I am again developing a fine set of "whiz-bang" nerves. I can hear the Jerry shells coming before they are even fired. And when it comes to maintaining a military stance . . . hell, I walk around doubled over like I had the crud. Wherever I go after the war, I hope it'll be free of loud noises.

Can't tell you where we are, or what we're up to. The matter is so hush-hush that I expect only the Germans know for sure. I figure their intelligence has to be better than ours since they have the whole Italian fascist network to gather info for them. My current job, and it is driving me nuts, is to make sure that we are unidentifiable – all insignia on uniforms and vehicles removed or covered; observing complete wireless silence; no contact with civilians, and etc. etc. And yesterday when I drove the temporarily anonymous Lulu Belle into a village the Jerries had left, but which our troops hadn't yet occupied, it was to be greeted by a chorus of kids chanting, "*Canadesi molto buoni, viva Canada!*"

I *can* tell you that I have billeted myself in a *palazzo* of magnificent proportions which is still occupied by an aged member of the Medici family. He is a sculptor and lives alone except for a butler as old as he is. And he chooses to hang out in the *palazzo*'s vast, glassed-in conservatory, which is full of potted palms and erotic marble bods. He beds down amongst these on a sort of hospital cot of gilded fretwork with the Medici arms on the head of the thing. All day long he hammers away at his nudes while Jerry hammers away at a bridge in the neighbourhood with heavy stuff – 17 and 21 centimetre. The concussions have bust out most of the conservatory glass, but the old boy carries on as if it was all in the day's work. He invited me to share a candle-lit dinner, served by his butler on family silver . . . in the conservatory. Did I accept? Did I, hell. Doc and I ate Spam and biscuits in one of the Duke's wine cellars.

In case I haven't mentioned it before, I've still got the Italian Trots and if I lose any more weight I'm like to blow away. Actually it hasn't seriously incapacitated me, except that I can't touch *vino* any more. Mother, if this is a judgement in answer to one of your prayers, please lay off. I don't feel any the better for this enforced abstinence, and not much the worse for the bug, except when the nearest latrine is in the open, three hundred yards away, and it is shelling out. I'll never get acclimatized. My new boss is making sure of that. He insists that Tac HQ has to be within shouting distance of the infantry. I think he means *shooting* distance, and I hope to God he develops a better sense of self-preservation before it's too late! The silly bugger *sleeps* in his office-caravan four feet off the ground. *I* sleep in a slit trench four feet *under* the I-truck.

[east of Senigallia on the Adriatic coast]

Aug 20

Sorry for the last week's silence but I've been very busy earning my seven bucks per day. The Intelligence racket has become the most bewildering collection of odd jobs one man ever told another about which. Between rounding up civvy spies at midnight (turned out to be an old geezer leading his mule to a safer place by lantern-light), lecturing on chemical warfare, keeping track of the order of battle, trying to second-guess the Jerries on our front, trying to mislead said Jerries about our own intentions, interrogating Jerry deserters, stooging for the Brig, and having to reconnoitre a new slit trench every day because we are now forever on the move, your one and only has become the busiest little critter you ever did see.

Mike Woods, our crafty staff captain, says he will wrangle a confirmation of rank for me from the doughheads in the adjutant general's warren. As is, my captaincy is listed as "whilst so employed," presumably as IO. Who knows? Mike might succeed. He is a great believer in the motto: Bullshit Baffles Brains. It would be a great relief to Doc. He has taken to mounting my third pips on my epaulets with dome fasteners, so they can be quickly and easily removed or replaced, as called for.

Another job of the Intelligence wallahs is to predict the future, and in the mess the other night I got tricked into betting that *la guerre* in Italy might be *finito* by November 15. If I'm right, I'm going to set up shop at Delphi. If wrong, I'll be a cinch for the job of military commentator on the *Toronto Star*. This *does* look like the year, but if by chance we don't make the grade in '44 the bloody war may run on well into '45.

The Second Front (hell, it's the *third* front – *we* opened the second front in July of '43!) seems to be getting all the press attention these days, but it may not be long before you again are hearing news from Italy. And that's a dinkum prediction, as the Aussies would say.

[Toronto]

Sept 2

Squib, Old Son. –

Saturday morning and The Building is closed and dead as a tomb so I'll have my weekly gam with you.

The three of us have been out for a week "doing" Welland and

Haldimand counties. We began at Niagara Falls and ended up at Simcoe on Lake Erie. A pleasant late summer drive and a lot of the worst public libraries in the world. Which is hard to understand since this is wealthy farming country. We could see why the farmers were wealthy, having bought a bushel of melons that were very nice on top and very rotten below.

This afternoon we are going for a "duty" sail. I have been promising to take Reg Saunders and his staff out for years, and they have certainly been very good to me. There will be about seven or eight of them and they'll all be underfoot, and it will probably blow like hell and the rotten old mainsail will rip to ribbons and all will be merry as a wedding bell.

Well, son, even you and I have to admit that the news from the front is really damned good at last. Of course, the broadcasters and newspapers are several weeks ahead of our armies. But this morning the breakthrough of the Gothic Line by 8th Army was announced. This was a shock to Helen, who had developed a theory that the Germans had withdrawn from Italy and you would be seeing no more action till the next war. She is keenly disappointed, and that is not as silly as it sounds because the war is already won as far as the civilian populace of Canada is concerned. This does not please everyone, for there are some who might have wished that it, and its accompanying profits, could have gone on for fifty years.

Mum sends her love, and Elmer wants to get going, so it's off to sway up the old red sails again. No word from you for some time now, but the reason is not far to seek. S'long, feller.

[Richmond Hill]

Sept 5

We were talking about your rank last night. I said we must pray that the war continues for at least six months after the date of your promotion to "acting" captain in order that it might be confirmed. I explained that if you were set to another task in the meantime, you would become a lieutenant again. This put Mum in a "quarry" (as *her* mum used to say) but on the whole she thought it would be better if the war ended tomorrow and you remained a subaltern forever after.

It is partly nice and partly upsetting to see the 8th back in the news again, however briefly. The *Globe and Mail* even got around to mentioning the units of the First Brigade this morning and the CBC last night referred to the "half-forgotten 8th Army." This made me very angry, considering what is owed to that army, but it is quite understandable. The news from France has been so stupendous that even I am permitting myself to hope that it may all be over in Europe within a year or so. But I'm waiting to see how the Huns do on their own soil.

By the way, have you seen Eisenhower's statement in which he takes the U.S. press to task for creating the impression that the Yanks have been doing the whole show in France? He stated that the British and Canadians had been given the hard task and that without its performance, the Yanks couldn't have moved a yard. Some of the Canadian press, which takes its cue from south of the border, seemed quite surprised to hear this. I wonder how long it will be before we become American in everything but name, or will we eventually lose even that?

The sail on Saturday was successful. It blew right smart and some of the male publishers deposited their luncheons, which had been mostly liquid, in Toronto Bay. Some of the lady publishers tried to use the toilet and turned the valves the wrong way and nearly sank *Scotch Bonnet*. It is all grist to the mill for my new book.

[south of the Gothic Line at the Metauro River]

Aug 25

Dear Parents:

It is now 2205 and at 2400 the 8th Army will strike the blow which ought to be the beginning of the end for the Hun in Italy. By tomorrow night we should know whether our war will last a month, or another winter. Now it's all in the hands of the gods of Valhalla, and may they smile upon us, particularly on the men of the PBI who at this moment are feeling their ways tensely through the black night towards the river which is the start line for the attack.

Yet the autumnal somnolence seems complete. No gun has been fired from our side of the Sangro River for days now – nothing done to disabuse the enemy from concluding that the Adriatic front remains quiescent, manned only by skeleton Allied forces, while a major offensive is being prepared on the opposite side of Italy. It has been part of my job for the past three weeks to help foster this illusion, and we'll soon know how successful we have been.

During the past week, an almost empty landscape of vineyards, orchards, ravines and dry river beds has become so densely populated that there hardly seems room for another truck, another platoon, or another gun. Brought forward under cover of darkness, masses of men and machines hide themselves from the view of enemy OPs by day, and at night again inch their way forward. Now, uncounted guns are lifting their snouts towards the north like hell-hounds sniffing the Jerry spoor, preparing to begin their cataclysmic outpouring of steel and fire. Sitting here at my radio set, I am only a few hundred yards ahead of the nearest batteries of twenty-five-pounders, and when they and the mediums and the heavies let loose, this truck will shake and shudder as if in the grip of a hurricane. Through the blasted night will come the occasional crump of an enemy shell as the startled crews of German guns frantically fire back at no particular targets but at a southern horizon that is erupting from the mountains to the sea with an opening barrage being fired by some four hundred of our guns.

Strange pauses, rather like those that suddenly silence the hubbub of a cocktail party, will occasionally quiet the billowing roar, and through these pauses will come the plodding, determined beat of Bren guns, and the hysterical chattering of answering Spandaus. The Very lights will burst in rainbow colours over the river and half-dressed paratroopers will scramble out of their deep holes, rush wildly in the dark to man their machine guns and mortars and then, as the full force of that awful barrage falls upon them, scuttle back to their holes. Some will pray. And some will curse. And some will cover their heads and scream. And some will die.

I don't know what kind of barrages you had in your war, but I can conceive of nothing like the obliterating concentration of fire that will descend on Jerry's positions soon. It seems incredible that any living thing will be able to live through the weight of metal which will whine and shrill above our heads. Tomorrow I think there will be many of the *Herrenvolk* for whom *Der Tag* has come. But there will also be farm lads from the counties, maybe a stockbroker from Toronto, and a host of others, some of whom may be friends of mine.

The ground is beginning to quiver now from the vibrations of hundreds of tanks still so far away as to be unheard, but only felt as they crawl up to join the infantry. And now there is true noise – the discordant drone of bombers winging their ways towards the petrol dumps, ammo stores, supply routes and reinforcement camps behind the Jerry lines. With the dawn, their ponderous drone will be joined by the skirl of fighter-bombers circling disdainfully in skies that are now always ours, searching for the fleeing staff car, the stubbornly resisting strong point, the wildly driven ammo truck, the hapless tank that has tried and failed to pretend it was a straw stack.

My God. The way I'm talking you'd think I'm anticipating with enjoyment what's soon to come – instead of being scared stiff. Right now my set is tuned to London and I am trying to concentrate my attention on the thin strains of a dance band. Also I am sitting at a typewriter banging out a letter to Canada in which I say *don't* buy me any more war bonds! Who the hell is crazy around here?

A flock of messages coming in now from the forward posts. Looks as if Jerry is getting restless – as well he might. I gotta go.

[overlooking the Foggia River]

Aug 29

This is the continuation of an airmail I wrote you three days ago while waiting for zero hour.

Three days later, the first stage of the offensive is over and there has come about one of those inexplicable lulls that makes the shift in the moods of battle so extreme. Last evening, the last shell of German defensive fire that had been going on for twenty-four hours burst not far away. Jerry was trying to silence our guns, which were pounding the bejasus out of him, and interdict our troops and tanks moving foward on the only passable road in the region. And our worthy Brig had chosen to establish Tac HQ beside a bridge on that road, in the middle of a concentration of our field artillery. Jerry stonked the area with from twenty to fifty shells every hour, with calibres ranging up to 17 cm. People were hit while talking to you. Radio sets were smashed while you sat beside them with the earphones on. Jeeps were blown off the road to land upside down in the mud. Even the Brig's precious caravan, parked cheek by jowl between two stone barns, was perforated (he wasn't in it), and our mess truck was riddled like one of the cook's own colanders. For twenty-four hours, my every thought was contingent on the flat crash of exploding shells. Then I went to bed and got up to a quiet Indian summer day. Sounds of battle have faded to a distant mumble, like a departing summer thunderstorm. We had canned bacon with real eggs for breakfast, eaten under a fig tree laden with fruit. Chicken stew for lunch, then an hour's sun bathing, then a hot bath in the open air, refreshed by a balmy breeze, and an evening drink and a good book to read. Jerry had decamped.

To be frank, I've never experienced such a terrific and complete contrast before. And I marvel at the adaptability of the human animal that enables me to write this, feeling perfectly normal, after a good night's sleep, and as happy as usual. However, I suppose we will pay for it later in our lives.

Last night I crawled into my slit trench cradling a bottle of rye. I was firmly determined that at the arrival of the first Jerry shell in my vicinity, I would up-end the bottle and so sink into a numbed slumber. Well, I kept waiting for the "crump" – and darned if I didn't just drift off, awakening this morning with the still-full bottle in my paws. And there is no excuse to drink it this morning. War is hell.

Spent a relaxed time sipping *vino* with Bill Boss, who is a Canadian Press war correspondent and a good type. His stories come from up front, and he tells it mostly as it is from the rankers' point of view. As a result, he is not liked by the high mucky-mucks. *This* evening we talked about the *paucity of good Canadian writing!* My God, we could have been sitting in a Toronto pub.

You will in due course read about this battle which, if it continues to unfold as well as at present, will likely be the beginning of the end of the Italian campaign. *The* brigade has certainly done its part and is now resting and licking its wounds while others chase after Jerry. We hope they make out O.K., otherwise we will no doubt have to help them out. We are *the* Shiny First, and no one doubts it when the going gets sticky.

Have had a lot of prisoners to deal with. One was a twenty-year-old *Hauptmann* (*my* rank, and him only twenty!) who was a red-hot Nazi and spoke good English. He worshipped *der Führer*, bragged sickeningly about the prowess of the Wehrmacht, deprecated Canadian soldiers to the level of guerrillas, and gave a short speech on world politics that might have been a commencement exercise for his class in dear old Hamburg High. I paraphrase it: Today I am more convinced than ever of the ultimate victory of the Fatherland. The Allied High Command has ordered that the war be ended this year, because they know by next year their armies will fall apart from exhaustion. The U.S.A. is ready to quit and go back into the isolationism which our agents have inculcated so well. England and her native troops are finished with war because they have been bled white. The English will sue for peace in six months and offer to join us against the Russian Beast. We will not need them. Russia has made her last, dying effort and will shortly collapse into a barbarian rabble, etc. etc. etc.

Apart from being highly incensed at being called "native troops," I felt a kind of horror at this specimen. Can anyone believe it will be possible to educate such creatures to another way of thought? The more I see of the Hun, the more convinced I am that sooner or later Germany will do it again. We should realize this and prepare ourselves for it so that we won't be caught with our pants down again. The Russkies know this, but I'll bet the Yanks and our lot will be having a love feast with Germany a couple of years after we've beaten the ass off them. So much the worse for us.

Perhaps a hundred years hence the bloodied remnant of humanity will, in its ultimate desperation, find a way to eliminate the twin cancers of greed and war, but I doubt it. It might be amusing to hear what the next dominant animal species on this planet will have to say about us. "Lord, what pitiable fools"?

Ah well, not to worry. The next twenty years are going to be good ones for me but I don't think I want to go through the agony of watching my children thrown into the next cataclysm. Ergo, I shall produce none if I can help it. But can I help it? Ain't biology wonderful? For rabbits, yup.

Just for contrast. Yesterday the Hasties sent me up a good-looking young Bavarian POW. He was scared witless. Can't say as I blame him since it was raining 105s when he arrived, but that wasn't what was really eating him. He had been told we Canadians killed *and scalped* all prisoners. When our interpreter finally convinced him he wasn't going to be hurt, he broke down and bawled like a kid. He is another type of Jerry, but unfortunately a type that is easily led. And there will always be s.o.b.s in Germany to lead him where they will. And not just in Germany.

Well, I think I'll go read *Brave New World* again and have my little laugh, along with Huxley.

[Richmond Hill]

Sept 12

Dear Brother. –

Your letters of Aug. 25 and 29, written just before and after the attack towards (I suppose) Rimini, came over the weekend. It's hellish decent of you to write so often these days, knowing that scraping woodwork and painting till we are too tired to see straight doesn't really do much towards allaying anxiety. Putting together what you are able to say, and the news dispatches, I get at least some idea of what is going on. There isn't much said about Italy and what *is* said is veiled, and some of it is just pure balls, like telling us on the radio this morning that the Germans are getting out of Italy, because a neutral diplomat in Milan said that five hundred trucks a day were crossing the Brenner

Pass laden with Italian art treasures! Helen now listens to the news upstairs while I listen downstairs because she can no longer bear my yips of anguish and bellows of rage when something as fatuous as the above comes over the air.

Your recent letters give me much food for thought. Our barrages were probably not so heavy as yours but, I should think, more concentrated as both sides were shooting at well-defined trench systems packed with men. Canadians killed amounted to about sixty thousand in four years, but I should think that if modern gunners had been working on us it would have been more like a hundred thousand.

You said quite a lot when you remarked that, in spite of the way you can apparently settle into calmness after a show, you'll probably pay for it in after years. Yes, you will. You'll feel the effects full force if you get hit, or if you come out of the line for any other reason, and know you aren't ever going back in. It's a delayed response and is very tough to take, and you've got to prepare for it. Different people handle it in different ways.

My cure was to immerse myself totally for weeks in Western stories, of all the damn silly things. And of course there are many who don't get over it. You see them in the beer halls today, scrounging drinks and bumming smokes as they've been doing for a score of years. To most civilians they *are* simply bums. And it is impossible to explain what has happened to them, unless you have been through it. People, even doctors, just look at you with raised eyebrows when you say that those fellows burned out in action and just fell apart like charred corpses in a sudden wind when the flames around them were doused. The navy and air force, with their generous leaves and breaks for combat troops are, I think, doing something to halt or at least retard the burn-out process, but it would seem that, as far as the infantry is concerned, nothing has changed. Anyway, your thoughts on the subject are so true they make me feel as if the years between the wars had never been, or the years between you and me.

But I don't go with your pessimism about the next war. Barring a bourgeois revolution there, a thing that seems most unlikely, the Russians certainly can be expected to ensure that Germany never again becomes a major military power. Mayhaps two generations of education would turn the Hun into a pacific people, but the effort required would be simply tremendous. Also, our own house is very much to be put in order.

Elmer, who is under the desk making dreadful smells, sends his love. He sniffs your letters and gets an intelligent look, as much as to say, "Hell's bells, of course I remember that guy, from Camp Borden days." Elmer was just a youngster then, and now he's getting up in years, just like your Pa.

[near the Conca River]

Sept 1

Dear Parents:

We are enjoying a couple of days in reserve although I am working twice as hard as when the brigade is in the line. And I am not so fond of this HQ any more. My principal grouse is that the new boss doesn't see eye to eye with me on how battle histories and official war diaries should be written. Somewhat to my surprise, I find that ill-informed (make that stupid) and inept literary criticisms of even such run-of-the-mill stuff make me excessively annoyed. The temptation to tell him to write his own bumpf, if that's what he wants, is almost irresistible. But then I'd be Lieut. Mowat again, and poor old Doc would cry.

Also I find myself surrounded more and more by people with whom I can get along only with great personal effort. Jobs at Div and even at Bde are being increasingly filled from the rear rather than from the front. It seems there is a fat surplus of non-combatant officers qualified for staff jobs. And a shortage of same willing to serve in combat. And a lot of the newcomers here are, you will have to excuse me, Maw, shit-headed. If I have to listen to one more Grade 4 dirty joke I'll throw a slug into someone's smutty mug. God knows I'm hardly a puritan, but slime is slime, and only to be excused in adolescence. One serious drawback to army life is the inability to choose your companions. This doesn't matter at the front, where circumstances select the best, but to the rear it can become a real malaise.

[across the Conca River]

Sept 5

Some mail got up to us today, the first in a couple of weeks, including a parcel from Molly Noonan whom I loved and lost so long ago in Kingston. Can't think why she should remember me at this late date, but mine not to reason why.

I wait patiently for the appearance of *Carrying Place* which, despite Pop's pessimism about the reading public, is sure to have a wide appeal. I am counting on this if only to free me from the drudgery of slaving for a living when I get home.

Speaking of writers. One Mrs. Ernest Hemingway arrived on my doorstep today in slacks, a bandanna, and a U.S. combat jacket strung with cameras and notebooks. The Brig and the BM were busy fighting a war so I got stuck with her and had to listen to and try to answer a lot of asinine questions ("I hear your troops are mostly Indians. What tribes do they represent?") and be properly impressed by The Importance of Being Ernest's Wife. By good luck I had a bunch of Turkoman POWs on hand (Mongols from beyond the Caucasus, impressed into the German army) whom I introduced to her as some of our Native Scouts just back from a sortie behind the Jerry lines. The silly bitch was enthralled, but her "accompanying officer" from Army HQ smelled a rat. Me. Hi ho, I did my best to give her what she wanted. God preserve me from females in slacks who think war is a grand and glorious game.

The BBC news says that Jerry is fleeing from us in wild retreat. Like hell he is! He is digging in his heels at every valley, every hill and casa, and staying put until we blast him out. Wish the silly bastards would listen to the BBC. Would save us a lot of sweat and grief. We've had just two days out of range of hot stuff since this campaign started, and I am welching on my bet about Nov. 15.

Have you heard from Susi yet? Maw, you had best start learning Austrian with a gypsy accent. And just wait until you meet Auntie. But before you have a fit, remember that monogamy is not going to be my style. I expect to have a house full of women which, I'm told, can be a paying proposition. I have decided to make my living *après la guerre* by writing for *Zippy Stories*, *Garter Tales* and *Forbidden Frolics*. I understand that the research required can be edifying. *And* I am growing a new moustache. I hope this one will be visible.

Sorry pals, it is getting too damn noisy up here in the I-truck. I think I'll make for a nearby cellar.

[Toronto]

Sept 20

Dear Squibbles. –

Carrying Place should be out by the tenth of next month. I'll send you an autographed copy. The price is $3, which you can remit by money order or bank draft. Reg has made a handsome book out of it. Advance sales are going well. One order of one hundred already, and several fifties and a number of twenty-fives. Though that doesn't mean a damn thing since the booksellers are buying it on Reg's reputation, not mine, and he has made it his leading book with two front pages in his catalogue, ahead even of Matthew Halton, the war correspondent.

The highways are full of servicemen hitch-hiking. I always pick up as many as I can until the poor old Dodge groans and creaks while the passengers argue fiercely as to which service is run the worst.

It's too bad things aren't so happy at your HQ. But there is nothing to be done except let the boss run the show as he sees fit. Do try and button down your mouth at least until you are confirmed in rank. Damn it, if you'd only learn to do a little more yessing, you'd get on better in the army. Lookit me! Oh the hell with it, I'd rather cling to the last few shreds of what I blushingly call my integrity, and I suppose you are tarred with the same brush. So the hell with you too then. It will be something to be the senior serving lieutenant in 8th Army when peacetime finally comes.

Is it coming soon? All the Ontario municipalities have been instructed to prepare plans for great victory festivities. Festivities, forsooth! As for me and mine, I guess we'll quietly sit down in what used to be the kitchen garden and think a little about those who won't come home, and those who come home maimed or burnt out, and the mothers and fathers and kids and wives who won't have anything to be festive about. Ho hum – there I go again, always in the minority. But I wish the end would come soon. Instead of being forgotten now, the 8th Army is only too much in the news these last few days and I have to keep telling Helen that of course the brigade is out "resting" but she's not so easily kidded as Martha Gellhorn (Mrs. Hemingway to you) whose book, *Liana,* is a lot of badly written nonsense about copulating in a garden, according to your Maw. I hope you were polite to her or you'll be in trouble again. You little burr!

[Toronto]

Sept 20

Why Hello Farl!

Here I am sitting down to a second letter in one day. Major Connie Smythe, RCA (and Military Cross in the other war), is back from Normandy badly wounded – him who used to run the Toronto Maple Leafs (or Leaves?). He has let loose with a long, front-page tirade in today's papers about reinforcements, saying he has talked to a lot of officers in Normandy and all agree that the new reinforcements are too few and don't know too much. Don't know how to fire a Bren gun, don't know how to use a Piat, don't know what to do with a grenade except pull the pin and wonder what the funny fizzzzing noise is all about. Anyhow – no good.

So out comes Defence Minister Ralston with a full denial. So shut up, Major Smythe, and don't go upsetting Canadian Parenthood and informing them that their sons mightn't have been killed if the reinforcements were more numerous and better trained.

I look at it in my usual dazed way and wonder what the hell. However, it is a very simple truism that as a war progresses, the quality of the individual soldier deteriorates. Bound to. The first are always the best, especially when they are volunteers. . . . But what a silly thing to be talking about the war to you, who would rather hear about anything else. Not my usual practice.

Colonel Yates is giving up command of the second battalion of the Hasties and I am told that I could have it if I so desired. I wish I could do it, but I can't. Not from here. But I do hope we can keep the militia

139

alive. It is now very well equipped and armed, indeed, and it would be a shame to return all that good machinery to stores when, who knows, it might someday be badly needed. Only for deer hunting, or partridge shooting, of course. I leave the scenario for you and your pals to write.

[Cattolica]

Sept 16

Good People All:

Sitting aloof and morose in my cluttered corner of the I-truck, I ponder on the ways of a dim and mouldy world. I have malaria again. Each time I get a jolt of it, I feel like Papa used to look when he had jaundice, discoloured and distempered. There is no sunlight on the green grass outside my window but only a dull, all-pervading and brackish mist engendered by large slugs of quinine, which substance I loathe and detest.

To make matters worse, I must shortly drag myself out of here, board Lulu Belle and, in company with Capitano Francisco Garibaldi Sacconi, perform a particularly distasteful part of my job. Who is Francisco? He is an Italian Army officer posted to us to liaise in such matters as Intelligence, Security, Procurement of *Vino*, and the odd (not so odd at that) accusation of rape by some local *signorita* against one of our Romeos. He is a rare character. Small and bird-like, he rises at 0500 daily, rain or shine, and does callisthenics, thereby setting a frightful example which we are terrified the Brig will order us to emulate. A veteran of the Duce's war in Abyssinia, he sports a monstrous black moustache, each end of which droops almost to his collar bone. To add to the general confusion, he also sports a goatee that tends to drift upward and become entangled with the underbrush beneath his nose.

Today he and I must dispossess, unhouse and otherwise remove three or four families of farmers who have somehow managed to survive in the ruins of a shell-shattered little village that has the misfortune to overlook Tedeschi's current defence line. Some bloody fool has reported seeing lights blinking from the ruins at night. Ergo, it is full of spies busy communicating vital secrets of our disposition to the

enemy. Balls and bullshit, of course, but they will have to go. Go
where? Well might you ask. We start them to the rear carrying whatever they can on their backs and heads, old folk, young folk, bambinos and maybe a goat or two. If they are lucky, they will end up in a
kind of concentration camp for refugees down around Bari. If they are
not lucky, they will be shipped by slow freight to *real* concentration
camps for collaborators, in Sicily. Poor, unfortunate bastards. All they
want is to be left alone in the wreckage of their homes and lives to try
and put things together again as best they can. But . . . *c'est la guerre.*

Francisco hates this sort of thing, and I have seen tears come to
his eyes upon occasion. Well, I can't say that it gives me much of a
boost either, even when some blighted staff officer at Div sends me
a memo of congratulation for having cleared "all the Wops" out of
our sector. Like I say, I'll be goddamned glad when this war is over,
if it ever is.

It now seems pretty certain that I am going to lose my bet. One
thing about Jerry, he is one tough s.o.b. But I've seen some radio inter-
cepts picked up by our lot in which the Germans give *our leaders* a lot
of credit for *their* success – they conclude our staff has made some
mighty blunders. Could you believe it?

But here comes the Capitano, and I must away.

[Richmond Hill]

Sept 30
Dear Farl. –

I've been driving the old car as little as possible these past weeks.
Trying to make it last longer than its makers intended which, as we all
know, is not very long. So I've taken to the rails again. The trains being
crowded to capacity, and the good people of Ontario paying the bill,
I have been using the first-class chair cars. However, I have only found
one fighting soldier in seven trips in first. Mostly the chair passengers
are male civilians of military age and, presumably, indispensable to the
War Effort, or else old bodies who have made their pile and ought to
have been painlessly oozed out long ago. So I'm going to travel coach
henceforth, where the infantry, tankers and other proletarians are.

They're a hell of a lot more interesting, and I gather quite a few stray clues and info about what has really been going on.

The news releases and war correspondents' stories are fearfully vague, but we can string a few facts and dates together and assure ourselves (wrongly, no doubt) that on such-and-such a day the brigade was doing certain things and on this day, therefore, is probably out of the line. Which is a great help in enabling your mother to compose her mind for sleep.

Of course we are wondering about the malaria now that you have casually mentioned it. Mum is reading it up in the fever book and even sees us heading to Saskatchewan again where the malaria doesn't grow, after you return. I had lunch opposite an old farmer from Saskatoon in the train the other day, who told me all about the wonderful crop on the prairies this year, and what the poplar bluffs look like, and what the coyotes and gophers are saying, and how the greenhead mallards are crowding the sloughs, until I got so fidgety I couldn't stay in my chair.

[Rome]

Sept 28

Dear People:

It is now 1230 hrs here in the Eternal City and I have had a medicinal *martini rossi* which has done me no good at all. I am p....d off for sure, so it probably behooves me to write my kith and kin.

P'd off in Roma? Well, here is how it came about. About a week ago, the Div came out of the line after the Rimini show, which was a bastard, not to say a débâcle. After eighteen days of continuous action, the brigade went into rest, which it badly needed, but on the day of our arrival in the rest area (another stretch of vineyards and olive trees) the BM informed me that I was urgently repeat urgently required to report to a base near Avellino (which is near Naples) to take part in a court-martial. There was no indication what said court-martial was all about or what role I was expected to play, whether president of same, witness or accused. The latter seemed most probable, so it was not without some trepidation that I hopped in Lulu

Belle (now Mark IV – Mark III got parked too near an incoming 105) and headed south.

Arriving at Avellino weary and dusty after an eight-hundred-kilo-metre endurance test, I reported to the proper office and found not a damn soul with any inkling of what I was wanted for, or if I was wanted at all. Nor could they have cared less. This being par in the old army game, I sighed wistfully and, thinking of the loss of my well-earned rest period, buzzed off down to Naples to work out my next move. It was beyond me. I was afraid to go home since sure 'n hell they'd call for me again the moment I arrived at the brigade.

Then, racking my somewhat atrophied brain, I dimly recalled an incident in Amalfi when I was there on leave, concerning a minor accident between two Limey trucks, of which I was, unfortunately, a witness. Since, improbable as it seemed, this was the only conceivable reason for my being in court, I hot-footed it back to Avellino and spilled the beans. And well, well, well, a snotty adjutant general's lackey from 8th Army did recall why I'd been sent for. "Frightfully funny, old chap, don't you think?" To make it even funnier, the Limeys had neglected to call the other witnesses to the collison. These, as I recall, were a couple of Special Service Desert Rats who by then were prob-ably mining Jerry trains in the Brenner Pass or somewhere equally remote behind the German lines.

"Awkward, what? But not to worry. We'll have them notified. Meantime, please hold yourself available."

Hold myself? I managed to *with*hold myself until I got out to the jeep. Then I whistled off to Rome where I have been for the past four days. Occasionally I telephone the AG chappie, but he either doesn't know who I am or, if he remembers, simply abjures me to be patient. Ye gods! And me with an irate brigadier who expected me back three days ago to write his damn and blasted battle narrative for him. When I do get back, if ever, I shall no doubt be a Lieut. again, and an unknown stranger to boot.

To top it off, yesterday I collected another bout of malaria and spent twenty-four hours in bed cursing the fates. One of these days I will tell the world to go to hell and go to hospital for a holiday.

From which you may gather that I am magnificently fed up. Moreover it now appears that another winter in this God-forsaken country is inevitable – a grim and gloomy thought to one who well recalls last Christmas outside Ortona.

Rome, incidentally, is like every other big city in the world – rotten. The crumbling rock piles that pass as antiquities do not compensate for miles of stinking slums. Nor do the *palazzi* of the wealthy few, including that lot holed up in the Vatican. Cities are not for the human kind; they are for the birds or, more accurately, the worms. Bad cess to the lot of them!

I shall now crawl back into bed there to dream fondly of T-bone steaks, curried veal, fireplaces and boats.

[Toronto]

Oct 13

Dear Mk II. –

The date is Oct. 13 and the place Toronto and I hope this letter is no. 121 or 122. We have had your letter about Rome and I'm shocked – again. I did so hope that the army in the field was different from the rabble in Canada. But it seems that as soon as you get past brigade, or maybe division, on the way to the rear, they are all tarred with the same brush.

However, it did give you a bit of a change, though an eight-hundred-kilometre jaunt in a jeep with malaria (not the jeep) couldn't have been much fun. Mum keeps asking me why you don't go sick with the thing and get into hospital and I'm damned if I know. Putting it on the lowest plane, I tell her that if you leave your present job before being confirmed in rank you lose your third pip. Then, soaring into the heights, I tell her that you don't report sick with malaria because it isn't done in places where people are becoming really sick with chunks of hot metal in their bodies. But I wish to God you could get a rest.

Frank Hammond has finally sent along the package of papers you gave him to bring home to us and we have read and re-read them with what avidity you may guess. I am fascinated by the battle narratives and stories. "Stephen Bates" is far and away the best thing you have ever done. If a publisher doesn't take that, then they are crazy.

Squibbie boy, you must fight like hell not to let malaria, the army, frustration or anything else get you down because you were born to write, and you've got to keep level-headed to write even though you may write the most un-level-headed things at times. Which we all do if we start young enough. Which was my great mistake, that I didn't. Damn it. Now here's a funny thing. In your verse you dip down into the depths and fling restraint to the winds and come out with things that are pretty much like "Strange Fruit" but lack conviction because, I think, they do lack restraint. But in your prose you get disciplined, and all first-class writing is closely disciplined. *Grapes of Wrath*, which is a masterpiece, is one of the most disciplined books I've ever read, and one of the most powerful. Why you should miss it in your verse and catch it in your prose is puzzling. My guess is that the verse is practice for the prose, although you may not see it that way at all.

So long, old feller. Keep a steady hand.

Stephen Bates

During the final hours before we made our landing in Sicily, I occupied myself with little things, with bits of scribbled paper, with meaningless reports that might be blown to bits in an hour or so. In the course of filling in some blanks in my platoon record book, I asked C 17948, Pte. Bates, S.E., who had come to me just before we boarded ship in Scotland and whom I had made my batman/runner, what his civilian job had been. He replied that he had been a coal miner when he was sixteen and had still been one when he enlisted at nineteen. There was an element of stolid pride in his voice which suggested that his father, and perhaps *his* father before him, had been coal miners – and damned good ones.

When we landed, Steve followed me through the surf then crawled into the barbed wire with a Bangalore torpedo.* He knew

---

* A long piece of pipe stuffed with high explosive.

1 4 5

explosives better than any of the rest of us. Then, when the Bangalore had blown a gap in the wire and I had taken the rest of the platoon through, he went back for the company sergeant major, who was dying at the water's edge, and dragged him out of the machine-gun fire. He was hit himself while doing this.

I did not see him again for a month. When he came back to us, there was a long, angry scar across his chest. We were in a rest area at that time, and one night I managed to scrounge two gallons of vermouth and gave a little party for the platoon. It turned out to be an odd sort of party. We all drank a lot but instead of singing the dirty songs and telling the dirty jokes whose words no longer had any meaning, we began to talk about the war and the part our people at home and our country were playing in it. It was strange that these men who had already fought several battles would talk of things like that because the talk of front-line soldiers is usually limited to a few superficial subjects and does not vary much. Yet we had somehow begun along this different line, and since we were all a little drunk we had no embarrassment in talking about things we normally kept deeply buried.

One chap was a farmer, who blurted out his resentment at the wages his cousin was getting in a munitions plant. There were two men who had enlisted in 1939 who groused savagely about the overseas conscription Canada does not have. Somebody else waxed furious about the trouble his wife and four kids were having trying to get along on his niggardly pay and allowances. A corporal started cursing his Member of Parliament, whose three sons were all sitting out the war at college. Then, as the moon paled behind Mount Etna, Stephen Bates spoke up. Instead of bitching, he began talking proudly about his people back home – coal miners in the Maritimes who, he said, were working as hard to win the war as we were. He got royally heckled for that, and laughed at too, but stuck to his guns.

"All right, you bastards," he said, "but my sort back their own in a fight. Back 'em all the way!"

There was no anger in his voice but a kind of glow of faith on him, and pretty soon the subject got changed back to wine, women and the rest of it.

We finished up the Sicily job and went on to Italy. Steve was my constant shadow in battle and at rest, unobtrusive and not memorable. Then one day we came to a little hill town perched like a filthy boil on the nape of the mountains; we fought for it through the week and finally took it, but the Germans continued to shell the blazes out of it – and us. Three things happened there that I do remember about Steve. One morning we were together in the cellar which served as platoon HQ. He had shovelled out the excrement of the enemy who had used this place for a latrine, but he had not been able to sweep out the smell or the vermin. Yet we lived there because we knew that we could go to sleep knowing that our chances of waking in the morning were good. Steve was sorting the letters that had come up with the rations. He handed me one from a girl I had not thought about for half a year, but I opened and devoured it as if it had been a most precious gift. And when I read it I was happy for a while, and I asked Steve what he had heard from his wife.

He had a letter from her in his hand and, so quietly that there almost seemed to be no trouble in what he spoke, he told me that she was not going to have their child, and that his hopes of one day returning to Canada to a son were gone. To cheer him up, I told him that they were both still young and that there would be much time that would hang heavily on their hands after the war, and not to worry. He smiled back at me and said no more.

The second thing occurred next day. It was a day to celebrate for we had had no men killed in twenty-four hours. At noon the regimental sergeant major came up to see us and passed out mimeographed sheets containing the news of a world from which we had been cut off for so many days. I took my copy down to the cellar and read it aloud to my section leaders and to Steve, who was cleaning his mess tins in the corner. I read to them about great air battles and about the Russians and the big events of the war. And then I read that twelve thousand coal miners had gone on strike in our own country, and that there was no coal coming out of the earth for the forging of our weapons.

My section leaders went off to tell the men what was happening, and Steve, who spoke so quietly and so seldom, came up to me and shook his fist in my face and shouted, "That's a goddamn dirty lie what you just read! It's a goddamn lie, and bastards who lie like that ought to be shot!" I was too surprised even to reply for a moment, then I said the things which a platoon commander must say. But, principally, I told him it was no lie, and I wish now that I had said it was.

An hour later the third thing happened. Steve and I were walking up through the stinking streets of the dead little town, and as we came to the square a signaller ran towards us with a message in his hand, and a shell hit ten feet in front of him. It's funny about blast. We were no more than twenty yards from the spot and we were not touched. We just stood like two omnipotent beings whom no power on earth could harm and watched as the signaller went backward from the waist, his legs firmly spread and his body hinging on a hand's breadth of skin and muscle that joined them to his torso. It was like watching an acrobat in a circus, except that this man's entrails came loose and rolled down over his feet in a steaming mass. I suppose all this took no more than a second, yet we saw it as if we had stood watching for an hour. We did nothing for him, because there was nothing to do, and ran for the shelter of a house. Inside, with the dust from the next explosion thick around us, we remembered to be frightened, and I clung against a wall with my heart thudding in a sick, irregular tempo.

Between the shell bursts, I heard Steve muttering one word that held within it all the poignancy of a terrible grief, though he said it so quietly. "Bastards!" he said. And I knew he was not thinking of the men who fed those shells into the guns, nor was he thinking of those other men whom he had accused of lying.

A few weeks later, we were in a quiet town in the mountains that had not been devastated by war. I was going out to dinner at another regiment and Steve was fussing over my cap badge, spitting on it and polishing it with his sleeve. I was trying to put on a crinkled tie, the first I had worn in months. As I struggled with it, Steve spoke.

"Sir," he said. "That thing in the paper about the miners a while back; I know why they done what they done. It's because of us when we come back and there ain't no place for us because the owners'll have all the dough and all the say. They did it for us, to make sure we get a square deal – and don't anyone think any different! I'm a miner and I know my own people, and they're fighting this war as hard as we are – like my old man who's in the pits."

I was busy with that tie and I only grunted. When I was ready to go, I turned to ask him for something and I saw with astonishment that he was crying. Then I thought of what he had said, and I curbed the ever-present bitterness in my own heart and looked away and replied that of course he was right. His people would not let us down. They had struck for a good reason, and more power to them.

He did not answer me.

I wish I could say that Steve was killed in courageous battle, but he was killed by a shell fired from a great distance. He was not badly smashed up and probably suffered little pain. I wrote a letter to his people.

What did I say? I said what I have said to a dozen parents and wives. I said what I shall doubtless have to say to a dozen more before someone perhaps writes one for me.

"Your son is dead, fighting for you and his, fighting for the great thing which is his country and for the greatness and freedom of his people. He died very bravely with the knowledge that his giving was a part of the great giving of all of us. You may be very proud of your son – as he was proud of you."

[near Riccione on the Adriatic coast]

Early October

My Dear Parents:

A bit of luck. Tac HQ has gone out into the blue looking for a new place to roost, leaving me in sole possession of the operations room at Main HQ, which is in a shellproof and rainproof (not quite sure which is more important these days) casa. I have nothing to do but monitor communications, and let the brigade major know by radio if any troubles brew. I have in fact just let him know of a report from Div Int, acquired from a POW interrogation, that the Hun has booby-trapped a number of local buildings probably including the ones in the place Tac HQ is heading for. The BM seems quite concerned and is enquiring somewhat querulously over the air: Do I realize it is raining? And where in hell are they going to go? I have no suggestions to offer. I am too busy wondering if there is a time bomb in the cellar under where *I* sit. Such thoughts are not conducive to achieving a calm and placid state of mind and they lead me into another quagmire: Should I or should I not go out to the latrine in the farm yard, there to relieve myself when, at any moment, the time bomb under the casa might catch me with my pants down? Weighty thoughts indeed.

I got back from Rome intact and was chagrined to discover that nobody seemed to know I had been absent. I don't know what happened to the court-martial. I just pretended it was a bad dream that had gone away.

Don't worry about the malaria. My attacks have been quite mild and the MO sees no reason to evacuate me (I am *not* referring to the use of an enema) as long as I am in a "sedentary job" (well, blue him! sedentary indeed!) and can go to bed when the bug strikes. Matter of fact, it's kind of useful. I can just put on a wan look and mutter that I'm going to bed-and-who-the-hell-wants-to-make-something-of-it?

Believe it or not, my confirmation of rank came through during my absence. Mike did it! And I now owe him my booze ration for the next six months. I was also recommended *again* for an ALO's job at Corps but was again turned down because: "This officer is only twenty-three and it is not felt that he has sufficient experience in the field to warrant his employment in this posting." Well, goddamn! Perhaps they think I need to be properly senile, like themselves, to be allowed around the young and virginal (?) fly boys. Anyhow, I was highly recommended for the job by Lord Tweedie, who is an aide to the army commander now, and who says he has challenged the G-1

Angus, Helen, and Farley aboard Scotch Bonnet *in Whitby Harbour, summer 1938.*

FM firing his homemade trench mortar in Trenton, 1941. Major Angus Mowat and the quartermaster pass the ammunition.

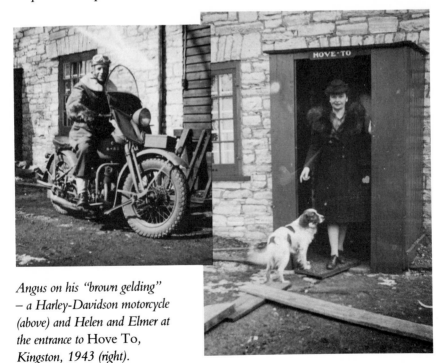

*Angus on his "brown gelding"
– a Harley-Davidson motorcycle
(above) and Helen and Elmer at
the entrance to Hove To,
Kingston, 1943 (right).*

Somewhat wiser, if not much older, FM suns himself outside his dugout near Ortona, in early spring, 1944.

FM in the doorway of the "Iron Pig" parked on an Ortona street (above) from which position he watched passers-by coming from the town well (right).

FM and two visiting officers paying their respects to First Brigade Commander's private outhouse.

FM preparing his "V-8" secret weapon for its first test, apprehensively assisted by one of his men.

FM at the wheel of Lulu Belle Mk.IV in Oostmalle. Accompanied by Lieut. Mike Donovan. Hotel de Kempen is in the background.

Members of Mowat's Private Army beside a German one-man submarine.

Helping the locals celebrate victory in Holland. FM stands at the front of this Nazi half-track. Doc McConnell is the rearmost "Jerry."

Italy, spring 1945.

Air to come out and do a patrol with me to see if I have enough field experience. That will be the frosty Friday in July!

My beloved boss has made it known that it is his wish that every officer in the brigade buy a Victory Bond, and them as don't have to submit a written explanation of why not. You can imagine my reaction to that one . . . and *his* reaction to *my* reaction. Mike says my confirmation just came in time, and he could be right. On the other hand, he could just be trying to squeeze another bottle of hooch out of me.

Is the war over? I am getting lots of letters from friends who either stayed at home, or have returned there from the navy and air force, about going to college and becoming consulting entomologists, chartered accountants, etc., and getting married, and raising mobs of little tots, or trots. They want to know what I am going to do. I tell them I am going to try and stay alive, that's what *I*'m going to do. Maybe the war *is* over, and we just haven't heard about it here on the "forgotten front."

[near Riccione]

Oct

This is a business letter. Simple and straightforward.

I am tired of bitching about what the war is doing to me, and crying poor pussy about it. If I've got to turn into a rusty old sewer pipe full of bad smells and stagnation, I've decided I'll do so only after a helluva fight *not* to. So the gloves are in the ring, whither I'll follow shortly. With some help from you two.

Send me, please, the following: *Pocket Oxford English Dictionary*; Fowler's *Modern English Usage*; *Roget's Thesaurus*; six of Mr. Remington's portable ribbons; an anthology of Conrad's best stories, and some sort of punctuation guide that will enable me to tell when not to use a semi-colon. Kindly oblige at the earliest instant or, as we say in the Ahmy, deal with soonest.

What's up? My back is, and if I have to go on floundering in this witch's cauldron I'm going to try to turn it to my own account. In short, I'm going to write and write like hell, not for publication, or future fame or peltry, but to keep myself afloat. I may not succeed, but I'll bust a gut trying.

Also I'd like Mum to nip out and buy something that a young and reasonably frivolous female might appreciate and dispatch it to a Miss E. Hickey, 216 Eglinton Ave., Toronto. And don't panic. I am not in love with the wench but for the past two years she has dutifully written to me every week when she probably had lots of better things to do. For an attractive lassie with all of Civvy Street to play about in, this is a Deserving Act, and I want to recognize it.

And, Mother, tell the Old Man to be sure and look after MY boat, MY house, MY car, MY dog, MY mom, and his cantankerous old self.

[probably Oct. 23 – north-west of Rimini]

Tonight the brigade is out of the line and luxuriating under canvas, mostly in various muddy fields, while a dirty grey rain drizzles chilly out of a sky that has become a permanent image of Mood Indigo.

But *not* your one and only! Mowat sits regally in his I-truck on a teak chair complete with built-in ashtray of mother-of-pearl. On his right is a compact little mahogany bookshelf sporting works of E. A. Poe, Damon Runyan, Rupert Brooke, Boccaccio, Jerome K. Jerome and sundry volumes on German Weapons, Order of Battle, Tactics and Military Organization. A catholic collection, don't you think?

Atop a small rosewood end table inlaid with birds made of semi-precious stone, sits a grim, grey German army radio from which is issuing, at the moment, the strains of the London Symphony playing "Danse Macabre," which seems singularly appropriate even though all is quiet in the black night beyond the reach of my gasoline lantern. Behind me sits a smallish cylindrical kerosene stove, of the kind once to be found in every Canadian summer cottage, and it is doing its best to heat my evening snack which will be creamed lobster on toast. Tastefully framed under sheets of talc (map boards for the use of) are photographs of you three and the *Bonnet*, and one or two females with whom you need not concern yourselves. The Mayor's typewriter is before me on a polished ebony writing case, looking rather shabby in such spiffy company.

Mowat is in his Office and, true to his word, *is writing a book.* Sort of. He is at least thinking about it. Meantime he is enjoying his creature comforts which are the acquisitions of three months of assiduous liberating by his Intelligent Staff. He is, in truth, almost independent of war and weather at the moment, at least partly as a result of having lived so much of his previous life in caravans and the cabins of small vessels. The one thing lacking in this snug little nest is an armoured outer skin. The tarpaulin which serves as roof and walls is adequate to keep the water out, but not much else.

Do you remember a long, lean drink-of-water from the RCR name of Ferguson? Fergie for short. Good pal of mine who soldiered with us at Camp Borden. Killed last week in a useless attack. Des Eagon got it in the same show, as did little Simms ("The Nose," remember him?). And so one by one they go away, and I feel as old as Neanderthal when I see how few of us are left. And I guess, in this present job, I stand a good chance of being "left" at the end of it; I'll be one of those guys who sits in a pub on winter nights mumbling the names of the "gone aways" into his booze. The business of facing down the shadows is going to be the hardest part – harder even than acknowledging the lost years.

It probably hasn't got a snowball's chance in hell of getting to me in one piece, if at all, but see if you can buy me a record of Paul Whitman playing "Slaughter on 10th Avenue." The Int-section has liberated a phonograph, but the only records we can find are Italian operatics, and the hell with 'em .

Did I tell you about my visit to the Repoooblique of San Marino, the postage-stamp little country up in the Apennines? The place is strictly *verboten*, being as how it is neutral in the war, but one of the Div IOs, a crazy Limey, name of Ken Cottam, who was a prof at Oxford before enlisting, decided he and I should check it out.

Ken weighs about 250, wears moustachios and looks more like a red-faced British general than any British general ever did. He is also fearless and mad as a hatter. In order to get past the 8th Army check-points on the switchback road to San Marino, guarded by a bunch of no-nonsense Gurkhas, Ken simply borrowed and put on a staff officer's red-banded hat, and a set of brigadier's insignia which he "just happens" to carry about with him. *Not*, I suspect, because he is expecting a field promotion to that exalted rank.

I drove the jeep and pretended to be his ADC and, well, you can guess the rest. Bullshit baffles brains! The Indian Army captain in charge of the guard post will be court-martialled if anyone ever finds out that he let us through but then, bah goom, so will we! So mum is the word. We brought back several cases of pre-war *vino* and cognac, of which I gave two to our mess. So now the Bigshot thinks I am just the cat's meow! But I intend to avoid Cottam in the future. Too hard on my frayed nerves.

[Richmond Hill]

Oct 27

Dear Squib (one B as far as I'm concerned). –

Today I got you off another box containing a set of the books you asked for, and *The Turn of the Screw.* Nothing like a little variety. The *T of the S* was included at Helen's suggestion because she feels that reading of the best is good for one's style. I dunno. All it ever seemed to do for me was muddy up any natural style. Certainly I was influenced by my constant reading in Conrad. So deeply influenced that nobody ever found out what my first book was about.

Yesterday afternoon Reg had a cocktail party for his two best-selling authors. The other one was Matthew Halton. Of course I got Halton in a corner and demanded to hear all he knew about the Hasties. The fellow has got a warped mind. He feels that the infantry is bearing the brunt of this war. He says (not over the air, or in print, because he can't) that all the advertising-agency copy about the navy and air force gives him a pain in the ass. Shows how dumb he is, what?

I'm beginning to look at our village of Richmond Hill with some suspicion. It is growing apace, not by way of the birth rate but by way of city people moving in. Practically a solid line of moving vans coming out from Toronto. And all bringing their city ways and their stupid little *petit bourgeois* ideas with them. Living in the village *all by themselves*, as people live in cities, and being a part of nothing. We may have to move back to the county after all.

In the meantime, I have to go off to Ottawa in a last effort to get the old dodos to do something about service libraries. An ordeal to be dreaded after my previous experiences there. But I'll bear up.

Nov 7

That trip was of a hecticness, as Helen would say. Days filled with meetings, and speeches by Mowat until he became very tired of the sound of his own voice.

Going on to Montreal, I spent all my first day at McGill's Library School. I started making them a speech, formal and standing. Next thing I knew I was sitting on the table swinging my legs. And then I was down in the audience, straddling a chair and the speech had become a general discussion. Oddly enough, there are six men at Library School this year, three of them veterans and, amazingly, one of them a Hasty. He remembered you very well as IO but I got so excited that I forgot his name.

That night I took your Aunt Fran and Uncle Arthur* out for dinner, and we made Arthur buy a drink! It was heavily watered. He is organizing a yacht-building company, just as if the war was well and truly over, and was quite hurt when I refused his offer to become an investor and a dividend-gathering capitalist. Fran has become my most brilliant literary critic. I was basking in praise from the local papers, and a radio review on the national hook-up that would have given Shakespeare a swelled head, so Fran said, "Thank you for the book. I read it." So I said, "Oh?" having learned to be cautious with Fran. "Yes, I read it. And in one place you said 'neither or' when you ought to have said 'neither nor'." With a family like ours, how could you and I ever manage to take ourselves seriously?

Well, I've been bulling along and haven't even mentioned your last letters. You're like your mother. Why won't you, just once, finish a sentence, or a story? You were going to have a boxing engagement. Well, so what happened? Then you went on a court-martial that hadn't materialized yet. O.K., did it ever? Perhaps getting your third pip confirmed has made you a trifle scatter-brained.

So all your friends who have survived the Boche are getting married? And you won't? To paraphrase: What do you know about

---

* Helen's spinster sister and her youngest brother.

being struck by lightning, you who have never been struck by lightning? I picture a strong-toothed, buxom squaw paddling you and the kids around while you sit in the bow of the canoe with a Remington (typewriter, not rifle) in your lap. Worse things could happen to a guy.

❖ ❖ ❖

ALTHOUGH THE GOTHIC LINE HAD BEEN BROKEN, THE ENEMY HAD NOT. He continued to fall back in good order from river line to river line, forcing us to mount a succession of set-piece offensives which became increasingly costly.

Then the weather changed. Towards the end of October, the infamous bora gales began sweeping across the Adriatic from Yugoslavia. They howled through days and nights black with driving rain. The coastal plain where we were giving battle turned into a morass of mud, and the countless canals and rivers flowing across it from the mountains to the sea began to rise, each becoming a foaming barrier to our further progress. Snow began to fall on the mountains, and any last hopes we may have had of breaking out into the Po Valley faded. All we could hope for now was that the generals would realize the stupidity of continuing this particular struggle and let the war wind down for the winter.

Brigade headquarters no longer seemed like a sanctuary to me. I was beginning to hope, with ever-increasing fervour, that I might find myself some place "far from shot and shell." I no longer simply wanted to escape the battlefield. I wanted out.

❖ ❖ ❖

[north-west of Rimini]

Oct 23

Chère Maman et Père:

Spent last night until midnight over a bottle of Scotch and a tin of your lobster (magnificent, by the way) yarning with Bill Boss, the CP war-co. You should look for his stories in the yellow rags and can be fairly well assured you are reading the truth.

Enclosed are some pictures taken last April in Ortona. They were taken by one of the Sigs officers, and it took this long to find a place to get them developed and printed. The "Iron Pig" you see in one of them is the very same one we use at Tac HQ now, and I love it like a brother. What a skin it's got!

Main reason for this short note is to let you know I'm going on a two-week Int course tomorrow. Which means, for this old soldier, three weeks, including coming and going. I wouldn't be surprised if I have a "mechanical breakdown" and have to stop off in Rome for a day – or two. So long for now. Will write from school . . . if I have time.

[Richmond Hill]

Nov 15

Dear Friend Farley. –

You have acquainted us with the information that you are going on an Intelligence course. Your mother, and Elmer, and your former schoolmistresses and masters are all in agreement with me as to the probable advantages of such a course, but with one accord they ask, "And how did he qualify?"

Mail about *Carrion Place* keeps trickling in and, fortunately for my *amour propre*, from people who like the thing. Those who don't like it don't write. Anyhoo, Reg is sold out of the twenty-five hundred he had bound and is trying to get another thousand bound. Macmillan in New York, by the way, is interested but slow to make up its mind.

I wonder how much of the truth you people are hearing about the reinforcements – or lack of reinforcements – mess here. It is all pretty heartbreaking. What it must be for understrength units trying to do their jobs at the front with fewer and fewer men, I do not like to think. What gets my goat even more than the spineless Zombies, or the spineless government and country which permits an outrage like this, is the volunteers in all three services who glory in being "Active" but have never been out of Canada and, if they can help it, never will.

Going up to Windsor in the train the other day I was seated beside a Lt. Col. in the ordnance. He must have been all of twenty-seven and had spent the first three years of the war at university and was now happily in charge of a major ordnance depot. He confided in me that he expected to become a full colonel (without ever having left Canada) if the war lasted another year.

I think you need a haircut. The picture taken in the door of your truck indicated the need for such. As that was taken last April, I shudder to think of your condition now. But no sign of the moustache.

Last evening we dropped in at the Bradshaws'. Alex talked at length about the circus you staged in our mutual backyard in Windsor in 1932 and of how you smooth-talked him into "lending" you enough canvas from his company's samples to make a Big Top. Which you then sold, after the circus closed because somebody's mother found out you had persuaded her eight-year-old daughter to display her talents as a nude dancer. He also reminded me of the time he stood at his apartment door, unseen, and listened to you describe in somewhat gruesome detail the sex life of the porcupine to some spellbound fat woman who had come to our door hoping to sell a subscription to some magazine. And I reminded him of the Hallowe'en when you went around dressed as a witch, chanting at people's doors:

> Oh, I'm the Witch of Windsor,
> And I'm hungry, tired and cold.
> Oh, kindly let me in, sir.
> Have pity on the old.

Have pity on Windsor, more like.

I hope shortly to finish typing out the stories you sent me and shall send them to *Maclean's*. Whether inadvertently or not, I think you are taking the right course. From verse to short story and then to full-length book. It has always been one of my sorrows to be bad on the short story. I can't get moving fast enough for it.

Be good, sweet burr.

[Naples]

Oct 28

Dear Parents:

You will doubtless be amused no end to know that your ever-loving son is in Napoli, back at school and liking it.

Following the battle for Cesena, about which I do not care to talk, Ken Cottam, the senior Div IO, concluded that I might do something injurious to my soaring military career and so wrangled me a course in Intelligence work being run by Allied HQ in an outskirt of Napoli. I, in turn, wrangled a jeep (they wouldn't let me have Lulu or Benny) from the transport officer and took off right smartly three days ago. The course actually begins tomorrow and ends on Nov. 13, but I am not *officially* finished until the eighteenth. Ain't it wonderful the way IOs look after their own! Maybe I'll go to Oxford *après la guerre* if it's still turning out characters like Cottam.

My most recent stay in the Eternal City (engine trouble) was much better than the last since I made a good civilian contact. She is the wife of a deceased Eyetie banker who operated in Shanghai, where she was born (relax Mum – no slanty eyes). He brought her back to Italy in '39 and promptly kicked the bucket, leaving her well-fixed but with two small bambinos. She's well-educated and well-read, and talks English perfectly. Not that this is anything to brag about, but it makes things the hell of a lot easier for me. My *vino Italiano* doesn't take me very far.

She has a nice apartment in the better part of Rome, large enough so I got a room to myself, with all the trimmings including hot water, honest-to-God linen sheets and laundry service from the *concièrge*. And, believe it or not, she has a swell radio-gram and loves Ravel, including "Bolero"! Seventh heaven! The only difficulty she has is food. And this is where I come in. Seasoned old codger that I am, I had stored my jeep as for a round-the-world voyage. Not just with comestibles (army issue) but with tradeables. So I look after the larder. A couple of trips to villages well outside the city have filled it to over-flowing and have been helpful to the wine cellar, too.

I begin to get some idea of the way things look from the Eyetie point of view. Not good, for sure. The condition of most urban civilians is really pitiable and the chaos unbelievable. The lady and her friends say those we have chosen to run the country are mostly slick former fascists who lick our boots but make life hell for their own people. The political scene is like cats in a house on fire. At least ten parties, each of which thinks it is the chosen midwife for the rebirth of Italy, spending all their time and energies clawing each other up and down while the fascist rats run away with the goods.

Canadians may bitch about shortages and costs but try this on for size. Eggs cost fifty cents each; flour three to five bucks a pound; meat runs from five dollars if tainted, to ten dollars if fresh. The few surviving horses all have haunted looks. No cat sits on the back fence and yowls at the moon – it'll get a knife, not a boot. A pair of boots will get you someone's sister for a week, or semi-permanently if you'll feed her and the family. Sugar costs up to six dollars a pound. And a lot of this stuff – sugar, flour, powdered milk, canned meat, etc. – is shipped into the country by the Allied control commission *for free distribution to the needy*. But what we then do is turn it over to the local racketeers who *sell* it for all the market will bear, as above. The Allied organization for the aid of the Italian civilians is about the lousiest excuse for a bunch of fat-assed bastards you could ever find. But, hoo boy! When they go home, they are going to be toting as much jewellery, gold, art objects, etc., as would make Hitler's SS robbers die of envy. *Noblesse oblige.*

I figure that within six months, Free Italy will be in such a state of anarchy that there'll be revolution and then we'll have to sit on them with guns and tanks or else the communists will take control. Hell, they'll be *given* control by a population fed up to the teeth with us and our democratic ways.

Hi dee ho, and there I go. I should stick to bird watching, huh?

[Naples]

Nov 7

Still in Napoli and very much enjoying an opportunity to use my head instead of my feet. Although I'd rather be studying deep-sea navigation, or tropical biology, this business of learning how the Nazi military system works is pretty fascinating. And somewhat scary. For a wonder in this man's army, everything is run as it should be, and on the assumption that we are adults. You attend classes as you wish, or not if that's how you feel. The "student body" consists of only twelve of us including Indians, Yanks, Limeys, and even a Brazilian – mostly capitanos with lots of "experience in the field." We live in a luxurious villa ten minutes from the Orange Grove, run our own mess, give periodic celebrations for whom and what we please and, strangely since there is no compulsion, do a lot of hard head work. Very refreshing.

Got out to a Yank Liberty ship in harbour the other night. She had just brought in a cargo from the U.S. east coast and had had a close call with a U-boat. Her skipper was a former small-boat sailor out of Rochester before the troubles, and knew *Scotch Bonnet* by sight! We had a great gam over a bottle of Lemon Hart 151 OP Rum, and he warmly invited me to sail back with him to Boston. Tempting.

I have also prowled around amongst the small craft in harbour and found amongst other unexpected things a couple of Ackroyd sixteen-foot dinghies made in Toronto! Also went for a sail inside the harbour (the frigging Royal Navy wouldn't permit us to go outside) in a Tyrrhenian bark (or *barca*, or *barka*). She was pretty old – you could have shoved a blunt paddle through her timbers almost any-where – and stank like she was the original ark. Her owner was another ex-emigré to the States who had come home in 1938 to enjoy his wealth. Boy, was he sorry now! He tried to sell *me* the *barca* in exchange for a fifty-pound sack of flour.

Had a presumably half-blind pavement artist do my portrait the other night after a session at the opera. Will send it along for Elmer's kennel. The opera was *Aida* and, though you enjoy that sort of thing, Mater, your son was not amused, or even entertained. The San Carlo Opera House is supposed to be the home of opera, but the hell with it. Damned if I can get enthused by the vocal contortions and postur-ings that go on – and on – and on and on.

Have done much less bumming about than was to be expected. Though the only laddie here with my own vehicle, I go out less than most. I did, however, spend a couple of evenings at the home of the

Contessa di Pozzuoli and her two good-looking daughters. Rather a run-down joint. The family had clearly seen better times – probably when the Fascists were in power. The eldest daughter, a sometimes blonde, got very pally but I don't know if it was my pristine charm, or the case of condensed milk I had in the jeep. Had. Somehow most of it got transferred into the establishment. Next day I stood for an hour on a street corner waiting to take the blonde one out for dinner. But I had to be content with a yammering of small boys (Signorina, Johnny? Very clean. Very young. She my sister!) and a scatter of shopworn wenches (Lonlee, Johnny? Make-a you happy?). I got stood up.

Haven't heard from you for a month or more and I wonder if any of my recent letters have reached you. Hope so – particularly the request for a thesaurus etc. I feel the stirring of a literary embryo. It'll probably be still-born.

[Richmond Hill]

Nov 22

Dear Lamby.

I took your present to Eleanor Hickey, a lovely silver bracelet price $10, a very wonderful present I'd say. Angus and I took it over and met Mrs. Hickey, who wasn't dressed (dressing gown) and was very flustered and voluble.

Had a birthday supper party for Angus consisting of the elder Gambles and Evie* and a bottle of rum. Angus read them one of your stories and we had a huge wood fire and sat and talked until after twelve. Ev expects her husband home by Xmas, and I wonder how things will be. He is evidently a good soldier.

So you didn't like *Aida*. You will like opera if you keep on hearing it and get to know the score. Don't tell me you take after Angus and only like the bagpipes!

---

* Bob Gamble was a former prospector who struck it rich in northern Ontario, then bought an estate not far from Richmond Hill. His daughter, Evelyn, was a close friend of mine although some years my senior. At this time, her husband was overseas with a Toronto regiment and the marriage was in disarray.

A Pauper Army

Nov 22

Dear Squibbles. – (All right – two b's)

Your uppity letter from Naples arrived yesterday. "Mercurial,"
Mum says. "Mercurial. Give him a few days away from that headquarters and the malaria," she says, "and he starts to effervesce." Well,
I finally got two of your war stories typed out in readable form and
added a few commas (and took out about three thousand unnecessary
ones) and, on my way to *Maclean's* magazine, let Reg see them. He says
they are too strong for *Maclean's* but he is going to talk it over with
Napier Moore, the big shot of that rag. What Reg really wants to do,
and I can see him edging around to it, is to make up a little volume of
your stories and verse. However, it would be too slight as yet.

The great thing, of course, for anybody who aspires to write, is to
get into print. Stimulus. It seems to engender a sense of responsibility.
You feel that you aren't talking to a brick wall any more and, having
been in print once, you simply *must* do it again and keep on doing it.
Nobody amounted to anything, or very few did, till they began to
achieve some kind of volume. Not that one should sell his birthright
for volume; that would, naturally, be fatal.

Anyhoo, I'm busting to see you in print as soon as possible. You've
got the knack and the flair for it, and you are so young that if you got
started now you'd have a long writing life ahead of you, trench mortars
and shell-fire permitting. And that is very important. I got started much
too late – in everything except getting married and having a brat.

I haven't put down a word since leaving the army. There doesn't seem
to be any time at all. Also I'm so damned sick at heart about this country
at war that I can't get thinking calmly. The public may be finally getting
mad about the Zombies but, goddamn it to hell, there are lots of Zombies
who are not even recognizable as such. The navy, and army and air force
are full of hidden Zombies. So is Civvy Street. So are the munitions
plants. All the little twerps who don't want to go into the infantry
because, forsooth, it is too hard and too dangerous, are filling the letters
columns with their excuses for staying home. Bastards! The impression
they give is that the infantry is a sort of low-down occupation, fit only

for the proletariat, not for the sweet little bourgeoisie. And unlike the navy and air force, the people at the head of our army haven't the brains to put the infantry where the Russians and Germans put it – in the public eye at the *head* of the Line of March, not at the tail end.

Oh well, I'm going to be cheerful, and whistle and sing and chortle and chirp. Indeed and indeed, we have cause for merriment. Prime Minister Mackenzie King says the war is won, though anarchy is at hand. And Air Minister Powers said he wouldn't support conscription for overseas duty because Eisenhower doesn't use the Canadian infantry right. He puts them in the line, and they get killed and wounded. So Powers has been discharging, right and left, unneeded men from his glamour corps* who have never even left Canada, instead of transferring them to the infantry in Italy and north-west Europe.

And the Zombies are on the march to defend their rights, tearing up or burning the flag and protest-marching with loaded arms against being sent overseas. And the universities are bulging with brave little men cowering away from the war. There are anti-conscription parades all over Quebec. Lots of reason to be merry.

The only dismal item I have for you concerns a "march" of 150 Zombies in Ottawa last night. They straggled out of their depot bearing anti-war placards and banners, and the poor fellows had just got nicely started when two sailors and a soldier, all recently returned from overseas, came along and broke up the parade.

The fun will really start when they begin trying to move the hypothetical sixteen thousand Zombies who have so belatedly now been booked as reinforcements, to the east coast for embarkation overseas. The authorities (ha!) will find it is like trying to move mercury with a canoe paddle. The Zombies will disappear into the woodwork like cockroaches when the light comes on.**

---

* The Royal Canadian Air Force.

** Most reluctantly, and only because the lack of reinforcements for the army overseas had become a national disgrace (and bid fair to becoming an international one), the King government at last introduced a limited form of overseas conscription. However, it was implemented in such a half-hearted way that few conscripts actually did get sent overseas, and fewer still ever saw action.

You fellows must all be very proud of your country. Bob Gamble told me, not long since, of the Young Officers' revolt you and a few others at Borden tried to organize away back in 1942 against the government for refusing to impose overseas conscription then. He said you came to him for financial support. You never told *me* about that! Bob said he led you on, making sure you didn't get into trouble, until you were sent overseas. He was afraid you'd try to get Mackenzie King. How could such young toads, still wet behind the ears, have been so perceptive?

I repeat (as you keep mentioning it in every letter) that your demands *in re* thesaurus etc. have been filled, and filled again. If they all get through to you, your I-truck will look like the office of a Professor of English Lit. Maybe that's a job you should think about after the war. You already have the motto to go with it. B.B.B. Well, the old desk is piled up with letters, mostly as foolish as this one. I must get to them.

[Miramare, on the coast south-east of Rimini]

Nov 19

Mes Chères Parents:

Home again, after having to fix a flat tire in Rome, a business that took most of a week. You've no idea how hard it is to find tube cement and patching material in Rome these days. Fortunately I had a place to lay my head – the Passeroni ménage on Via Cavour, of which I have previously spoken. Sadly, I think it may be my last visit there. Luigi, the six-year-old and heir, has taken to calling me Papa.

The OC of the Int school invited me to stay on as an instructor, which would be good for my skin. I haven't definitely said *niente* yet, but hell's bells, after all the things I *have* said in my time about Base Wallahs, how could I in good conscience become one myself?

Once again I have the feeling of coming home to an empty house. With the departure for Canada of the '39-ers*, there are few souls still left in the brigade that I landed with. And it is such a hell of a nuisance having to explain to the newcomers that I really *am* over the age of

---

* Those were men who enlisted and went overseas in 1939. Most of the few surviving '39-ers in front-line units were shipped back to Canada during the later part of 1944.

puberty, despite my youthful air. On the other hand, the BM says I am beginning to look my age – but still not acting it.

A little close figuring now suggests that if the Russkies are prepared to take on the onus of occupying and pacifying Tedeschiland, I may hope to see my native shores by 1946. Maybe. Though to be completely honest, apart from seeing yourselves and Elmer, I seem to be losing any great desire to return. Guess I've been away too long, travelled too far in time and space to ever feel "at home" in Canada again. Not in the Canada I knew. I have the scary feeling that *it* is gone for good.

Anyway, I find umpteen letters from you and two food parcels plus some books, for which *molto grazie*. The canned giblets from the lady in the county will doubtless be particularly tasty. I'll save them for Xmas eve. Thank heavens (and yourselves) for the socks – I've been riding on my rims for weeks. So far no sign of a response to an aspiring author's dream – no, I don't mean *Carrying Place*, although I hear it is a helluva yarn – I mean the books on how to write a book. They'll probably be in the next mail. Hope so; my enthusiasm is dwindling.

Have been doing a lot of wondering about how we are going to cope when we get home. I think the difficulties to be faced by our lot are worse than they were in your time. After the last war, there was some possibility of returning to a kind of status quo. This time there is none. Perhaps the best solution is to send us all off to Burma to fight the Nips and, if any survive that, send them to the Antarctic to civilize the penguins.

You enquire why I don't send you any more poetry. Let us say that the junior Mowat has finally realized that his poetry stinks. I have some pride. No fooling, the more I read it, the lousier it sounds. So I have accepted the fact that I can't write poetry for beans and have stopped being asinine about it. Doggerel is another matter and I enclose another dose of same.

Slow March

Experts hesitate to say which is the fleetah,
The Greyhound, Antelope or Cheetah.
But they are not the least bit loath
To say which is the Sloth.

Nocturnal Etiquette

When dining on a Mouse or Rabbit,
Owls have the most disgusting habit
of glutching hair and bones and all,
which forms an undigested ball.
So, after Owl has had his sup,
he turns his head and brings it up.

Perhaps it's staying out so late
that makes the Owl regurgitate.

Yak Yak!

"Pigeons on the grass, alas!"
is a poem by Gertrude Stein.

"The Yak is out of whack, alack!"
is mine.

So when, oh when does *Carrying Place* arrive?

[Richmond Hill]

Dec 1
Darling Bunje.

Elmer and Angus trudged through the snow before breakfast to
the post office and came back, both faces beaming. Two letters from
you, so we settled down to read, oblivious to the fact that Pop was to
drive in to work. You didn't mention malaria, which I'm always worrying about. I *do* hope you take that job as instructor if it comes up
again, because you've earned it and Pop thinks the same, but you do
what the old conscience says.

I really shouldn't give you advice. But my whole instinct is to
put you in a pouch and carry you around like a kangaroo – carry
you, not the kanga, if you see what I mean. And I'd put Elmer and

Angus in another pouch and then I'd be happy.

We've had the first heavy snow and it is fairyland. You know how it looks with the branches heavy with new, white snow, everything hushed and quiet, footsteps padded. I love it, but it always makes me sad, I don't know why. Angus has been shovelling the walks and now is resting by the wood fire in our cozy living room and I am listening to Brahms' First Symphony, which you would love.

Write to your grandmother, like a good boy, and to your Aunt Fran. They have both sent Xmas boxes, as did Isobel. A lot of parcels for the troops came to grief as usual. They were burned in a big fire in Halifax. Hope yours escaped. My Anglican intercession group goes on as usual, and we pray for you always.

[Toronto]

Dec 4

Dear Squib Mk.II. –

Life in Naples certainly seems varied. But I suspect your Contessa was the kind we used to meet in France. Anybody with a house and a couple of girls and a few bottles of bad wine (cider laced with sulphuric acid, usually) was always a countess or something. Hell, I knew one in Bailleul who was a duchess. Her girls were patently in the last stages of syphilis, in fact I think she used to keep them in the woodshed, they looked so badly. But she did have access to red meat, probably French army horses that had died of old age, and could do *pommes de terre frites* that were edible. Also she used to have a fire in her house, which was unusual in northern France, even in the winter. But I guess our French *dames* couldn't hold much of a candle to your Neapolitans. Neapolitans have pink streaks in the centre, or is that only Neapolitan ice cream?

Now about veterans' rehabilitation. It'll be worse this time than in my time, as you suggest. The men have been away longer and the worm has bored deeper. Also, as you say, we came back cheerfully to what at least looked like the status quo. Maybe things will be different – better – for you fellows this time, but I'm not so sure. The old gang, politicians and owners, are pretty damn strong and they control all the propaganda agencies. They'll throw you a crust or two, then put you out of their minds and try to keep you out of the minds and memories of the people as a whole.

Well, for a more cheerful topic. I got your revered mother on skis yesterday for her first lesson. At first she did not take kindly to the idea, moaning like a Hebrew dirge and wondering out loud how she could have married such a crazy devil. But once out into the deep, soft snow, she caught on quickly and now is talking about the hills she is going to ski down next weekend. I think, as is so often the case with her, I may have bit off more than I can chew.

[Miramare]

Dec 2

Dear Folks:

The restraint imposed on your pens in describing the Presentation of the Bracelet does you proud. But I can well imagine your real feelings as the door to the Hickey mansion gaped wide before you. In fact, I can see it all. A voluble, frumpy and excited female encased, as far as it is possible to encase Mrs. Hickey, in a rumpled dressing gown opens the door and behind her is disclosed a scene of several weeks of housekeeping postponed. I can hear your thoughts: "Oh, Lord, let it not be that Farley has gone and got himself tangled up with *this*!" and, later, "Well, if he has, we will bloody well have to bear up under it, and may Heaven be merciful."

Rest easy. The story is as follows:

When you were in Kingston in '42, and I was in Borden, Jerry Austin introduced me to the Hickey ménage when we were on a weekend leave to Toronto. There were three buxom, blonde sisters and Jerry was much enamoured of the eldest. There was no Mr. Hickey (I never heard what became of him) but the family lived in a nice house in Forest Hill and the doors were always open to all in uniform. Of a naturalness, a multitude of such hung out there, and I did too for the brief remaining period before being posted overseas.

Was Maman independently wealthy? Not. She earned the family's keep by selling . . . wait for it . . . life insurance to guys in blue and khaki who were bound off for the wars. The deal was that *until* you'd bought a policy from her, she was always hanging about when you came to see the girls. Once you'd signed on the dotted line, she would become invisible. Well, hell, the temptation was irresistible, which is why I have a $5000 policy with the New York Life which I will be paying for *ad infinitum*. Ah well. We do live and learn, sometimes. But to the bracelet. Despite the fact that there was little between us, Eleanor, the youngest datter, wrote to me and still does, almost every week, for which I am extremely grateful. The bracelet is simply a token of gratitude thereof.

No sign of the writing books. Please repeat the order. If both lots should arrive, I have a pal who also thinks he wants to be a writer. As for the publication of "my war stories," don't bother trying. In fact, *don't* try. After reading your last letter, I read them over and was appalled by my inept treatment of things I had thought I felt deeply enough about to describe accurately. Maybe I should go back to writing Fourth Form essays for Miss Izaard at Richmond Hill High.

❖ ❖ ❖

"IN SPITE OF THE UNPROFITABLE STRUGGLE AGAINST AN ENEMY aided on one flank by the barriers of rivers and waterlogged plains, and on the other by strong mountain fortresses on which the winter snows were already falling, fighting was to continue without abatement."

So did G. W. Nicholson in his official history of the Canadians in Italy sum up the situation as the last days of November darkened the skies over First Canadian Division which was then, after twenty-eight days of continuous action, in "rest" a few miles behind the quagmire that was the Adriatic Front.

The currents of rumour that always precede battle began to flow again. Vague at first, they began to acquire substance as the plan for a grand new offensive, designed to break out of the wedge of swamped landscape before Ravenna, was slowly revealed to us. The

First Canadian Corps, consisting of First and Fifth Divisions, was to lead the way into something grotesquely named Operation Chuckle.

First Division was required to attack across three major rivers, several large canals and innumerable swollen ditches draining reclaimed swampland which, under the impact of winter rains, had reverted to something like its original state. The water courses all ran between high embankments, some of which stood thirty feet above the plains. All were in spate and their waters, fed by mountain torrents, were bitterly cold.

Operation Chuckle began on December 2. By the fourth, First Division was stalled before a high-dyked river called the Lamone. At dawn the acting Divisional Commander, Brigadier Desmond Smith, ordered First Brigade to cross that heavily defended barrier – in darkness and without even prior reconnaissance.

What followed was a débâcle which very nearly destroyed the Regiment and did result in the dismissal of our own brigadier, together with the COs of the Hastings and Prince Edward Regiment and the Royal Canadian Regiment. These were the chosen scapegoats for an operation which can best be described as a suicidal shambles. Its effect upon all of us was cataclysmic, yet the letter which I wrote home on December 7 tells little enough of the terrible events I had just witnessed. This was in part due to the restraint imposed by army censorship, but even more to self-censorship.

❖ ❖ ❖

[Lamone River west of Ravenna]

Dec 7

This letter is very hard to write. Something hellish has happened but all I can say for the moment is that the regiment has been to hell, and only part of it got back. Was *sent* to hell. Most of the few old friends I still had there are gone. I'm too flaming mad to dwell upon it now or I might do something we'd all regret. Perhaps I'll be able to talk about it later on, but keep the name Lamone River in your minds. It is seared into mine.

Meantime I must try to cling to the belief that time goes on, and memory is not indelible. For now I simply have to bury the event, even though that may turn it into a delayed-action bomb that may lie dormant until long after the war when the shield of indifference we build to protect ourselves in action has melted away through lack of need. I know that I and many like me are going to have some bad moments one day. Was it like that for you, Squib, when some chance thing brought back a flaming memory of horrible events hardly accepted at the time? Or is the limited sense of pain and loss, which is all the conscious mind permits us to feel in action, the end of it? Maybe it is some of both.

Enough of that.

The news you send of *Carrying Place* gets better and better. And why in hell won't they buy it in the States? We know the answer to that one. Because it isn't *about* the great U. S. of A., around which the sun and moon, planets and stars, all circle admiringly. "When this bloody war is over . . ." as that old song of yours puts it, somebody is going to have to take them down a peg or, as Granny used to say: "They'll get so uppity they'll fall through their britches and hang themselves."

But maybe Hollywood will buy the rights to make a movie. I can see it all now. "A Sizzling Story of Forbidden Love with Errol Flynn and Dorothy Lamour – a Saga of Searing Passion in the Cold Heart of the Great White North . . ." On second thought, maybe it's a good thing the Yanks don't want it. Otherwise Pop would likely lose his iron self-control, as he did the summer day in Saskatoon when he was writing *Then I'll Look Up* in the dining room, and Mutt and I got into a vocal fight on the lawn outside the window, and he fired four volumes of the *Encyclopaedia Britannica* at us.

The "Iron Pig" is not *my* truck, nor does it suckle its young. It doesn't have any, but was born like the phoenix, springing full blown from the head of a boffin in some military version of a witch's cauldron. I know this because I have never seen a juvenile or even an immature Iron Pig. What the hell am I talking about, anyway? I'm really thinking of Stan Ketcheson who was acting CO when it happened. He wasn't hurt in the body, but I doubt if the rest of him will survive. And it was all so goddamn stupid!

Change the subject. Did I ever tell you about the urinals in the San Georgio Opera House in Naples? Banks of them made of Carrara marble, and each with – at the exact correct point of aim from which there will be the least splash-back – a large, purple fly (the *flying* kind) embossed. And the attendant, a nicotine addict, who posted the following handwritten sign over the majestic curve of urinals: Pleez to not putting cigar-ette end into toilet is make almost impossible to smoke. Or words to that effect. I'm quoting from memory.

And I bet I haven't told you about how Mepacrine (the military version of quinine) has become every Canadian soldier's best friend. It is a terrific hit with the Italian signorinas. On approaching a target, the soldier holds out a handful of the pills and announces: "*Niente bambino, niente* clap" or words to that effect. Those clever *Canadesi!* Inventing a contraceptive pill that doubles as a cure for the pox. *And* also, but merely as a side effect, controls malaria.

As to the Int-School instructor's job, it doesn't look as if I am going to be allowed to accept even if I wished. This may be as well since I would probably go nuts being a base bum when the brigade went into action. Fact is, I've been here so long I'm developing a phobia about leaving. Maybe it's the only home I've got, this side of the water at least. I've even withdrawn my application for a staff course. Real noble, except that there isn't a chance in hell of getting it anyway until I'm twenty-five.

As to the reinforcement situation. Yes, we get the news. Stories in the home papers such as "Conscripts stage mutiny and are warned they will lose their pay and allowances for the time they refuse duty," and "Conscripts tear down Union Jack and burn it. Are fined $11 each" and "Quebec volunteers for overseas beaten up by home service conscripts." It is not good news. Especially since we are suffering such heavy casualties, and the reinforcement drafts don't begin to make up what we have lost, either in numbers or in training. Con Smythe is dead right, and if I'm going to get court-martialled for saying so, they'll have to court-martial the whole damned Canadian Corps in Italy! You should hear the German propaganda broadcasts about the

Zombies! What a windfall for Goebbels! I have to tell you that we are becoming so ashamed of our so-called country that some of us don't give much of a damn if we ever see it again.

Well, having got myself lower than a snake's belly all over again, I guess I'll quit and go see if Doc has any of my rum ration left.

[to Servais Rahier, Carlton, Sask.]*

Dec 11

Dear Servais:

Your Xmas card and letter arrived today and I was most pleased to hear from you. I haven't written as often as I might have, but you will understand that time for such personal pleasures is scarce.

I'm really tickled that at last you've had a good crop and hope the prices are good. Thirty-three bushels to the acre is like the old days in the West before the great drought began, and with wartime wheat prices like they are you should be able to make up some of your long string of losses. Here's to you and yours!

The war progresses but gets no pleasanter for the infantry. Mud, rain and more mud seem to be our lot for Christmas celebrations, but we hope (as we have hoped for three years) that next Christmas we will be at home to make merry in the old ways. One of my first visits will be to you and family at Carlton, and you and I and the boys will go out after Hungarian partridge and prairie chicken. They should be nice and plump about then, and my shooting eye should still be in good practice.

You know, Servais, I'd sell my left hand right now to hear a chickadee singing in the diamond willows by the Saskatchewan and watch a magpie cussing out the crows, or see a flock of honkers going by overhead. About this time of the year I get badly homesick, except of course when I read the papers and see what Canada's infamous Zombies have

---

* Servais was a Belgian immigrant who settled on the prairies in the early years of the century. He and his family had made Angus and me welcome when we were caught in a blizzard while on a hunting trip from Saskatoon in 1935. The Rahiers were one of the good memories of earlier days which helped sustain me during the war. I went back in 1946 and, although Servais had died, the family made so much of me that I almost felt I had come home again.

done to Canadian prestige, then I'm almost glad I'm over here.

I have the picture you took, and enlarged yourself, of the ice going out of the river last spring, pinned over my table. I often look at it when I am feeling particularly low.

Well, I have to go to work, so Merry Christmas to all of you.

[Toronto]

Dec 6

Dear Cap. –

I am chuckling with glee at a resounding joke that has befallen my son. You will remember him – little Farley Mowat who used to live in Saskatoon and edited a mimeographed magazine called *Nature Lore* that had a column headed "Little Bitch of Laughter"? Well, some time ago my son sent me three terrible attempts at storytelling, but the one called "Stephen Bates" was accepted by *Maclean's* magazine and should appear in about six weeks.

Now here's where the joke comes in. Mr. Maclean goes to Defence HQ and can't get permission to publish the story under my son's own name. This joke can be made to backfire, however. Mr. Maclean and I shall just invent a pseudonym (look that up in your new dictionary, which I assume you have got by now). Something like "Pink Skunk" or "Low Lifer" or I may even appropriate Elmer's new nickname, "Smallballs."

But the real joke about it all is that under army regulations, a member of the Canadian Army (Active) cannot accept remuneration for *anything*. This is done so he will not get rich and forget about fighting a war. You see the joke?

However, even this can be made to turn around. Mr. Maclean is going to pay *me* the money. It's one hundred bucks. Just think of that! One hundred berries for a little short story, when I only stand to clear five hundred for a full-length novel that wins wide acclaim and takes two years to perpetrate. So this part of the joke is on me, or would be, except for the fact that *I* get the dough for your story.

But hark ye. Even as I wrote that last line I began to see another side to the joke. *I'll have to pay income tax on your damn money.*

So, in the end the joke's on all of us.

And I had to submit to letting Mr. Maclean take out most of the "damns" and all the "bastards" and "sons of bitches." He says his great journal is for the home, not the barrack room. Maybe you'll forgive me. The piece bleeds a bit with the language purged, but the great thing is you've got your start. Just keep on hewing at that block of wood you call your head and my prophecy about the Remington (typewriter) in the bow of the canoe will come to pass.

Your mother and I are more thrilled than we have been about my two books combined. If you come through this war, son, you can make yourself free! FREE – got that? You may be free to semi-starve, but you'll be free to live. Gosh, how I am excited!

So *au revoir, competitor.*

[Richmond Hill]

Dec 8

Dearest Bunface –

Can you believe it? Two authors in one family. Next thing Elmer will be writing his life. And you getting a cheque for one hundred bricks. And fret not, it will be put into your account, Helen Mowat (in trust).

What I am most glad about is that in writing you will be able to get away from the war, in your imagination anyway, and have the interest of writing for "your public" to distract you, too. Poor old Pops has been put right in the shade. But we are busting with pride and can hardly wait to read it in *Maclean's*.

Yesterday was a trying day. Angus had to speak to two hundred busty women about The Novel, and then we had tea and had to shake hands for hours it seemed. After that a drink at Reg Saunders' which helped pull me together, because I get as nervous as Pops when he speaks.

We are having two Xmas dinners this year. The Gordon Inces in Toronto on Xmas Eve, and your Aunt Jean in Oakville for Xmas Day. Don't care about going to either without you, and we had so hoped it would all be over by this year. Jack Campbell has arrived home from overseas, and his brother Bill is back, too, and at Camp Borden. Everyone, it seems, but you.

[Toronto]

Dec 9

Dear Farl. –

A brief note in haste. It's not "Stephen Bates," but "Liaison Officer" that *Maclean's* will publish. Apparently the bitterness in the Bates story, which was not your bitterness but that of many thousands of fighting men, is not considered to be conducive to Canadian Unity and to the War Effort. This is your first experience of censorship of literary people by the Establishment. Please take note that it will not be your last, although it will probably not be called by that name once the war is over.

[Richmond Hill]

Dec 14

Why hello Bunje. –

While I was racking my brains for a good pseudonym for you, your momma got it. She said, "Why, 'Bunje,' of course!" Of course. So Bunje you will be when "Liaison" comes busting out in print. They didn't say anything about illustrations, but if they want some I'll draw them. I'll use as a model the photo of you and me and Quartermaster Sergeant Trounce outside the Trenton Armouries in 1940, setting off that contraption of an imitation three-inch mortar you invented out of a piece of sewer pipe, some condensed milk cans and a lot of black powder. I had a chuckle over it the other day when it fell out of a book. You look like Houdini on the completion of a particularly difficult trick; me looking worried; and Trounce looking as if he had just done something in his pants and was afraid to bend over any farther.

Speaking of *Carrion Place*, which I wasn't, but am now, your Uncle Jack Thomson wrote from England saying of my heroine, "Bloody good show. The bitch got what she deserved." What a swell review that would be – I wonder if I can get it into print. Reg says not a damn copy is left in any bookstore in the country. Perhaps the booksellers have buried them in their cellars.

[Richmond Hill]

Dec 20

Dearest Bunface –

I wonder if by this time you have heard about your story selling to *Maclean's*, and if that helps to get you away in your mind from the sad and terrible things you have recently had to endure.

Sometimes I know you feel that you cannot go on but, my darling, Angus and I are with you every step of the way. We can't help directly, we can't suffer the physical, but when we sit on Sundays in front of the blazing logs with the radio playing a symphony, the curtains pulled and all most comfy, we look at your picture over the fireplace and our spirits are miles away with you. Only our bodies bask in the heat and comfort.

Sometimes I just can't bear it, but then I think how proud we are of you, so enduring, and of the spiritual in you – call it guts, it means the same thing. Anyway, in spite of everything, of pain and even loss if it should come to that, I'm glad you have done what you have done.

We are not only proud of our son but perhaps we've learned to know you better, and you us, than we would ever have done in peacetime.

But to get off this high plane, which probably embarrasses you no end, you are quite right about our reaction to the Hickey ménage. But Angus firmly remarked – "He can marry a Hottentot (whatever that is) if he wants to, and it is all right with me."

Tell us as much as you can and want to about your life, and don't mind getting the blues off your chest. God bless you and bring you home safe and sound, my lamb.

Hove To. Christmas Day 1944

My Darling –

Our thoughts are with you on this day and always. We dropped in on the Sandersons yesterday who have lost their only son. Dinner with the Inces last night and they tell us your pretty cousin Janet will be home from England for New Year's. I phoned Ev and found her husband has come home, so I do hope they can get along together and be happy now. Your Uncle Jack writes that he'll be home shortly, too. All of this seems to make Christmas even emptier for us.

So we are writing this short note to you together. Angus will tell you how we started off for Oakville but had to turn back because of a storm and luckily the Pocknells phoned to ask us to help eat their eighteen-pound turkey as their guests were unable to get to them.

We hope and pray that next year this will all be over and only a bad memory for all of us.

Well old Boy.

I suppose hell is being raised somewhere up north of Bagnacavallo and the Shining First is right in the middle of it. We were all so proud when the army commander mentioned the regiment the other day, and I must say the papers and the CBC all carried the story. But I fear that it was like the recognition accorded a successful hockey team, transient and shallow. The death, and loss, and misery of it will only be understood by a faithful few.

I have just now opened the Xmas bottle of rum and I am taking the first drink to you, old son. . . .

And now the second, to the regiment. . . .

Slough of Despond

❖   ❖   ❖

OPERATION CHUCKLE BROUGHT THE FIRST BRIGADE PERILOUSLY
close to dissolution. Throughout December its regiments were
ordered again and again to attack across yet another canal or river,
and each time their numbers dwindled until, towards the end of that
fearful month, the strength of most units had been reduced by half
or more.

Reinforcements came forward in such small numbers that they
could not begin to stem the wastage.

In Canada, the Zombies rioted.

By Christmas, First Canadian Infantry Brigade had become a
mere shadow of its former self with, as the CO of the Hasty Ps said
grimly: "Only enough strength left to lean against the Hun," as he
slowly withdrew to new and seemingly ever more impregnable
defence positions.

With the beginning of 1945, winter struck full force upon the
saturated plains about Ravenna. Snow mingled with the freezing
rains. Heavy frosts coated the muddy sloughs and the contorted
skeletons of shell-torn trees. And finally the war sank into desultory
exchanges of artillery fire, patrols, raids and sniping.

Nothing more could be attempted until spring came. There was
nothing to be done – except endure.

Bitterness began to grow upon us like fungi sprouting on forest
trees that have been swept by fire but are not yet dead. We grew
angrier at our fellow citizens at home in Canada than we had ever
been with the German soldiers with whom we traded death wounds.

One evening a former English teacher, now a gunner in a field artillery battery, was visiting me in the frigid casa we called home. As he huddled over a little kerosene heater warming his hands around a cup of rum, he turned to me and grimaced.

"If there is a Slough of Despond, Squib, we're into it, up to the ears. Up to the fucking ears! And I'm going to remember all my life, whatever remains of it, who put us into it. And it wasn't the Jerries did it."

As the winter months dragged on, my inner vision began to clear and I started to see the world as it really was – and to recognize the real enemies of humankind. The incentive to do so had come from the war; the guidance had largely come from Angus. It was not the least of the gifts he made to me.

[Toronto]

Dec 28

Dear Captain Mowat. –

Pappy has just had three beers, and for all the good it has done him, it might as well have been three Cokes. But, old boy, when you arrive home and I get a claw-hammer in my hand and begin wandering around the storeroom trying to remember where the hell I nailed down that forty ounces of pre-war Quebec *rhum*! That'll be the day.

Today at lunch time I went down to Ashbridge's to look at your boat. There she sat with two feet of snow on her deck and frozen in as snug as you please. And hardly a drop of water in her bilges. Which is just as well. The sewage is best kept on the outside where, I am told, it is so powerful it will preserve the wood forever.*

So I take your writing too seriously? Nuts to you, feller. I didn't say, did I, that you are a Thomas Hardy or an Anthony Trollope or even a Mr. Tolstoi? I only said that, bar getting yourself killed by a stinking mortar bomb or shell, you can plan for a life after this hellish

---

* Ashbridge's Bay was then the recipient of much of Toronto's (untreated) sewage.

business is over, based on something you can do. And be a free nigger into the bargain. But all kidding aside, I understand full well that the *Maclean's* acceptance, which your mother and I considered terrific news, would appear to a fellow going into action for the Nth time about as relevant as the price of eggs in Rosthern, Saskatchewan. Do you recall the shopkeeper there telling your maw the hens weren't laying, "And darned if I blame 'em, with eggs at ten cents a dozen."

I took with a large dose of salts all the phooey the radio and press gave us about what a perfectly swell time the Canadians in Italy were having at Christmas. I'll bet it was swell. Dear God, the blather they feed us. What really enrages me is that they think we are so bloody dumb we will believe it all.

Doug Reid went back overseas on his own insistence. I knew he was unhappy with the way things are in Canada. One day before I left Kingston, I stopped beside him on the m/c to ask him how he was. He gave me a sad look (like a borzoi) over the tops of those trees in the woodlot he has around his mouth and said he didn't take much comfort in being surrounded by so many elderly folk, even if some of them did drive motorcycles. His parting shot at me was to have his photo taken sleeping on a couch, evidently sent to the arms of Morpheus by the copy of *C.P.* lying on his chest. Good fun, Doug. Will I ever forget him trying to learn to "snap to attention" while on parade with you other subbies in Trenton? Him and the box of Kleenex he used to carry under his arm because of the sniffles. Well, he could never have made a parade-ground soldier, but he made a damned good airman.

[Russi, west of Ravenna]

Dec 14

Mes Amis:

Day before yesterday came a parcel containing an autographed copy of *C.P.* Here's what happened. To begin with, Chapter 1 got skimmed through very quickly to the tune of some very untuneful shelling, while I let my eyes (as if I could have stopped them) rove from the written page to the four walls (and ceiling) around me. I occasionally thought the book's narrator was interjecting comments about wall thicknesses and muzzle velocities into the more philosophical stuff. Anyway, I retain no more than a hazy idea of what the first chapter was all about.

Chapters 2 to 5 got slightly more of a sporting chance. I read them aloud (or parts thereof) to half a dozen Germans. There was only one lantern available in the casa the Int section was inhabiting and it wasn't deemed either fair or wise to take it out of the room where our erstwhile opponents were being held in durance vile. So I had to come to the lantern. And I was so darn tired that I couldn't keep awake, so I tried reading *C.P.* aloud. I regret to tell you that before dawn's early light allowed me to douse the light, my audience had all slumped into peaceful slumber against the surrounding walls. But you should not take this as in any sense being in the nature of a critical comment. The circumstances were unusual. Besides which they understood little if any English.

I completed the balance of the book this evening in relative peace, while sipping at a dollop of rum. This greatly confused things. When I should have been full of woe at the final clash between Eric and his nemesis, I was instead beaming happily through a rosy haze which kept coming between me and the page. And when I should have been joyfully praising the War Department for its rumish generosity, I was instead weeping bitterly to see the bottle upended, and not a drop remaining with which to toast the author of the epic.

Seriously, the conditions for coming to grips with the book were inauspicious in the extreme. I haven't been able to see it as an entity in its own right. It contains so many vignettes of things that conjure up throat-tightening memories for me that I can't see the forest for the trees. Mutt and the skunk in the cellar quite eclipse the rest of the chapter. Incidentally, I now understand why I have been accused of plagiarism by the Senior Mowat, but I didn't *know* Poppa had written the skunk episode first.

I realize you are both anxious to hear my assessment of the book but I can't offer anything in depth as yet. It is like the rice pudding thing but in reverse – do you remember how I used to dig the raisins out of my rice pudding and save them to eat later after the bowl was empty? This time I dug out all the treasured memories and gorged on them and on all the colour and atmosphere for which we out here are quite starved. This time I've saved the *pudding* for later.

[Toronto]

Jan 11, 1945

Dear Squib (b) Mk.II. –

Looking back to find out when I sent you the box of literary aids (never did find out), I found instead that at one time you were in quite a dither about a gypsy lady named Susi.

Ah, these women, and ah, also, we men who believe everything they say. Like the time when the Depression was still on and I picked up a wench on the highway and ended by lending her $2 to buy a housemaid's uniform without which she couldn't get a job as a housemaid. I had some difficulty persuading Helen that the $2 really was for a uniform. That was in 1938. She hasn't paid me back yet but I daresay she'll think of it one of these days and send me a cheque.

What do you *do* with typewriter ribbons? I have sent you enough so that they would stretch, if unrolled, from here to Italy. And still you keep yipping for more. If it is ribbons you want as a means of assisting Italian wenches to decorate their housemaid's uniforms, say so and I'll send proper ribbons. Or improper ones, if I can find them. Any kind would be easier to find than typewriter ribbons.

Was in Midland on Tuesday making a speech to the Canadian Club (women's section). A dandy audience in beaver and seal-skin coats. I was supposed to be talking about libraries, but somehow got off on the war and what the front-line soldiers think of us and why. I thought they would get mad as hell. I was. But, oddly, they were interested. It had never occurred to most of them that a soldier can be wounded or deeply damaged by anything except bullets and shells and that sort of thing. Or that a man who had been immersed in battle for a long time might need anything but a few buckshee "war bonus" dollars and a loan to buy a farm or go to university, in order to be perfectly at home again, and grateful into the bargain.

What they don't know about is the burning out process, and

nobody – not our gabby retired generals, nor our great medical minds, nor, certainly, the politicians and their mouthpieces the press and radio – is telling them. And for good reason. It would be one more "bad" aspect of war and would help to make it even less acceptable both to those who are needed at the front, and those who have to see them go.

There hasn't been any mail from you for some time, but we comprehend the reason. We follow such reports as come through from Italy very closely, and with much sadness. The casualty lists are very long and although they don't tell much of events, they at least give us some true idea of what is going on, and our hearts ache for the misery and unendingness of it all.

Yesterday I ran into a couple of wounded tankers, one from Italy, one from Belgium. They were in a low and mutinous frame of mind because both had overstayed their homecoming leaves by a few days, and their pay was being docked as a result. A couple of fellows home for the first time in years, wounded and going to be discharged, overstayed their leave a bit, so they had to be punished. Hell, that's not like the Zombies going over the hill in droves all over this country and getting away with it. Hardly. But that's the rules, and they aren't bending where they ought to bend. *And they have to be bent for the returning veterans.* These, as you will too well know, are men who have suffered grievous damage, if not to body then to the soul, or spirit, or whatever damn thing you want to call it. They won't know where the hell they're at for a long time. They are filled with disillusionment and on top of all that are suffering the frustration of men who have, for a second time, lost their homes – their units, their communities. My God, those two tankers were homesick for their units. I still remember that feeling myself.

So what's to be done with them? I'm just damned if I know and perhaps nobody does. But, by God, we in Canada should be straining every nerve and exhausting every resource we've got to find an answer.

Do you ever feel us pulling for you? It's there all the time, boy.

[Richmond Hill]

Jan 16, 1945

Dear Lamb –

Last week was not so good. No letters, and Angus and Elmer return from the PO with long faces every evening. But you are so good about writing that we know this isn't any of your doing. Angus is working on the new Library Act and we are putting a box together for you. I'll put in a couple of *Atlantic Monthlys* although I don't like it as much as I used to before they turned down your poems.

Young Bob Endean from across the road dropped in tonight for a talk. He feels so out of it, being crippled, and all his friends away, many of them overseas. It is so hard on young men like him who would like to do their part and can't be accepted, especially when there are so many healthy young chaps about who have found excuses to stay home and have a good time.

You are wonderful the way you write so cheerfully, but I know. So just write the way you feel if it helps, and thank you, darling, a thousand times for writing so often. Even a short note helps. Some mothers and wives hardly hear from their men overseas, and it is killing for them.

[Bagnacavallo, east of Ravenna]

Dec 23, 1944

Dear Parents:

Still Italy, goddamnit!

Unless this blankety-blank war gets itself over quickly or unless I get the hell out of Italy, this sunny disposition of mine is going to sour beyond all recovery. Particularly now that those goddamn goody-goody politicos back in Zombie-land have concluded that issue rum is bad for our morals (never mind *morale*) and so has now been replaced with something called "medicinal rum." This *looks* like rum and even smells like it, but has an additive which makes it taste like the contents of a honey bucket, and which, if taken in any reasonable quantity, engenders a ferocious attack of the Eyetie quick-step. Can you imagine the petty, weasel-mindedness of those fat-assed s.o.b.s who, safely hunkered down in Canada, have deprived us of one of the very few little pleasures in our lives? I hope the militia hang on to some of those useful bits of equipment. We may find a bloody good use for them later on.

This morning I got out a Haig and Haig bottle that's been nestling in my kitbag for a month with one drink left in it. I drank it out of pique, and feel worse. Why I should tell you all this, I can't rightly say. You'll probably again assail me in your next letter with accusations of drunken habits. God, how I wish I had the opportunity and where-withal to *be* a drunken reprobate. But on one twenty-six-ounce bottle of Canadian or British booze every two months, supplemented by *vino cara armato* (armoured car wine, because the juice has been squeezed out of the best grapes in the vineyards by the treads of tanks), we are almost automatic members of the WCTU.*

What with the news from France, which is only a temporary depressive, and the news from Zombie-land, which is a permanent emetic, and the fact that the third Xmas in a row is destined to be spent doing things I don't like, and the possibility that the next Xmas may be similar, plus the lack of letters from home, instead of which we get a flood of "Merry Xmas" cards, "Wish you were here," "Thinking of you," "You are with us in spirit" sort of balls . . . well, you add it up and it all spells balls, balls, balls!

Hey, this is doing me good! When I gnash my little milk teeth at the Things That Be, I frequently end up with the giggles (sort of) and feel better. Catharsis yet. But someday *I am going to find* the slimy bastard who decided to doctor our rum. And then . . . !

Had a long epistle from old pal Bill Campbell. For quite a time he and I have nurtured a dream of establishing a little Utopia in one of the fiords of northern British Columbia. The idea had kind of got lost in the shuffle, but now he has resurrected it and I must say it sounds good. So see if you can get someone who lives on the west coast to check into what might be available, and how we would go about getting our mitts on some land up there. Which reminds me, any ideas

---

* Women's Christian Temperance Union.

I may ever have had about wanting to do my bit to make Canada a better place to live in when I get back have gone overboard. Most of us long-term exiles feel increasingly cynical about our Mother/Father Land. The other week I actually heard a Lieut. Col., who shall remain nameless, advocate a military take-over of Canada after this is finished, in order to send all the war profiteers and political yellow-bellies and that ilk to Baffin Island with one-way tickets, and one match each. Furthermore, I think he really meant it. In any case, he was cheered to the rafters.

C.P. has been going the rounds to enthusiastic responses. The Brig just returned it, with very complimentary remarks and says he is instructing his wife to buy several copies to send out for delayed Xmas presents. Fame! Can Fortune be far behind?

Got to quit. A bunch of very muddy Heinies has just been delivered by a squad of RCRs. Ought to be some good souvenirs in their dirty pockets, if nothing else.

[Bagnacavallo]

Jan 4, 1945
Dear Parents:

My heart rejoices! The box of writer's aids has at long last arrived. Visitors to my stone crypt in the casa Brigade HQ presently occupies are at last showing a decent respect for the cloak-and-dagger boys, as we I-blokes are called, usually with ridicule intended. When they look at my bookshelf and its shining new contents, they now salaam reverently and swallow their usual lewd jests. A dictionary! A thesaurus! A punctilious punctuation manual! *And* Fowler's *Modern English Usage!* These provide a formidable demonstration of our right to be deemed Intelligent. Whether or not or for what purposes we use said intelligence is, of course, a horse of a different texture. But I've already discovered how to spell sucess – or is it succes? I doubt it.

Perhaps you know I have a new boss. It's hell. I just get one broken in and, zingo, I have to do it all over again. I wonder, do the higher powers think I have nothing better to do than break in new brigs? This one is going to take a lot of work. He is picayune (thank you,

Mr. Roget). He says I am too pale! He says I must get more outside exercise. So every day I take an hour's stimulating exercise in the fresh air . . . letting the winter wind blow into my face over the hood of a speeding jeep. And if you think Lulu doesn't move along right smartly when she and Benny are out of their shellproof cellar, you just don't know. Hell's Angels have nothing on it! But I still remain pale, and though I explain until I am hoarse that I was born pale, have always been pale and God Made Me That Way, little good does it do. Please include a couple of pounds of rouge in my next parcel. And some eye pencil. If people could only *see* my moustache, they might conclude I am old enough to be allowed a little decadent pallor.

I am not going to talk about the past month, except to say it may well have been the worst in my life. I know you expect some explanation, but I can't do it yet. I don't want even to think about it. Sorry, but that's the way it is, for now at least.

My ornithological inclinations have been stimulated by the acquisition from an Eyetie kid of a nondescript and rather ragged linnet, at a cost of one chocolate bar. It is a sad, dispirited little bird but it twitters now and again, and it can hear an incoming shell whistling miles away. By observing its attempts to hide under its birdbath, one is alerted to impending whumps. Like the canaries in coal mines, it gives warning of trouble. And it has given me a great idea. I am writing a submission to Higher Authority suggesting that my linnet be taken on strength Canadian Forces; provided with a lot of lady linnets; and, under my direction of course (should be worth at least a brigadier's rank), encouraged to produce numerous offspring which can then be trained as Early Warning Devices, Soldiers for the use of, and issued to all front-line units as part of their War Establishment. The new BM has tried to dissuade me. He says such a suggestion will get me nowhere among the Brass Hats. But he is wrong. If nothing else it could get me a medical board, and a referral to that happy hospital at Basingstoke where military nut cases live in some comfort *and* in safety. Anyhoo, my linnet answers to the name Tucker-Burr V, so-named after a U.S. Army intelligence officer attached to my section for experience. He is Tucker-Burr IV and is from Boston. A nice enough chap, but he tends to twitter.

I have also acquired something for which I have always longed. It came as a gift from the Fourth Estate, namely Bill Boss of CP. It is a seven-foot ostrich (stuffed, I hasten to add) which Bill liberated somewhere. It too now shares the Int cavern and may to some extent be undoing the effect of my library. Some people have begun to spread the word that I am a bit of a character, after coming into my office and being accosted by the beady eye of Benjamin, he of the long and dusty plumes.

Your patience in not asking me to reveal the details of my work is appreciated, so here is a little reward. One incident in the day of a brigade Int section.

It came about that just before we were pulled out of the line to have a little rest, a certain company of Hasty Ps was holding the dyke on our side of one of the steep-walled canals that make this country just about impassable in winter. Jerry was holding the opposite dyke, about fifty yards away, with neither side daring to show their noses over the crests. However, downstream a bit the canal made a U-bend into and then back out of Jerry territory, so they held *both* dykes along this stretch and were able to cause the neighbouring Plow Jockeys some little trouble, since they overlooked our guys.

One night our duty officer (a lowly LO) roused me to report that there had been one hell of an explosion on the Hasty Ps' front and the Brig wanted an explanation pronto. The LO had called the Hasties' duty officer but all he could get out of him was something vague about "enemy action," so the word was, "Get up, Squib, and do your job."

Which I did. I roused out my Int-Cpl and sent him off into a sleet storm in a jeep. About an hour later he came back, half frizz, but laughing fit to kill.

The explanation he'd been given at Hastings' BHQ was that the enemy had fired a giant shell, probably from a railroad gun, that fell into the canal on the battalion's front. Nobody had been wounded by the explosion, though a number of our men who had been on a "patrol" nearby had been concussed. So that was that.

There was just one hitch. There are no railroad guns on the Adriatic front, and the story was a lovely lie. As my Cpl was climbing back into the jeep, one of his pals from the battalion I-section sidled over and spilled the beans.

It seems Baker Company's sgt. major is a hard-rock miner from up around Bancroft way, and a devil with dynamite. He talked his company commander into letting him make an unorthodox attempt to eliminate the Jerries holding the bend in the canal. The plan was simplicity itself. He took a forty-five-gallon drum and filled it two-thirds full of gun cotton and other such potent stuff. Then he calculated how long it would take said barrel to float down the canal from Baker's positions into the loop in German country, and fused it accordingly.

The final step was to have one of Baker's platoons roll this monster up to the top of our side of the canal bank on a suitably stormy night when nothing could be seen and enemy sentries would be hunkered down for shelter, then let it roll down into the raging waters to be floated into enemy territory. Eureka!

The CSM ought to have got a medal out of it. But there was a problem. It was the coldest night of the year, and the canal had frozen over.

So what did I tell the boss? I am a Hasty P. I said it appeared that an aircraft, perhaps one of our own, had jettisoned a thousand pounder on the Hastings' front. I told Div the same thing, and everyone was happy. A few days later a bottle of Scotch from the CO of the Hasties was delivered unto me, with compliments. Not being entirely heartless, I split it with my Cpl.

[Toronto]

Jan 24

Dear Professor Mowat. –

So thank God the books arrived. Lose not one of them by anything less than a direct hit. The thesaurus and punctuation guide cannot be replaced, even from the publishers.

I told Mr. Hoover, my elderly bank manager, about your linnet.

Whereupon, swaying slightly and with closed eyes, he proceeded to recite the whole of Wordsworth's "Green Linnet" for me. Well, I waited him out, but humming to myself "The Road to the Isles." Who would have thought that old Hoover would spend a lot of time every winter memorizing poetry. But he does.

Mum has a new idea about a book. A poppa's letters to his son and vice versa! But published letters must be either inspirational, or funny. Mine, being usually just plain mad, would not do at all. "Liaison Officer," by the way, has not yet appeared.

The *Globe* quoted a moving editorial from the Lindsay paper this morning which said in effect (and all unconsciously patronizing) that we must be sympathetic and understanding towards returning men. Now, goddamn it, how these fools do get things back-assed! What I'm trying to tell the dolts is that *they* must try to *earn* the understanding and esteem of the returners. That they must shake themselves out of their bloody complacency and take the community to the veteran – and not vice versa.

How I do rant.

So you talked yourself into an ostrich? My God, what'll you be after doing next? Is it a he ostrich or a she one? Try to bring it back with you. It will look well on the front lawn of Hove To and nice long legs for Elmer and his pals to leave their calling cards on. Yes, indeed, I can well believe that you might be regarded as something of a character.

Yesterday, a little cold Pop's been cherishing got a bit ahead of him and he was persuaded to see Dr. Rolph, who gave him some bad medicine and ordered him to bed. So here I lie on my little truckle-bed with Elmer lying beside it, snoring and making smells. He eats too much. Helen will sail in in a minute, make a horrible face and shoo him out of doors where he will trot, in the zero cold, from Gracie Thompson's garbage can to Janet Cooper's, and so on down Elizabeth Street, shaking his paws with the cold (some people say they have seen him blow on them) and building up a good bellyful of future odours.

As for me, I expect I will shortly try and sneak downstairs in my pyjama top, extract a Christmas cigar from its hiding place under the couch and smoke it up the chimney where Helen can't smell it.

My, what a nose that woman has!

It's a somewhat trying time of life, Farl, when you're not young enough to do what the young men have to do, and not old enough to sit on a bench in the sun with the other old men. I am now revealing my feline streak – poor pussy Angoos.

[Richmond Hill]

Jan 23, 1945

Dearest Bunface,

I suppose you are following the Russians' progress with great interest. How I hope it means the end is coming but I'm afraid to count on that or look ahead. Do we seem unreal to you, Bunje? And all your old life? The correspondent Matthew Halton said something on the radio that made me wonder. He said (after six weeks in Canada and then going back), "This is the only reality, over here – the other is a dream."

I can't bear to think of you so pale and tired and sleepless, but this is no way for the mother of a brave boy to be acting – forgive me.

The Reverend Captain Burnett is back from Italy, with the MC which he won for bringing in wounded German soldiers as well as our own. He was dangerously wounded but looks fine now. Mrs. Brown had a big reception for the poor man, who had to stand and shake hands with fifty people and looked as if he would have rather been back in Italy.

We had an evening with your pal Andy Lawrie. Angus was confined to bed with flu when Andy phoned and invited us to see Noel Coward's play, *Blithe Spirit*, with him in Toronto. I said I was sorry but Angus was sick, whereupon Angus bellowed down the stairs that we would go anyway, and Andy said he would bring some special navy medicine. So we drove into Toronto, picking the Lawrie family up on the way.

Andy has had jaundice and looks thin, but will soon go back to Halifax to join a ship, a corvette, I believe. He is very keen to get back to university and says there will be a great future for biologists. He says the government will pay $60 a month to servicemen while they are at college. We went back to the Lawries' after the show and I had a rum and brandy liqueur, which didn't do me any good. We talked of you muchly and I tried to get Andy enthused about cruising in *Bonnet* but he seems a little tired of the sea! He brought us three bottles of rum which he got in Trinidad for seventy-five cents each, and we pay $7.50 if we can get it at all, which we usually can't. Angus says he is jealously guarding the bottles for your return, which *should* be soon, the way the Russians are driving the Germans back towards Berlin.

[Bagnacavallo]

Jan 17

Chères Parents:

Several letters from you both, smelling somewhat of depression. Is it because of the gloomy tone of voice of my December letters? I hope not, but this *has* been a rough time and it has been hard to keep a light touch. Or is it just that time seems to be stretching out so interminably and the war has just gone on too long?

Anyhoo, I had a hell of a (unintentionally) funny letter from Arthur Thomson. It was a carbon copy, addressed "Dear Farley/ Jack" (non-applicable name to be deleted). It was full of complaints about the discomforts caused by the war, including the fact that shop girls were "becoming very impertinent." From which it leapt to an ecstatic prospective of Art's new yacht-building venture – "There will be many affluent people after the war and therefore a booming market in pleasure boats," and concluded with an invitation to invest now, and make our future fortunes. Jesus H. Keerist! Sorry, Mum, I know he is your kid brother but he's also my "kid" uncle, being only nine years older than me, and I couldn't contain the expletive. Shouldn't someone tell him what's been going on? I shall answer: "Dear Sir/Madam – Yours of the last inst. recd. and contents ntd. Yr attn is drawn to K.R.O.16(iv)3 which states that the m/n subject be not repeat NOT discussed with serving members of H. M. Forces for fear of causing apoplectic consequences, and thus giving comfort to the enemy."

I wonder how Uncle Jack took it? I'd expect him to blow his stack loud enough to be heard from London to Montreal! But I suppose that, for many if not most Canadians at home, the continuation of the war, now that they have made their pile, is seen simply as a disaccommodation to be endured, albeit not quietly, until they can all get back to the lotus-eating life.

I'm looking at a copy of *Saturday Evening Post* and considering what it tells me. "She's Beautiful! She's Engaged! She Uses Ponds Rich and Creamy Face Cream" . . . "An Exquisite Diamond Ring Will Show Her That You Value The Most Important Things In Life" . . . "Post-War America Will Give You Everything You Ever Wanted" . . . and so on, *ad nauseam*. Well, what I mean, goddamn it to hell – I can't stand it! And I bloody well won't! *This* is the Brave New World we're fighting for? Not me, brothers and sisters, not me!

I am considering transferring from the Regiment to which, of course, I still belong, though on detached duty, to the Intelligence Corps. I'd be out of the infantry as well as out of the Regiment, but I'm getting to the point where a little physical security begins to look irresistible. On the other hand, I'd probably feel like a bloody traitor. So at the moment I just don't know which way I'll jump.

[Richmond Hill]

Feb 6

Dear Urchin –

That's a good name for you. It suits you somehow. Your letter about changing to the Intelligence Corps just came and I hope you do, if it means a break, a change, a rest and some place out of the sound of guns. Angus and I have become very worried about you because it has been too long a stretch for anyone to bear. We thought of writing General Graham who is now very important in Ottawa, but then I felt you'd never forgive us for taking a hand, even if it did do any good.

I see today that the Legion is telling our lousy government to send home the men who have had a long *active* service and replace them with the ones who have held the cushy jobs in Canada. Perhaps the war won't last much longer with the Russians doing so well, but even so please do your d____ to try and get home on leave, or get out entirely. This long strain is hard on us too, so don't feel you would be letting the side down. No one would dream of criticising if you took a safer job.

[*Richmond Hill*]

Feb 5

My dear Fellow. –

Yesterday, while clawing through some files, I came across a "Billy"* Mowat folder. It held clippings from your bird column in the *Saskatoon Star Phoenix*'s "Prairie Pals" section, including the famous one where you wrote so glowingly of the underwater love-making of the Ruddy Duck, and got yourself sharply taken to task by several irate ladies in the *Star*'s letter column. There was also a complete file of *Nature Lore* (all four numbers) and your first editorial announcing that a "five-cent bit" contributed in buying the magazine would be used for the betterment of the birds and beasts of Saskatchewan. Well, God be thanked, those were happy days, and we had enough sense to savour them while they lasted.

There was also a copy of your letter to the Windsor *Border Cities Star* asking for support of the scheme you and Hughie Cowan had dreamed up to cover Canada with sicamore (sic) trees which, you said, were the "rarest and beautifulest trees I have ever seen in my life, and should be spread." I think you were nine at the time. And there was a story about Jitters, your pet squirrel, and a collection of your bird columns in the *Richmond Hill Liberal* written just before the war. Well, Squib II, if you don't make a writer, it will have to be because there is nothing left in your head to write about.

Fergawsakes, did you expect the old man to jump out of his skin on hearing you may transfer to the I-corps? If he did jump, it would be in joy and relief. Naturally any such move must always be spoken about with the utmost levity, but I can certainly feel for you in making such a decision. There is a tug about any soldier's unit when he has been through things with it that is very hard to escape. But it doesn't bother my conscience to see you make the break, and you don't have a conscience anyhoo, so what the hell? You don't owe anybody a goddamn thing, so go to it, brother, and let's hope it

---

* "Billy" was the name I adopted when we moved to Saskatoon, in order to avoid the obvious variation on "Farley" coined by some of my schoolmates in Windsor.

comes quickly so all three of us can take a new lease on life.

I *have* been worrying about more than mortars and shells. I *know* what happens to people who stay up there too long. It is past time you removed yourself or were removed from that hell's brew. I'm just praying that it comes off. Helen and Elmer, too.

And listen, my brother and my son, you just keep on writing exactly as you feel. It wouldn't be any easier for Helen and me if you were to write pretty letters. We wouldn't believe you, anyway. And what would be the use of having at your back a couple of people who can take it, if they didn't take it? The very fact that you can, will and do open up to us is perhaps the greatest help we have these days. It keeps you closer to us than anything else can. So let her fly, Squibbie old son, and I hope this doesn't have the same effect upon you as Mum's oft-repeated injunction to me. "Be funny, Angus."

I've sent you a copy of *Maclean's*, containing "Liaison Officer."*

At last. The story is better than you think, though not nearly so good as the untouchable "Stephen Bates."

[Richmond Hill]

Feb 13

Darling Peanut –

Ev came and spent yesterday with me. She is not living with her husband, and says she can never do so, and wants a divorce. Very sad for him, and not much of a homecoming after being with the Highlanders almost as long as you with the Hastings, but Ev says she has tried her best, but cannot live with him again. Bill Campbell is back in Canada now and just sort of "dropped in" that evening and the three of us sat and drank Ev's rum and looked at the fire and talked a good deal about you. Bill seems to be of one mind with you about going to B.C.

Just you grouse as much as you want, but keep your head down. We so hope you can get the Intelligence job, and that right soon. I know it is so hard for you to write so often, but it means just everything to us, just to hear once a week, then we say, "He was all right then."

---

* The published version was titled "Battle Close-up."

[Richmond Hill]

Feb 20

I've been wrestling with that awful coke in the furnace and stove. First one goes out, then the other, and Angus is away. We can't get any real coal. Oh, the hardships we poor civilians have to put up with. Your letters are taking much longer to reach us now, and you say ours are very slow to you. But we write every week, and sometimes twice a week.

Bob Campbell just dropped in for a cup of tea and says brother Bill is now engaged to a nineteen-year-old who works in a bank in Toronto. I wonder how Evie will feel. Or is that all over? You three were such close companions once, I used to think of you as being a little family of your own. But the war has broken up so much, and not just things. I don't suppose Bill will go back overseas now and perhaps you three will get together again when the war is over.

[Bagnacavallo]

Jan 20

Dear Parents:

Re your queries about the new Brig. He would be at home as vice president of any big business. He has lots of "push" and "drive" and is determined to get to the top. He was well on his way until he overreached himself last month and got busted down a grade. He doesn't like me much, but then he knows that I have the *real* story of the disaster that bad planning and overweening ambition brought upon our lot last month. But I do not care to pursue this subject.

The new BM and staff captain and the rest of the gang are mostly good souls, but the Brig's appointees. This, plus the fact that I am now the senior surviving officer of this HQ, sometimes makes for a bit of strain. So my best pals are not here, but amongst the Int laddies at Div and elsewhere. We form something of a breed apart.

Stan Ketcheson is in England. His wound, which I am convinced he got while deliberately seeking the quietus after the débâcle referred to above, is not serious, but he'll never be back here. You might see him in Canada. And you just *might* get him to tell you what happened in December. If you do see him, let him know that he is not forgotten and that some day the truth will out. As for the rest that you might know – there's nobody left who served under the "Maj" at dear old Camp Boredom or in Trenton, and precious few of *my* old pals and peers either.

I did get a phone call the other day from Frank Banfield who, as you'll recall, was one of our determined trio of budding biologists (Harris Hord was the third) who spent the summer of '39 harassing the birds and mammals of Saskatchewan for the Royal Ontario Museum. Frank is a meteorologist at Corps HQ and so is far and away out of my usual sphere. But I invited him down for a visit on the assumption that a tour of the slums would do him good. I think it did. I managed to get the two of us stonked by some eighty-eights which, since he had never previously heard a shot fired in anger, is a memory he will no doubt long nurture. We also went bird watching in a swamp behind the lines and shared a bottle of his Scotch one evening.

His visit had an amusing consequence. Things are pretty quiet on our front now, with both sides mostly willing to live and let live until the sun comes back, and things warm up and dry up. The new boss thinks differently. He thinks it is our duty to "keep the Jerry on his toes." This means we have to send out a lot of patrols, and otherwise keep him stirred up and inclined to be nasty. I am in charge of the "otherwise" in this war of nerves – not by choice but under orders. It is a task that brings me into ill repute with the boys up forward, who tend to reap the whirlwind when somebody's brainstorm gets Jerry mad. However orders is orders. Frank? Oh yes. Well, the meteorologists have a supply of giant hydrogen-filled balloons which they send aloft bearing weather instruments. And I thought I saw a way to use some of same to bewitch and bewilder Jerry without inciting him to take revenge on our guys in the slit trenches.

Result: The V-8 Secret Weapon. It consists of one met balloon, inflated with hydrogen to a diameter of about six feet, to which is attached, in a sort of gondola, the illuminating flare from a three-inch mortar starshell; a green signal-light cartridge; some safety fuse; and a detonator. I built the first one in the Int office, somewhat to the distress of my staff, most of whom found urgent reasons to go elsewhere. A successful test (with tethered balloon) was conducted next day. All that was then required was a dark night, a favourable wind and a long sales pitch to a 48th Highlander company commander who was extremely suspicious that whatever I did on his section of the front, it would be trouble.

And then we did it. Over Jerry's lines just after midnight, a blazing white Star of Bethlehem suddenly and noiselessly bloomed as the time fuse set off the flare. But *this* flare, instead of slowly sinking as is normal, began to *rise* – spiralling faster and faster as it mounted like a crazy rocket into the black firmament and illuminating an ever-greater expanse of landscape behind Jerry's line.

That must have set them staring. At length the brilliant light went out. There followed a moment of dramatic darkness and then, from about two thousand feet up, came a brilliant green flash (the Very cartridge), followed instantly by a huge red explosion (hydrogen explodes very satisfactorily – remember the *Hindenburg*?) Then came the *pièce de résistance*. Coinciding with the big bang, the Corps heavies – 7.5-inch howitzers – brought down an almighty stonk on what my photo-interpretation pals at Div Int believed might be a Jerry brigade or maybe Divisional HQ.

Oh, *mamma mia*!

I save the really delicious bit for last. Tedeschi reacted speedily. Our wireless intercept chappies reported the air was full of confused and apprehensive German voices wanting to know what in hell kind of a hate we had unleashed on them. They decided to retaliate, not as usual upon our innocent infantrymen in their slit trenches (most of whom must have been as amazed as the Germans by the show) but on several targets which *they* may have suspected were *our* HQs. And one of these *was* the HQ of the Shining First! The boss was seen to move very smartly from his luxurious caravan to a "better 'ole."

Next day the BM informed me that I was to cease and desist forthwith from engaging in acts of unorthodox warfare because, he said, and gave me a long wink, the boss feared it might be contrary to the Geneva Convention.

I don't believe it was. Do you? But what I had in mind for an encore probably was.

This would have involved a highly original use of issue contraceptives, Durex by name, salacious soldiers for the use of. Not long ago we captured a lewd poem (of dubious literary quality) from a Jerry Feldwebel. Its burden was a complaint about the shortage of condoms and the lengths to which the German troops were being driven to find substitutes. Well, we still had an almost-full cylinder of hydrogen, and my plan was to inflate several hundred Durex (inflate them *gently*) and release them to go bouncing over the canals and into enemy-held territory. I assumed the first few would be shot to pieces by a bemused enemy, then someone would get the drift (ha) and there would be a frantic chase to retrieve the rest of these priceless gifts from the thoughtful Canadians.

War is a terrible thing.

Each of the condoms would have been invisibly coated with a substance procured by our QM (who is a practical joker) during a recent trip to Rome.

Itching powder.

[Bagnacavallo]

Jan 25

Don't for heaven's sake let Postmaster Mulehead tell you how marvellous the mail service is to "our boys over there." We have had only one letter mail in the past six weeks, and it was a thin one. Or maybe Canadians are so busy converting to civilian life that their pen hands are paralyzed. But I suppose Italy is small potatoes these days, and we are the forgotten potato weevils. Maybe *we* should forget about Canada. After reading the latest news about the exploits of our Zombie "comrades in arms" in Montreal, it might seem like a good idea. But the betrayal isn't confined to the French Canadians. I've felt for some time that they are being painted just a leetle bit blacker than life to emphasize the sterling qualities of the rest of our citizenry.

Don't pay much attention to this letter. I'm just damn tired at the moment and my carefully nourished spark of ebullience burns low.

I still wonder if I am right to let you in on my low spells. But the business of writing cheery notes whether you are in the depths or not is just silly. It doesn't fool anyone.

I am becoming more than ever determined to do the hermit stunt *après la guerre*. If I can ever find a decent draftsman for my Int section, I'll have him draw up a set of plans for the cabin I intend to put up and have already built in my mind. Small, compact like a ship's cabin, comfortably fitted out (I've had enough of discomfort not to want any more for its own sake), and with plenty of distance between it and the nearest neighbours. Not that I would intend to stay in it for ever and aye, but it would be a base from which I could sally forth as and when I was ready.

Have overcome my fear that a corrosive bitterness might be my heritage from *la guerre*. I know my point of view has changed dramatically from the dewy-eyed visions of earlier years, but I don't think the way I see things now is necessarily all bad. Caution, suspicion and selective intolerance are not evil of themselves, as long as they are not directed at the true beliefs and honest actions of others. A blindly benevolent "love thy neighbour" attitude, as prescribed in the best circles, is too much like living on a surfeit of sugarplums. Tasteless and cloying after a while, I should think, though Mum will probably take violent umbrage at this. But I'm just rambling.

The books you sent are useful and greatly appreciated but unfortunately can't do my writing for me. I guess that any real attempt to carve out a career as a free-lance author will have to wait until I get back. It is just too much heartache to try to write under these conditions. Every time I try, I seem to end up in an airless place where I can hardly breathe, feeling helpless as a kid.

The linnet sends her love to Elmer. And tell him I have a guinea pig now. Name of Desdemona. The ostrich also has a pal, a (stuffed) golden oriole.* The Int office is now being referred to by one and all as Mowat's Zoo. Like old times in Saskatoon when my room was filled with snakes, gophers and magpies, hey Mum? And I'm spending more

---

* The ostrich never made it back to Canada but the oriole did. I have it still.

and more of my spare time training my binocs on birds and beasties rather than on Jerry and his works.

This has led to some odd incidents. Some suspicious blokes from 5th Div observed me observing ducks behind the lines on the flooded plains south of Ravenna and concluded I must be some kind of spy. They sicced (sic? sik? sick?) a posse of MPs onto me and, would you believe, I actually had some trouble convincing them I wasn't one of Hitler's Finest in disguise. *Bird* watching? On another occasion I came across a gaggle of staff wallahs from Corps HQ bogged down in a couple of jeeps in the same swamps. They were draped about with guns – but they weren't hunting Jerries! Uh uh! *Shotguns.* For killing birds. In the middle of a bloody war they were indulging themselves in what I am fast coming to believe is one of the most atrocious aberrations of our kind – the butchering of other critters for "sport." As you see, I've come a long way from the days Pop and I and old Mutt used to hunt mallards in Wakaw Lake. But being shot at by one's own kind tends to give you new perspectives on a lot of things.

[Bagnacavallo]

HQ 1Cdn Inf Bde Can Army CMF Feb. 7, 1945

Long Suffering Ones:

This will be the last time I will use the above address for a while. As you know, some two months ago AFHQ asked for me as an instructor at the AFHQ Int School. Now it has gone through, and none too soon as I had a pretty good set-to with the boss a few days ago and am definitely feeling my neck, while Doc is muttering darkly about "not *going* to unsew them captain's pips again." I will be leaving here within a week. I am now quite serene about the idea of getting out of the battle zone for a while – hell, I'm tickled pink. Apart from growing weary of being perpetually scared to death, I look forward to maybe being able to do some writing.

My new duties aren't onerous and this will be a pleasant enough way to finish up the war. And I am not a little proud of being selected for the job. The six instructors at the school are chosen from the entire Mediterranean theatre and the school is considered in Int circles as the best of its kind anywhere. Though the Jerries might argue the point.

And yet I'm surprised to find that I don't seem to be experiencing any excitement or strong emotions about the move. I don't feel either happy or unhappy. The wrench of departure may be somewhat eased by the knowledge that I served the Bde at a time when it was just about the best place in the army to be. Now this isn't true any longer, yet I do feel a need to justify myself in leaving. I tell myself that I am one of the very few combatant officers who has served in every battle the First has ever fought – nine months with a battalion, and ten at Bde HQ. The only times I've been away (on leave or courses) were when the Bde was out of the line. Apart from being blown up a couple of times, I've pretty well escaped the physical consequences so far, but eventually everyone's luck runs out.

P.S. My recent contretemps with the Brig just *may* have had something to do with the enclosed Int Summary. You think he's jealous of my literary skills?

Weekly Intelligence Summary – 1 Cdn Inf Bde

Feb. 1, 1945

1. It is drawn to the attention of all ranks that success in battle does not depend solely on a knowledge of tactics and weapons. It is at least equally important to have an understanding of the psychology of the enemy. To this end, this week's summary offers the following illuminating commentaries on the German psyche.

2. *Home Front Morale.* Source: Printed document recovered from the wallet of an Unteroffizier of 21 Panzer Grenadier Regt. Translation of text as follows:

Dear Front Line Hero:

When will you come back on leave?

When will you be able to forget the hard duties of a soldier and exchange them for a few days and nights of joy, happiness and love? Here at home in Germany we all know of your heroic struggles. We also understand that even the bravest gets tired and that he needs a soft pillow, tenderness and healthy pleasures.

WE ARE WAITING FOR YOU.

For you who have been compelled to spend your leave in foreign places without the solace of a soft hand on your brow; for you whom the war has robbed of his home and bed; for you who stand alone in the world without a wife, without a girl.

WE ARE WAITING FOR YOU.

Cut out the badge printed on this letter. Display it visibly on your glass in every tearoom or bar near a railroad station. Soon a member of our *League of Lonely War Women* will take charge of you and the dreams you dreamt in the front line and the longings of the lonely nights will find fulfilment.

WE ARE WAITING FOR YOU.

It is *you* we want – not your money. Therefore ask for our permanent membership card at once! There are members everywhere, since we German women understand our duties towards those who defend us.

Naturally we are not entirely selfish. For years and years we have been separated from our menfolk and we long to hold a real German boy against our bosoms. Don't be shy. Your wife, your sister, your sweetheart or even your mother may be one of us.

WE ARE WAITING FOR YOU.

We think of you, but we also think of the future of our country. Remember:

HE WHO RESTS – RUSTS!

    League of Lonely War Women
    (Verein Einsamer Kriegsfrauen)

3. *Soldier's Comforts.* Source: Captured documents from HQ 1 Para Div, and POW interrogations.

These sources indicate that the official Wehrmacht policy of supplying mobile brothels (motor vehicles hauling trailer-caravans, or specially converted railroad coaches) to front-line troops of the German Army is not only to be continued but is to be considerably reinforced in view of the general state of morale amongst combat troops. During an interrogation conducted at this HQ last week, an Oberlieutenant of a GAF regiment who was being queried on this matter wished to know why the Canadian Army does not supply similar amenities to its troops. The interrogators were temporarily at a loss for an answer, but the query has been referred to Cdn. Military HQ, London.

4. *Officer/Other Rank Relations*. Source: 2nd British Army Intelligence Summary No. 18.

It is reported that, as a result of the débâcle which took place at the Falaise Gap, several senior German officers, including a Generalmajor (Canadian equivalent: brigadier), were summarily executed by troops under their command for dereliction of duty. In the case of the brigadier, German GHQ has taken no disciplinary action against the executioners, but on the contrary has commended them for "having the courage to eliminate a senior officer whose manifest incompetence clearly demonstrated his criminal tendencies."

5. *German Opinions of Canadian Army*. Source: Interrogation reports at No. 3 POW Cage. Following are representative comments from a variety of captured German soldiers.

"Canadians are good fighters. It is too bad that their staff work is so atrocious."

"I fought against you in Italy. You were good soldiers, but why did you never have enough ammunition and men? Is it because you are such a small and unimportant country?"

"We have been told that in order to become a general in the Canadian Army you have first to be a stockbroker. In Germany we choose our generals on the basis of merit."

The foregoing comments will demonstrate how deluded the German soldiers are by Herr Goebbels' propaganda machine.

Farley Mowat, Capt.,
I.O.1 Cdn Inf Bde.

Feb 22 and Feb 24

Dear Teach. –

An hour ago Mum called me from R. Hill. Knowing her distaste about spending ten cents on a long-distance telephone call, I thought, "Well, here it comes. The house has burned down, or Elmer has been eaten by a cat." But that wasn't it. All she had to say was that you had written on Feb. 7 to say that in one week you would be posted to the Intel. Trng. Cn. Well, *that* wasn't anything to spend a ten-cent call on. So I just went on working. That is to say, I read through all my correspondence again. But it seemed to have been written in Chinese because I didn't understand a word of it, so I left the office and went out to a pub I know about where a fellow can study up on his Chinese.

(Next day)

Now this is really something, eh? To be the first "colonial" appointment at ITC. You must have made something of an impression when you were on that course. Are you getting to be an earnest little worker? You aren't, are you?

As for any qualms you may feel about leaving the Shiny First, don't be an ass! With your record, you could walk out on 'em and walk all the way back to R. Hill, and still keep a clear conscience. If you had one.

So Helen and Angus will sleep better now than they have slept since 10 July '43 when you went ashore in Sicily. We nearly always have a little chat about you before starting to read in bed at night and Helen always asks such a lot of hard questions.

> i.e.–
> How near is he to the shells?
> How often do the shells fall?
> *Where* do they fall?
> Does he go up ahead of Brigade? (I haven't yet figured out what she thinks a brigade is.)
> How often does he get his meals, and are they nutritious?

[Richmond Hill]

Mar 1

I have been at home with a cold for the past few days, and when staying in bed got too much for me (and Helen was absent at a Red Cross meeting) I got up and went rummaging through a lot of my papers looking for the log of my famous trip down the Saskatchewan River in the *Coot* – the voyage you announced to the *Star Phoenix* would "sail with the morning tide." I had thought of making it into a story for possible publication, but I didn't find it.

I'm really going to try and get in some writing this summer. The urge came over me all of a bang the second day after we got your letter about going to Int. Trng. Cntr. I think the next book will be about your generation. That would round out my original intention of having a book about Dad's generation, one on mine and the third on yours.

But now to hike over to Christie St. Military Hospital and see if I can sneak two or three of the lads out for a lunch and a few beers. I'll try and get one or two out to Hove To for a weekend, too. They are pretty unhappy.

[in reserve at Cesenatico on the coast]

Feb 15

Dear Folks:

Cancel last order!

My address remains as it was. I guess I knew in my innermost self that the new job was too good to be true. And so it was. Some Great Grey Father far to the rear has lowered the boom. I wonder a little if my effort to join the Base Wallahs' Guild was frustrated in the same way as was a friend of mine's selection for a job in Egypt. In that case, my pal's CO received a screed from somewhere back near the equator to the effect that, due to a shortage of combat-trained junior officers at the front, the transfer to the rear of the m/n officer could not be sanctioned.

Ah well, I'm not as disappointed as I thought I'd be. And I am now again installed as IO of the Shiny First, complete with a brand new

Lieut. from the 48th (who had been posted to my job), now acting as my 2 i/c. Either nobody has the heart to send him back to his unit, or *somebody* doesn't expect me to regrow roots in the job. We'll see. Meantime I have Lulu back; the rain has stopped; I'm due for a leave, so what the merry old hell care I? However, I *am* pushing for a transfer to the Int Corps – a step that nobody can block, apparently. This won't mean an immediate change of jobs. It will simply mean that when I am fired from here, I will go into Int work somewhere else.

Who knows, I might even be lucky enough to have begun with the brigade and stayed with it to the finish. One of my better prophecies, made a year ago, that the war in Europe would end by August of this year seems likely to be fulfilled. If we are then asked to go to the Pacific . . . well, I wonder. I'm sure there must be tens of thousands of healthy young and youngish Canadian males at home who would be hellishly put out if we old sweats were too hoggish about opportunities to fight for Freedom, Democracy, and etc. They may even have children some day (the science of artificial insemination being sufficiently advanced) whom they may want to impress when asked: "What did *you* do in the war, Daddy-o?"

I've written, and torn up, a couple of short stories. They served a purpose, if only to demonstrate that I will likely not be in a mental condition to write a good story of any sort until some years after the pax.

At the moment I've got flu and am ensconced on my safari bed in the middle of the room which serves as the Int office, where I can supervise the winning of the war. I'm nearly better, thank God. Being bedded by a bug in the army is small pleasure. However, I at least don't have to sneak downstairs with my bare fanny hanging out to smoke a cigar up the chimbley.

I continue planning the cabana I will one day build on the northern fiords of B.C. and will soon send a sheaf of draftings of same. I figure that living on my capital (a shudder goes through the whole capitalist world) I can exist for at least five years, and by then my typewriter ought to be earning me sufficient pennies to go on with which.

Long letter from Doug Reid yesterday. He is back flying, but is still depressed about his trip home. Says he doesn't want to go back to

Canada – not ever but, like me, has no other place in view to which he feels he could "belong." I think a lot of us probably feel the same way, exiled as it were by some kind of slow attrition of faith in our own people. If it weren't for you two, and the nature of the land, and its wild critters, I don't think I'd come back either. No, Elmer, not even for you.

It's amazing, the strength of this urge to retreat to one of Nature's hideouts. You did it in your time – fire-ranging in the Nipigon. Do you think it might be the same instinct that sends wounded animals into hiding looking for healing?

I like what you said, Pop, about "taking the communities to the veterans – and not vice versa." Makes a lot of sense. Of course, there are some, like Mowat Minor and Co who don't *want* the community to come to them, but they are the born misfits, as opposed to the misfits produced by war who desperately want, and need, to get back into the communal womb but don't know how to do it. They are victimized misfits, and the cure for them is going to require that the devil of a lot of time and trouble be taken by the community. Maybe this is too much to expect from a society composed so largely of the Seal Coat battalions; the "I'm doing dandy, so the hell with you" and the "Here's a dime for a cup of coffee, now don't bother me" brigades. And there is another point you never mention – maybe because you are one of them? – what happens to the *physically* wounded who will have to live with one arm or leg, or *no* arms or legs, holes in their guts, other parts shot away, etc., etc.? Once the war is over and the "hero" bullshit has evaporated, the civvies are going to just want to avert their eyes from such as these. Maybe this is something you learned by experience? And maybe this is why you have always acted as if your right arm was as good as your left. If you don't *look* normal, people are going to turn their minds, if not their gazes, away from you.

[Toronto]

March 5
Dear Laddie. –

Mum has just telephoned from the Hill that she has your letter of Feb. 15 in which you break the interesting news that some base-wallah seems to have bilked you of a just reward. Another sock in the jaw for the Mowats all around. And no doubt the doing of some smug swine who has kept himself fatly out of harm's way right through the show.

I have now heard the grim story of the butchering of the regiment at the Lamone, which you couldn't talk about. Several sources have described it, and the bitching of Stan Ketcheson, made into a scapegoat by others in higher places. It all makes a fellow pretty sick. I had clung so desperately to the belief that the army in action was run on different principles than at home, but am afraid that the fellows who are back here in hospital have pretty well shot down that illusion. You'll know who most of them are. They were lying in their cots the other evening when I came in and were chanting "Up the revolution" in unison, and neither the orderlies nor the nursing sisters were trying to quiet them. But, poor bastards, they aren't in a position to "up" anything.

More and more I see the urgent necessity for the lowly ones to stick together after it is over. If we can. But I doubt that, too. The forces, political and capitalistic, that will be arrayed against us are damned powerful, and very clever indeed. I fully expect that they will split us several ways, just as they did after the last war.

In my heart I am at least thanking God you had the guts to be an infantryman. Let the fancy services come home heroes after a tour of duty, or get hung with medals and honourably discharged without having been in action or even overseas. At least we of the infantry have the inward satisfaction of knowing that we are able to take it, and *did* take it – and so the hell with the rotten bourgeois world that rode to "victory" on our backs. And bones.

And I am looking forward to some sassy letters from you in view of your latest disappointment.

[Toronto]

March 12

This having been a particularly bothersome day, I haven't much idea for a letter to a permanent IO, but tomorrow is going to be worse so I'll do what I can.

To the Gambles' for a drink of rum the other night. They are feeling pretty low about son Bob who went missing during a raid on Bremen almost three months ago. The plane was seen to explode in mid-air but Edith hasn't given up hope of his survival, which is the worst aspect of a "missing" report.

There hasn't been anything about Italy in the papers or on the radio for days, and we are wondering what has happened to the forgotten men. A parliamentary delegation is just back from north-west Europe and reports that the troops there are in a fog of mis- and lack of information about things in Canada. Sure they are. Who the hell isn't?

[to Susi Szeny]

Feb. 1945

Dear Susi:

I'm afraid I've lost touch with you somewhere along the road. Have written twice to the Camp Ontario address in New York with no response, and so assume you hadn't yet arrived there.

Was in Rome a while ago and went looking for you but was told you left the Refugee Centre in August. Nobody could tell me where you went. But you left Rome at a good time. It is a desolate and dreary place in the grey pall of an Italian winter. I hope to God this is my last winter in Italy – another one will leave me no alternative but to emigrate to the South Seas for the rest of my life.

In my more despondent moods, I recall that afternoon in July with more pleasure than seems reasonable. Most experiences in war are either terrifying, grotesque and ugly, or tawdry. But out of the tangled skein of these, our brief moment of understanding remains clear and well-remembered. Perhaps it is as well that it ended so abruptly – to me its perfection was absolute and immutable – and very wonderful. The freshness of it, and the happy clarity with which I still see it, were all your doing. You have the magic touch of quicksilver.

There is not much chance this will ever reach you. But if it does, and if you can find time in the hurly-burly of a new life, I would truly love to hear from you.

With fondest hopes for you,

Squib.

United States
Department of the Interior
War Relocation Authority
Emergency Refugee Shelter
Fort Ontario, N.Y.

Captain F. M. Mowat
HQ. 1 Canadian Infantry Brigade
Canadian Army, CMF

Dear Captain Mowat:

Susi Szeny was not among the group of refugees brought to this country from Italy. I understand from people who knew her in Aversa that she was on the list, but circumstances arose which made it impossible for her to join the transport. The last that was heard of her was in August of 1944, at which time she was in Aversa.

I am sorry that I can give you no further information, and I am returning a letter to her which was received from you.

Sincerely,
Jos. H. Smart
Enclosure   Director

[Cesenatico]

Feb 19

Dear Progenitors:

Enclosed is something to while away the long winter nights with, trying to figure out what the hell I'm talking about, and why.

A Thumbnail Biography

In 1940, after a more-or-less pleasant youth mostly spent doing the things he wanted to do, rather than those other people wanted him to do, Mowat enlisted in the army and in due course was sent overseas. When he arrived in England, he had just sufficient horse sense to know when to come in out of the rain. Because of his upbringing, he thought of himself as a free agent, surrounded by hundreds of thousands of youths who had already been pretty well moulded into the patterns their lives would inevitably follow. The feet of most of them were already on paths which would eventually become ruts. Mowat distrusted ruts.

During a year in England, Mowat learned a little about life, including how to be more tolerant of his hide-bound (as he supposed) comrades. This knowledge was acquired at the cost of a few split lips, bloody noses and bruised tail bones. He also learned that there are ruts and there are ruts, and that the kind associated with bull moose not only have a legitimate place in nature but can lead to exhilarating interludes.

When the war really began for him at the time of the invasion of Sicily, he could have been described as follows:

Callow, but not innocent, although undoubtedly naïve. Strongly opinionated, but with a sufficient sense of humour to be able to laugh at some of his own pretensions. Although possessed of little practical experience of living, he had unlimited theoretical knowledge of what life was all about. His moustache was still invisible unless seen in a strong light after he had downed a foaming pint of stout. He may have resembled his father at the same age more than either of them would ever admit. He was, however, not enamoured of the army as his father was, and was in it only because of a high-flown and probably fallacious theory he held about the role democracy plays in the survival of mankind. His contention was that man could continue to evolve, and therefore continue to exist, only if differentiation of cultures, races and individuals could take place in the future as it had done in the past. He regarded regimentation, assimilation and homogenization as deadly threats to human survival. Surprisingly, he still held much of this point of view, and thus retained his original purpose for being in the army, three years later. The difference being that, while still an idealist, he was no longer such an insufferable one and had tempered his high-falutin' theories with a somewhat reduced regard for the ability of his fellow men to grasp the Truth.

However.

Leaving England, Mowat took part in the invasion of Sicily and thence to the final destruction of the German armed forces. He spent only a relatively short time as a fighting soldier but was close enough to the fighting troops thereafter to retain, and develop, a remarkable ability to keep his head down. In truth, he was scared silly most of the time.

During this period of his life, he developed a taste for issue *rhum* (Demerara, 150 proof) and as a consequence could not give any coherent description of what or how he felt by the time the war was over. "I was very muddled by it all," he said. By the time he got back to Canada, he was still muddled but since issue *rhum* was no longer available, he couldn't blame it for his ongoing confusion. He finally concluded that unless he wanted to end up as a permanent ornament in a Canadian Legion bar, he had better start to "do something with his life."

So he decided to be a tramp, with trimmings. He did not intend to be a mere "bum" for he understood (or thought he did) the importance of work as a *function* of existence. Which meant that he wanted to do what *he* wanted to do without suffering too much opprobrium (thank you, Mr. Roget *and* Mr. Oxford) thereby. The solution seemed to be to keep a sharp eye peeled as he tramped through regions and amongst people who interested him, and then write about these things. He was canny enough to realize that a writer doesn't need to make a fortune in order to be tolerated by society, and doesn't even have to be much good as a writer. He just has to *look* good, and Mowat figured he could handle this *if*, and it was a big *if*, he could ever grow a suitable moustache and/or a beard. He wanted to be, as he was often heard to say, "happily hirsute."

Mowat arrived back in Canada before Xmas, 1945. He made much of his parents, in a restrained way (it was typical of his family that its members never did say much about how they felt about one another) and was made much of, in a restrained way. Mowat's father, who was a bit of an eccentric, gave Mowat minor the keys to his car and told him to go off and make a damn fool of himself for a while.

Within a couple of months, Mowat had become engaged three

times; had had a number of inconclusive fights with other young men who believed, and were foolish enough to say aloud, that only dog catchers and railway men would be caught dead wearing a uniform; had done his bit to drink the pubs and liquor stores dry; and was becoming somewhat bored as well as exhausted. Thereupon his parents took him aboard their boat and, together with the dog Elmer and a young skunk Mowat had adopted, sailed aimlessly but happily around the Great Lakes for a season.

Then one day Mowat said: "Well, I think I'll get on with it now." His parents blessed him, and away he went.

He went first to British Columbia where he mooched around on fishing boats, bumming his way northward up the coast until he found an extremely remote and well-hidden fiord inhabited solely by non-human critters. Here he built himself a little house . . . somewhat "littler" than he had intended in his grandiose wartime dreams. It was twelve feet square, askew and off plumb, and it leaked. But it was home for the moment. Only for the moment though because, having parked his war medals and army boots in it, he took off for Alaska, and thence into the Yukon where he wandered about like a migrant caribou, pecking at his portable typewriter whenever he stopped migrating. He wrote a number of terrible stories which he traded to the Indians he met for provender. It is not recorded what use they put his stories to, but paper was always in short supply and high demand in those distant regions.

One day he woke under a wicky-up on the side of a mountain feeling peculiar. It was some time before he realized that the last of the psychoses he had been zealously nursing ever since leaving the army had sneaked away during the night. He made a frantic effort to recall some of these old companions which, for a long time, had given him an excuse to be a drifter but no luck. So there was then nothing to do but head back for his lonely little cabin on the fiord and go to work.

In 1948 he wrote a story about the north woods that sold to a magazine for what anyone else would have considered a pitiable sum, but which was enough to restock Mowat's cellar and encourage him to go on to greater endeavours. It may also have encouraged him to propose several things, one of them being marriage to a young woman who was cook aboard a salmon fishing boat that sailed into his fiord one day. She said "yes" to everything then so that, as she explained later, she wouldn't feel badly about saying "no" for the rest of their years together.

Mowat published his first book, about his northern travels, in 1950. And the rest, as they say, is history. . . .

❖ ❖ ❖

MY CRYSTAL BALL WAS A TRIFLE CLOUDED. IN THE EVENT, I NEVER DID go to British Columbia. Instead, in 1946 I journeyed by canoe into the northern parts of Saskatchewan, and the following year travelled widely in the sub-arctic tundra and taiga of Keewatin Territory to the north and west of Hudson Bay. In 1948 I wrote an angry account of mass starvation which had occurred because of our neglect of the Eskimos of that region. It appeared in *Saturday Evening Post* and these same people became the subject of my first book, *People of the Deer*, which was published in 1951.

❖ ❖ ❖

[Ripatransone, on the Adriatic coast]
Feb 26

I think I've been taking your letters too much for granted this past year or two. Today I calculated that I get an average of two letters a week from the pair of you, and surely that is something to shout aloud about from the heights. As you no doubt long ago appreciated, the mails are verily the breath of life to us. God, how we curse when they are delayed – and how we sneak away into private corners with gloating expressions when they do arrive. It is a grim thing indeed to be the lone mammal in the mess who doesn't even get an honourable mention on mail days. Thanks to my ever-thoughtful parents, this doesn't happen to me.

Ref the career of F. Mowat. The Int school job has fallen through without any hope of rescue, due to circumstances I can't reveal. They have nothing to do with the boss. He is probably hiding his tears of chagrin that fate keeps me here. I guess I am, too.

I really have reached the point of not giving a good goddamn which, unless altered, will probably get me right back to a rifle platoon. But you know me. I tend to exaggerate my petty problems.

I gather from one of Ma's letters you've been thinking about approaching Howard Graham on my behalf. Well, I sure and hell haven't much pride left, or not enough to compel me to accept the current status. If you think he can or would do anything, then go ahead and ask him. My only trouble (and yours) is that we make such a point of disdaining wire-pullers that when the time comes that it's a case of pulling, or being jerked, we don't seem to have the knack. Well, I'm learning. And if Howard can't do anything, you might talk to Reg Saunders ref me becoming a war correspondent. I'm practically an honorary member of the press camp here, being intimate with several of the characters who spend their time recording the exploits of the Shiny First. They have several times suggested the idea, but till now it hasn't interested me. But it could be an "out," and I can write anything the papers might want, yea, though it maketh me to vomit. The drill is to find some paper or magazine that wants a war-co, then they accredit you and arrange for your discharge, and that is that.

I now have to go and bawl hell out of a poor guy who has been found by the camp commandant to be carrying (secreting was the word on the charge sheet) a pet dog in one of the supply trucks. I'm going to hate this – but not as much as I hate that effing camp com! I'd like to give him a rabies vaccination – with a Sten gun.

The Guns
Go Silent

❖ ❖ ❖

OUR PART IN THE WAR IN ITALY DID NOT CONCLUDE AS THE RESULT OF
victory achieved against the Germans; it ended because of a victory
gained in Canada by General A.G.L. McNaughton. An ambitious
man, he had commanded the Canadian Army in England in 1943
when the British General Staff detached First Canadian Division and
sent it to join 8th Army for the invasion of Sicily and Italy. Later it
did the same with 5th Division, and McNaughton was furious at the
diminution of his command. Conflict between him and his British
superiors became so acute that he was returned to Canada. Here he
became Minister of National Defence. From this position of political
power, heavily backed by Prime Minister Mackenzie King, he was at
last able to arrange the transfer of the two Canadian divisions from
Italy to north-west Europe and so again bring into being a Canadian
army in the field.

By early February and despite stringent security, most of us
guessed what was afoot. In late February, we left the Adriatic for the
second and last time. And now we knew. On March 9 we boarded
U.S. landing ships at Leghorn and sailed, uneventfully, to Marseilles.
There followed a five-day drive north through France and into
Belgium.

The secrecy surrounding this move was so intense that we vanished from Canadian civilian ken from mid-February until mid-
April. Nothing about us or our whereabouts appeared in the press or
was heard on radio – and none of our outgoing letters or cables was
delivered. For two months, friends and relatives could only guess as

to our whereabouts. It was thought by some that we had been shipped to the Far East, then the rumour spread that we had gone to France. During the long hiatus, those who cared about us suffered mounting apprehension. It was a difficult time for my parents.

Leaving Italy was hard for me. I had spent the best part of two years there. I had grown accustomed to the place and fond of its people. Perhaps most important of all, Italy was where I had come of age, so it would be forever part of me.

I was leaving more than Italy behind. My time with the fighting troops was also at an end, and I was about to embrace a vastly different way of life in which I would gradually come to have some significant control over my own destiny.

And the war itself was fast winding down.

❖   ❖   ❖

[Richmond Hill]

March 15

Dearest Lamb.

Have just got my new glasses, and the first thing to do is write to you, though where this fountain pen came from full of green ink is more than I know.

Yesterday Betty Campbell came to dinner and stayed all night as Angus was in Chatham. She is so soothing, with her grave, quiet manner. I can see why you are so fond of her. After dinner we walked to the post office to see if there was any mail from you. There wasn't, so back in the lovely, warm spring evening listening to the early robins. Afterwards we played some records including Paul Robeson's "Sanders of the River," which I bought for you.

The tulip bulbs are up and the snow nearly gone. I sat out for two hours yesterday it was so mild and lovely, and I spent the whole time hoping and praying that you get that instructor's job in Intelligence, or something different from what you do now. I can never properly form the "Q" in Headquarters, which is of course why I so much want you to change your address.

Do send along your plans for your cabin but, as Bett Campbell says, "When he sees this house again he will want to settle down right here."

March 24

We have suspected for some days thru rumour, and the fact that your letters have been held up, that you were in Germany and that the final test is near.

Farley, darling, we don't talk like this often but you know how we love you – part of ourselves, and the best part. I know how unhappy you have been, my lamb. I know what you have gone and are going thru. Angus says I can't really know, but there, you may remember how good my imagination is. I don't see how you have stood so well all those days and weeks and months under fire. Don't get discouraged now. You are strong and good, and our prayers surround you night and day. God is truly with you. When things get too hard to bear, turn to him for help.

Have you a Bible? Then read Psalm 91 – and St. John 14th chapter, and Psalm 121. I have learned to know Him better, to feel Him near me, to be comforted and supported through all these anxious days. He has been my strength, my refuge and ever-present help. I am speaking to you, my darling, from my heart. Let Him comfort you, too.

We had quite a day with Ernie Butler in Toronto this week. He was on his way back to Saskatoon and was feeling very low because of his son being killed just after the invasion, so he got very tight and insisted we stay with him as he couldn't bear to be alone. So we had luncheon and dinner in his hotel and finally put him on his train. He remembers you well, which must have made it even worse for him.

There is good news. Luke Reid is out of prison camp and on his way home. He was rescued by the Russians, bless them.

March 26

Squib, my Son. –

I may be all wet, and I have little or nothing to go on, but have arrived at the theory that the reason your Int. Trng. Cnt. appointment was cancelled is that you and the others are on your way to foreign parts. I have rather expected same ever since McNaughton came to the throne in Ottawa as Minister of Defence. If he can't be a general (field marshal would suit him better) commanding a Canadian army, he can at least bring the elements of that army back together in one place. And it would make some sort of sense. But if I can figure this out, and I am not even in Intelligence, surely the Germans can, too? In which case all the security of mails and etc. would seem to serve only to distress the troops, and those of us who wait patiently, more or less, at home for word.

Although chagrined that you lost out on the Int. school thing, we are relieved that you are apparently still at brigade and were not pitched back into the unit where you would probably have had to go platooning again. You will understand how all this uncertainty affects us. How we rush for the radio for each news report. But most of them are terrible beyond words. Only the BBC seems reliable and worth listening to as far as news is concerned. I am confident that all our so-called Canadian news is filtered through (1) New York and (2) the propaganda office of the Liberal Party.

I keep pointing out certain areas on the maps for the benefit of your Maman, all of them, naturally, miles distant from any actual theatre of war. But me, I'd like to know for sure where you are. And to get a few of the letters we know you are writing. The one and only topic of conversation amongst those who have any connections with the phantom army is, "When did you last hear?"

[Richmond Hill]

April 5

Darling Bunje.

It is such a long, long time since your last letter. Feb. 6 it was written, and every day, and twice a day we go to the PO, but no word. I dread to think where you may be.

Angus is digging in the garden although it is a bitterly cold evening with light snow blowing past. Then he is going to enamel an enormous electric stove we had given to us. I will do the dishes while we listen to the BBC reporting from Germany. I sometimes feel I have spent most of my life having to listen to news of war and killing.

Your school friend Mac Cowper is on embarkation leave. After four years at college, he is finally going overseas, in the Dental Corps. Was married last week and has bought a house close by. Angus does not speak very kindly to him, and I have to admit I don't much like to, either, although he is really a very nice young man.

[Livorno]

March 2

Dear Friends of my Youth:

Although written on the a/m date, this letter won't begin its journey for some unknown length of time. Security being what it is. So by the time you *do* get it, the contents will be old hat.

Much has happened, and we are on the move in a big way. On Feb. 23 the bde was pulled out of its holding positions and withdrawn to the inevitable olive groves and vineyards, this time not far from Ancona. We were supposed to believe that we would be out for a ten-day rest then become part of a new 8th Army push into the Po Valley. But my Int tentacles work towards the rear as well as towards the front and I got wind of what was up. Our time in Italy, that's what was up!

A cloud of secrecy then descended on 1 Cdn Corps and it was so intense that all connections with the outer world were cut. No mail in or out. No contact with Eyeties under *any* circumstances, and only stringently restricted contact with other Allied troops, including the rest of 8th Army. Well, you can imagine the problems that all this entailed, and they were *my* problems as far as the Shiny First was concerned. So I was busy, busy, busy. So busy I forgot my own problems; and the Brig forgot to glower; and you will now understand why I didn't get the job in Naples.

On March 1 we got underway, with a seemingly endless succession of convoys, all identification painted out or removed, headed westward back across Italy. I can tell you the route now, but when we made the move it was so secret even we didn't know more than a day in advance.

Reads like a Cook's Tour of northern Italy! Foligno – Perugia – Arezzo – Pontassieve – Florence, and finally an enormous transit camp outside Livorno, an hour's drive from Pisa's tottering old tower. All the way across, I got about five hours' sleep, being on the go night and day and especially at night, trying to keep our lads and the Eyeties apart.

If there was a town near our night camp, I'd go into it after dark with a section of military police in tow. We'd collar the local mayor and/or AMGOT* officer and get him to take us on a guided tour of all the brothels. Then it would be my delightful task to search each of these joints looking for horny *Canadesi* who had sneaked off for a little recreation. Well deserved, but *absolutely verboten*. It was an education. And I would have won no popularity contests either with the *soldati* or the ladies of the night. I especially remember one Cpl. of the RCR fixing me with an aggrieved glare and sputtering: "Jesus H Christ . . . Sir. I never even got my boots off!"

But, since mine was a roving commission, I had a wonderful chance to enjoy springtime Italy without fear of getting my head blown off, and free to drive wherever I pleased and at my own pace. I'll never forget it because it brought home to me just how much Italy had worked its way under my skin. Despite all my gripes of the past two years, I have become right fond of the joint, and of the Eyeties, too.

Ken Cottam (remember him? From Div Int?) and I took a little detour into Florence – on duty, of course – and I visited the old Count's *palazzo*, but it was empty of everything except his statuary and a lot of broken glass. I guess a Jerry stonk had come too close. Ken distinguished himself by getting surprised by an irate husband who bloody well didn't want a damned Englishman putting horns on *his* head and chased my worthy compeer down a cobbled street, stark naked (Ken, not the husband) waving an old blunderbuss. If it had been me, there would have been a sort of poetic revenge in it for the poor sods I chivvied out of brothels on the way west.

Our final Italian destination is called Harrod's Camp (God knows why) and is the usual army hell hole. A million tents pitched

---

* Allied Military Government

cheek by jowl in the remnants of a pine forest jammed with men and machines with nothing to do, and given really rotten Limey grub. Life grows tedious indeed, and we are hard put to it for entertainment and amusements.

The boss unintentionally provides one lighter touch. From the window of my Int truck, the view is dominated by a fine, upstanding privy of the kind Chic Sales wrote about in "The Specialist." This is the boss's personal backhouse and bears on its door a large sign saying BRIGADIER ONLY. It is an impressive piece of functional architecture, noble in concept but sheathed in corrugated iron which gives it a certain grimness. It travels from place to place on its own truck but, gossip to the contrary, its single hole is *not* fur-lined. I think its owner finds it a mixed blessing since it is a unique establishment at Harrod's Camp and so is usually surrounded by a crowd of admiring soldiery from neighbouring units. Though he has privacy once inside with the door shut, the owner has to run the gamut to get there. At any rate, he acts even more constipated than usual. We have a new signals officer, an irreverent and outspoken chappie who, after his first look at BRIGADIER ONLY remarked loudly: "Maybe he thinks *his* shit don't stink."

There is a general atmosphere of disgruntlement about this place. Even though we are going off to new fields, and should feel some exhilaration, most of us leave Italy with marked reluctance and this despite the pasting we've taken in the past few months. The prospect of coming under command of First Canadian Army – after two years with 8th Army – is a sour one. We have been part of a real fighting force for far too long to easily accept the imbecilities of a lot of red-tabbed amateurs who are still wet behind the ears. Our new bosses are already flooding us with orders governing dress regulations, the length-the-hair-will-be-worn and other such trivia. Uniformity becomes the order of the day. The Staff Capt predicts that at future short-arm inspections it will be required that foreskins be rolled back by numbers.

Some of us visited Pisa yesterday incognito (no badges) and a major who was well tanked up on *grappa* was overcome by an attack of vertigo while standing on the top balcony of the leaning tower, and lost his upper plate. It went sailing down like a falling leaf describing the most fascinating aerobatic evolutions. A spry Eyetie kid snatched it from the gutter, thereby earning *molti lira* as a reward.

[at sea aboard U.S.N. Landing Ship 738]

March 9

Sailed this morning from Livorno (Leghorn) after the usual snafu of loading. I have the feeling we have entered an alien existence. The U.S. Navy does not come from the world we've been inhabiting for the past two years. Instead of the usual ragout of bully beef and dehydrated spuds for lunch, we had fried chicken, ice cream, green peas and apple pie! It was too refined for the plebeian stomachs of some who deposited it in the scuppers as the afternoon waned and we plowed through a short and nasty chop.

Could still see the high mountains of Italy a long way astern and many *soldati* stood at the rails gazing nostalgically aft. So many things came to mind. I found myself thinking of the beaches of Pachino in 1943, and CSM Nutley lying beside me on the sands with the sea foam curling over his head and refusing to answer me because he was dead. The dusty Hades that was Sicily. The high mood that was on us during the first months of action when nothing seemed able to stop us and most of us thought we would live forever. Monty with his damned fly switch, ranting at us from the hood of a jeep and telling us that, under him, we could not fail. The first winter in Italy and the mood beginning to darken as casualties rose. News from home of strikes amongst the industrial workers for higher pay, and riots amongst the conscripts. Then the blood bath of the Moro and Ortona, with the rifle companies reduced to platoon strength as the supply of volunteer reinforcements from Canada dried up. Alex Campbell leading the thirty-seven remaining men of Able Company into an attack that should have been mounted by a full-strength battalion, and lying on his back in a shredded vineyard, weltering in blood. That first Italian spring, with its revival of hope and of belief. The slow growth of our own roots into Italian soil as our isolation from Canada became stronger and our bitterness against the

Judas-politicans in Ottawa grew more intense. Then Cassino, and the May day when *we* broke the Hitler Line, and the bitter-sweet pride of that victory. Summer, and the announcement of the Home Leave Scheme promising that all Canadian soldiers who had been overseas three years were to be repatriated before Christmas. And the truth of it when eleven men out of the entire brigade were, in fact, sent home – for one month before being returned to action! Eleven out of three thousand. The winter of 1944. Wallowing in the mud at Rimini. The Lamone and Montone disasters. And the Tri-Wound Scheme – if you'd been wounded in action on *three separate occasions*, you could apply for leave to Canada! You could apply – but you probably could not be spared, because the Zombies were rioting while the prime minister remonstrated with them. . . . There was much else to think about. Out of the growing sense of betrayal came a remarkable in-drawing of the spirit until we became that very "band of brothers" that King Hal led and close kin to that other band which followed young Alexander. We fought our own war, remote from the world. For company we had other exiles – a Polish division, a Greek brigade. And every last man amongst the lot of us a volunteer. *We* knew who *we* were, if the world did not.

Arrivederci to all that; now we go back into the world again.

[Oostmalle, near Antwerp]

March 16

Your wandering son has now wandered into Belgium, there to sample the *estaminets* held in such high repute by his wandering father before him. The beer certainly *is* good. The Belgian women leave him in awe. Come to think on it, I didn't ever hear Papa speak of the women here.

I am still the Shiny First's IO. We are billeted in and around a small town of considerable sleepy charm, centred on a big chateau which is somewhat the worse for wear after having been long occupied by Jerry. Security remains tight and since I have to keep the screws turned down on everyone else, I can't tell you much of what goes on. Suffice it, mother-mine, to know that I am as safe as a toad in a pond.

I do, however, have an excellent view of the buzz-bombs* as they hiccup their way towards the channel ports. I taunt them. I sneer at them and thumb my weather-beaten nose at them, but they cling sullenly to their destined courses and do not deviate. Except when their none-too-reliable motors fail, whereupon they fall to earth with one hell of a bang.

Now it can be told. Crossing the Tyrrhenian Sea in a fleet of Yankee LSIs was like a holiday cruise on Lake Ontario. They served us fried chicken, Coca-Cola and ice cream, and some of us like to have wept at the memories of other days. By the Lord Harry, the Yanks do live well! Landed in Marseilles and took another Cook's Tour north. An eight-hundred-mile road journey through Lyon, Dijon, skirting Paris, Reims, St. Quentin and Cambrai, the last three of which will have been familiar to the Major. Many fields where the poppies still grow between the crosses of his war. The convoys moved with the utmost secrecy (it says here) and yours truly was a busy little bee trying to keep about three thousand guys from seeking forbidden delights and practising their French. Again Benny and Lulu and I rode herd, and in consequence saw one heck of a lot of springtime France. It looked pretty good, and tasted even better!

I expect to go on a seven-day leave shortly and will take it in Blighty, though I would have preferred France. Unfortunately, France is forbidden to the *Canadesi.* "Security," *They* say. "Bullshit," *I* say. May stay a while with Al Helmsley (one of my bird-watching pals from Toronto) who, with English wife and offspring, lives in a cosy cottage in Devon when not navigating Lancasters over Germany.

We find this new war distinctly weird. Our worn-out vehicles and equipment, our outlandish garb and customs make us feel like oddities. We are beset by gilded staff-wallahs from Canadian Army HQ, yapping at us like a bunch of Pomeranians. Canadian Army has high standards of "dress and deportment," and we must measure up! The unbelievable plethora of war *matériel* astounds us. An endless procession of aircraft overhead; acres of modern tanks filling entire fields;

---

* The German V-2, a winged, flying bomb driven by a pulse-jet engine.

artillery convoys that seem to have no end; and gargantuan dumps of ammo and supplies – these are things to make our eyes pop.

We are to be completely re-outfitted and then, so we are told, we shall be "allowed to take a hand in the final phases of the war." Nice of them to let us share the victory. Somehow I doubt that any real bonds of affection will ever be established between us and the lads who run *this* show. There is a healthy spirit of rebellion in our hearts and a strong disinclination to take this new aspect of war very seriously. Well, we've learned to take nothing much seriously, including death and ourselves.

In the peace and quiet which now obtains, I have re-read *Carrying Place*, or perhaps I ought to say, have really read it for the first time. My impression of it is clearer but the little descriptive passages that are so goddamn reminiscent of personal doings have affected me so much that the story itself sometimes got lost. I could wish the book had been set in a world I didn't know so well, and peopled by strangers. I wouldn't then have had to approach it through a turmoil of memories which upsets my easily upset ability to concentrate.

Frankly, Pop, I don't like the hero much. Eric espouses a moral code that seems somewhat idiotic to me. I think he acted like a simp towards Mona. He would have benefited from a couple of lectures on "What Every Young Man Should Know About Sex and How to Handle It." But then he didn't belong to my generation and may have been representative of his. I wouldn't know.

To me the most important person in the book is the Narrator. I admire his open admission that he is a malingerer from life. His philosophy suits me perfectly. Having been gassed at Ypres gave him a lousy pair of lungs, but a perfectly beautiful excuse for bumming his gentle and dreamy way through a very difficult age as an observer rather than another tattered and beleaguered participant.

Mona is my favourite. But I have to tell you that, as with Eric and the Narrator, I haven't been able to gain much understanding of the motives that jerked her along her incredibly erratic path. Was she nuts? Or was it that she was driven to distraction by smug and moral Eric Dalton?

As I've said, the minor characters impressed me most. Take Little

Cap. I don't think I've ever read as short a passage that gave as brilliant an image as the one describing him. I wish he'd been in the book more often. And I wish Mutt had been. The old fool had me in tears with his "thump-thumping" on his kennel floor outside the window.

What appealed to me most, I think, was the way the whole story came to nothing in the end (as does all life) but without an accompanying sense of futility. The Narrator, last of the Daltons he, sitting peacefully in front of the fireplace of the empty house on abandoned Waupoos Island contemplating the inscrutable games the gods had played with his family . . . without anger, and without recriminations against the fates.

Well, you will realize by now that I missed most of what you probably intended, Pop. But the hell with that. *CP did* succeed in rousing me from a mental lethargy of many months' standing.

So now I must write a letter to my trunk, which has been reposing in an attic in Darvel, Scotland, since I left it behind to sail for Sicily in June of 1943. I wonder if it will still remember me. I hope so. It contains, in addition to my serge uniform, a bottle of pre-war Scotch. The combination should make me well nigh irresistible to the dewy-eyed damsels of dear old Blighty.

WRITING TO ANGUS ABOUT *CARRYING PLACE* WAS VERY DIFFICULT. The fact was that I was uncomfortable with both his novels. I found them emotionally overwrought and heavily overwritten. The people in them embarrassed me. But loyalty and, it may be, compassion prevented me from even hinting at such an assessment, then or ever, as long as my father was alive. Peter Davison, my editor for thirty years, suggests that the conflict between what I felt and what I felt I had to *say* about Angus's books may have prejudiced me against writing fiction on my own. An interesting idea.

[Toronto]

April 16

Dear Squib. –

At last, some letters! The first, written from Belgium. I'm chuckling with sheer joy over your attempts to rationalize *Carrying Place*. Give it up, brother. Nearly all the reviewers had a shot at it and got lost as hell. So I'll confess to you, as I would to no other, I got lost too. From the moment Eric met Mona coming out of the theatre, I realized damn well that neither people nor life can ever be rationalized (except in biography, which is death) so then I just let the characters go where they would, as people do go where they will. And, of course, that's what you said in your critique, which I may say is more perceptive than any other has been.

I hope you will one day realize the intense pleasure a writer gets from reading the comments about his brain children. Eric Dalton, as far as I know, was just an unlucky devil who got ground up between an uncontrollable passion for one woman (not so rare a thing as the sophisticates would have you believe) and the fundaments of his inherited and early-trained character. As simple as that. And in any well-engineered thesis he would have found his way through. But in life? Hell no. The real Eric, and he was utterly real to me, followed no man's thesis. He wandered and vacillated in obscure and human ways. And he comes back to me from the reviewers as "a strong, silent man," "a moral weakling," "a simp" (that's yours), "a good man gone wrong," "a bad man trying to make good" – and a lot of shades between. Which leads me to the conclusion that he must at least have been a living person for most of the commentators, or he wouldn't have bothered them any more than if he'd been a stone figure on a monument.

But enowp, enowp. Your comments remain the most interesting I've had on the subject.

Mr. King announced last night that you and your friends don't have to go to Japan since twelve thousand Zombies are now available for overseas service (except for the four thousand who have already deserted). What citizenship will you adopt after the war? Russian or

Scots? I should lean towards the latter. There's an honest vigour in the Scots that runs all the way from their rough tongue to their love of usquebaugh.

Some time later.

I went to Christie Street and in the officers' ward I found Lieut. Smith still flat on his back under a huge cast, poor lad. Then I had another shot at trying to find Al Park, and this time was successful.

When I came into his ward, he was dozing on his bed wearing a huge head bandage that made him look like a Turk. I went up to the bed and remarked casually that I was Squib Mk. 1. "Oh my God!" he cried, and leapt out of bed and embraced me. I think you may have a friend there. He kept muttering all through the visit, "Old Squib! If I could only see old Squib again. And give him some good advice." He wanted to know everything about you and I may have enlarged on the fact that you aren't getting any more popular with your superiors. He opined that was natural. He thinks you may be somewhat indiscreet, and that you'd get ahead faster if you could give over being a couple of jumps ahead of your boss. Which, as he sagely pointed out, can't be helped sometimes, and does no harm – as long as the boss doesn't get wind of it.

He also remarked, as somebody else did not long ago, on your physical toughness in battle and otherwise. This has given me some food for thought. Actually you aren't so tough physically but you seem to have created an impression of being constructed of catgut and sulphur. I have some idea, you know, of what that kind of an impression can cost.

[Oostmalle]

March 23

Dear Folks:

Mail's finally caught up with us today after we've been weeks in Coventry. Three from you, in the first of which you happily congratulate me on the new job in Naples, and in the last of which you weep over my having had it snatched from under my nose. I wasn't much disappointed since I have long since learned not to expect much of anything good from the army. I am seldom disappointed.

Today I signed an application for transfer to the Int Corps. If it comes through, the Hasty P flashes will have to come down. That'll be sad, but if I want to retain any semblance of self-respect and personal integrity (read sanity for the aforementioned), I must get out. I could, of course, do this by collecting a court-martial but that could be, as they say, counter-productive. Did I tell you about my last tiff with the Brig? Paul O'Gorman (our new staff captain, and a Hasty), tipped me off that the chappie was going to have me on the carpet, tell me he had no confidence in me and suggest that I return voluntarily to the Regiment. Well, I got a small skinful before the meeting and, before he could open his yap, I saluted smartly and informed him that I no longer had confidence in him as my commander and could I please have a transfer to Intelligence. I think he was too surprised to think, so all he could do was bellow "No," and that is where it stands.

By the way, did I ever tell you about the time I *was* under close arrest awaiting court-martial? It was aboard the troop ship *Derbyshire*, coming out to Sicily. One night I got into cahoots with a Limey sapper Lieut, and he undertook to show me how one of their newfangled electric mine detectors worked. Problem was, of course, the whole damn ship was made of metal, to which the detector responded enthusiastically, and noisily, and continuously.

Then inspiration struck. I bethought me of the officers' mess, which was the former saloon lounge of the ship when she was a luxury passenger vessel and had a loverly *hardwood* floor. It was the evening drinking hour when we got up there and the place was jammed with officers from a score of units – Canadians, Limeys, Indians, commandos and you name it. Lots of big shots too, including a major general and a bevy of brigadiers. The plot was that the sapper would deposit a couple of metal objects somewhere on the floor, and I'd strap the amplifier on my back, put the earphones on my head, and taking a firm grasp on the detector (which looked like some kind of mechanical mop) do a sweep of the joint.

So far so good. My odd appearance and actions elicited a certain amount of curiosity from the thirsty mob as I worked my way in amongst them, diligently pretending to seek for mines but, what the hell, you get used to strange sights in any place where serious drinking is going on.

And that was the trouble. Everyone was drinking but me, and I got thirsty. So I stopped beside one crowded table, raised the detector head and passed it over the assembled glasses, at the same time turning up the volume control until a shrill squeal was heard from the instrument. Thereupon I seized somebody's glass of rum and orange and tossed it down. After which I said to the table's occupants: "You can thank me, chums, I'm from the Rum Disposal Squad, and that one would have murdered all of you."

Good humour being the order of the day, they went along with the gag. So did the sapper and I. Together we detected and disposed of a good many highly dangerous liquid mines, and all was going swimmingly, as you might say, until we came to the piano.

It was a grand and was bolted to the floor in the middle of the room. And standing at the silent end, leaning forward with his elbows on it, was the Limey brigadier responsible for troop discipline and physical training aboard ship. He was a gung-ho type and everybody hated his guts. When I looked up from a table I had just swept clear of mines and saw his large posterior directly ahead of me, I got carried away. Yes, I did. I slowly brought the detector head up to waist level and pushed it gently foward, unaware that a hush had descended on the mess and that all eyes were now upon the little tableau by the grand piano.

The hush was shattered as the sapper reached foward and turned the volume up to max. The resultant squeal was like that of a stuck pig. The brigadier stiffened as if shot but before he could turn around to see what we were doing, my pal touched him on the shoulder and in a loud voice said: "Excuse me, sir, but I think you should know there seems to be a booby trap up your behind . . ."

Shortly thereafter we found ourselves under close arrest and confined to quarters pending the constitution of a court of inquiry, pursuant to a court-martial. The CO of the 48th Highlanders – a good guy, indeed – eventually got us sprung, probably because we were due to do an assault landing three days later and couldn't be expected to do it properly when in irons. But I've always regretted that we bothered to warn that brigadier of the danger he was in. We should have let him detonate.

You are worrying, it seems, about my mental and spiritual condition. So am I. I am not, as you put it, Pop, "burned out," but I seem to be in some kind of a state of suspended animation. It is unsettling to find you have to *force* yourself to react to things of beauty, of horror, of pleasure, of fear. You know you should appreciate something – but you don't. You know you should be enraged by something – but you aren't. It's like watching a frozen hand drop off. You *see* it going and are curious, scared maybe, but you don't *feel* it. What especially interests me is the question of whether frozen parts ever come back to life. Or does emotional and spiritual apathy go on spreading until the whole organism has become a numbed mass of insensate tissue?

Well, curiosity is a good sign. It's the last of the rats to leave. As long as it is still around, the ship has not yet foundered. Another point of interest. The full effect of all of the above was not to be felt as long as gun barrels pointed in my direction. Only now that there is not much likelihood of ever again having to face them are things getting numb.

You express a certain wonderment about my lack of interest in the story in *Maclean's*. Well, I'll tell you. It stinks, my fond parents, and you and I all know it does, but you won't say so. However, that isn't the trouble. The trouble is that I can't either fix that story or write anything new. I've tried like blazes to write, just for the reassurance that putting words on paper gives me. But after a para or two, my interest just can't be flogged into further action. I haven't quit trying but I figure I might as well.

Hi ho. All very pitiable, ain't it? But a little self-pity is probably good for one. Anyhoo, I'm off to Blighty next week. I can't locate my RCAF pal, so I'll just play it off the cuff and maybe look up a girl I used to know. Or maybe not. It's a funny feeling, as if I've been exiled from *two* homes – Canada *and* Britain – for so long I hesitate to go back to either for fear I won't know them – or they won't know me.

April 10

My Dear Squib (Mk II). –

And the day will live long in the minds of men and will be by the generations remembered because it was on this day twenty-eight years ago that the Lord spoke to Squib (Mk I) saying "shiver the bottle," whereupon the waterbottle of rum that was being lifted up was shattered into a thousand fragments, and the arm that bore it became paralyzed with a blight, and from that day on no strong drink could he lift to his lips no matter how parched they might become . . .*

And on one other occasion twenty-seven years after this, the loud-speaker of the Lord blared forth among the ancient ruins of the Coliseum saying, "that young captain is standing just where the lions will come out" and the Young Captain looked with afright over his left shoulder and said to his driver, "Benny! Get me and Lulu the hell out of here!" And that took place after the Young Captain and his driver captured the Italian village single-handed and had been treated to much champagne therein by the grateful villagers, according to the account of the aforesaid Benny . . .

So yesterday, Ninth of April, I went to the hospital early to have a gam with Al Park. I use me as a sounding board on which Al can practise his memory. I look back through your letters written home while you both were still with the unit, pick out an incident and give him a lead with it. I did that with the incident of the mouse that made her nest and hatched her young in your box of ties in the Scots billet you two occupied before you went to Sicily, and then I sat back and watched him struggle through the mists until suddenly the whole thing came back to him and he burst out laughing.

So I was late getting to the office, and Sam, who works for me, said a young gentleman was looking for me. So who should walk in but Benny Bennett himself. You had not told me that, having survived for five years, he was coming home on leave. Too bad he couldn't bring Lulu Belle, but himself was quite enough. I simply gave up, told Sam

---

* It was on this date in 1916 that Angus had his right arm shattered by machine-gun fire.

to take over the shop, and went away with Benny. We got a case of beer and hastened out to R. Hill where we sat and sipped and talked. There is not much about you I don't know now, although Benny was not indiscreet. What does surprise me is that so many of his stories jibe so closely with your versions of them. Or vice versa.

It did bring you a lot closer, to be talking to someone who had been with you so recently. And Benny admitted that he did have a piece of pie the day you lived the liaison officer story. And he laughed and laughed over the time you promoted him to captain in order to get him into the officers' leave hotel, though admitting he was badly scared at the time.

So that was my day. How was yours?

[Oostmalle]

April 5
"G" Intelligence
HQ 1 Cdn Army
Dear Parents:

This must perforce be very brief. Have just arrived back from leave in Blighty, of which I will say more when I get time, and find myself under orders to report for duty at Army HQ, S.A.P. Yesterday, in fact.

Not sure what it's all about yet, but the BM tells me my transfer to the Int Corps has gone through. So I'm probably bound for a pool of Int officers God knows where. Whatever. I am no longer "of" the brigade, nor "of" the battalion. I'll worry about that later, no doubt.

Don't want to be a wet blanket but you should maybe not get too optimistic about a quick end to the shooting. In London these days you'd think it was all over but the cheering, at least to hear it from the civilians. Eisenhower puts it straight when he says that *unless* (and this is very uncertain given the nature of the Nazi Beast) some sort of formal surrender can be arranged, it may drag on as a sort of guerrilla war for several months. In any case, it would be a mistake to expect us home much before the end of the year. The point is, though, that we *will* be back by then, *if* King Mackenzie sticks to his promise for a change, and doesn't send us home by way of the Far East.

Got to pack now. Old Doc is coming with me, thanks be, but it is a sad farewell to Benny and Lulu Belle and the rest of my little gang of IQ kids.

[Richmond Hill]

April 20

Darling Bunface.

It has been so good to hear from you at last, and we do hope you had a good and well-earned leave. Did you see your Uncle Jack? He should be due for a thirty-day leave in Canada by now.

Angus and I have just come back from a jaunt to Owen Sound. Bad weather and poor hotels, so it was delightful to come home. Do you ever think that this is the first home we have ever owned? After all those years of gadding about the country living in other people's houses. Angus says he is now too comfortable in Hove To even to write another book. It only lacks you being here, which is a very great lack. Your room seems to be waiting. Angus has put your wooden name board from Camp Borden over your door: "Lieut. Farley Mowat" and his own over our door "Major Angus Mowat." I don't quite know where I come in, if at all.

There has been no mention of the First Division being in action in Holland, but we see in the casualty lists that the CO of the 48th Highlanders was killed in action lately, and also Molly Kidd's nephew, so I think you must all be in it again. If only the Germans would give up! But surely they cannot last much longer.

[Eindhoven]

April 8

Dear Folks:

You will remember how, in Chapter 1 written three days ago, the Hero of this epic returned from leave to find he no longer belonged to the Shiny First. Thereupon, after some lachrymose and spiritous farewells, he piled into a lorry complete with all his worldly goods and his trusty batman and began his ascent to realms on high. There was no fooling about, either. No stopping at Division. Nor at Corps.

Straight to the top our Hero goes, intent on reporting directly to the Army Commander.

He didn't get to see the Army Commander. Instead he paraded in and out of about a hundred swanky offices trying to find some member of the gilded (gelded?) staff who would accept him, give him a hug and welcome him to his new home. No such bloody luck. So, after two days of this run-around, he made his own arrangements for a comfy little flat in a nearby town, stocked it with stimulants and food scrounged by the inimitable Doc, then sent a note to the Army Commander saying where he was and settled down to await events.

Yesterday, a pompous staff captain arrived at my door to inquire if I was Captain F. M. Mowat and, if so, why hadn't I reported for duty two days ago, as instructed. Oh, Papa, I did you proud. I rent him from crown to sole until he fell off his high horse and condescended to introduce me into the Mysteries of this sacred place.

My new title is Technical Intelligence Officer (IO [Tech] Material), a very rare sort of bird, and my task is to scour the battlefields and beyond for examples of new military horrors being deployed by the Jerries against our lads. The Germans are a damned ingenious lot who keep coming up with cunning and deadly new weapons, or variations on old ones. I am supposed to track these down, assess their capabilities and figure out how they work so that our troops can be taught how to deal with them.

As you will remember, all my army life I have had a macabre curiosity about enemy weaponry and a certain way with the beasts (says he modestly). Therefore this promises to be at least an interesting job. And it has advantages. Not least of which is that nobody else in the whole bloody army knows *exactly* what I am supposed to do, or why, and what little they can gather tends to make them keep their distances for fear one of my finds might decide to go "whump." In consequence, I am being encouraged *not* to hang around the HQ offices which, as an acquaintance here put it, will keep me "from being smothered by all the chicken shit." Amen.

In defiance of Army HQ Standing Orders, I have retained my little flat, from which I amble to work around nine, or ten, or even eleven in the morning. Also in defiance of said orders, I retain my regimental and First Div flashes, refusing point blank to have Doc sew on the Army flashes. And I come and go anywhere and anytime I see fit on the whole army front, and to the flanks, in one of a fleet of vehicles at my disposal, including a jeep (Lulu Belle Mk. V), an HUP, an armoured half-track, a couple of 15-cwts* and – wait for this one, Pop – a Harley! I do not, however, ride the Harley. The damn things are too ruddy dangerous. But I've saved the best for the last. My nominal boss, and the person to whom I am directly responsible, is . . . Ken Cottam. Now *Major* Cottam, GSO 3 Int, and a big shot in the palace. Ken won't say, but I suspect he engineered this posting for me.

But, my Gawd, you have to see this place to believe it. Everybody over the rank of corporal seems to have his own private billet, and to drive around in a staff car. Even the sanitary men wear collars and ties and sport shiny brown brogues. People sit down to tables to have their meals . . . off real china and snowy linen. The whole place crawls with recent staff course graduates, most of whom wouldn't know how to tell their arse from a hole in the ground. These types massively outnumber us exiles from the fighting front and tend to treat us as pariahs, but they are easily handled. Ken gave me the word on this. "Bear in mind, Squib, that you must always treat these sons of bitches *as* sons of bitches. Then you can walk all over them."

I guess it's O.K. to tell you now that this move came just in time. I had become so fed up that I was ready to up and quit. Resign the old commission and return to the ranks. I figured the worst that could happen would be that I'd be sent back to Canada for burial in some reinforcement unit or the like. I still felt much the same way when first I got up here to Army. But things look a hell of a lot brighter now and so I'll stick it out if the Brass Hats leave me alone and let me get on with doing what comes naturally.

---

* Heavy Utility Personnel – a glorified van. 15-cwt – fifteen hundred weight – the army version of a one-ton pick-up.

[Eindhoven]

April 16/April 20

Things have been so hectic that I forgot to tell you about my leave. Here are the highlights. Crossed the Channel on a ferry on March 25 and came back again on April 3. Went first to Scotland to liberate my trunk – a long, weary hike on slow and unbelievably crowded trains, and in rainy, bleak weather. My heart had sunk before getting to Darvel and then it went through the floor. Nobody there cared to remember the days when this was Canadian country. Replaced now by a couple of thousand Yanks who, as the saying goes, are "oversexed, overpaid, and over here." Got my trunk and found it had been plundered. But my serge uniform was still intact so I cleaned the brass and climbed into it. It fit, barely, and felt pretty weird after the last couple of years wearing nothing but battle dress.

Giving the back of me hand to Darvel, I rattled south for a rendezvous with a lady – one I did not tell you about before, mainly because I thought you wouldn't approve. I met Hughie at the Overseas League in London in March of '43. She was in the Women's Auxiliary Air Force and married, her husband being a tanker with 8th Army in North Africa. That was the bit I knew you wouldn't approve of, and I didn't approve of it myself. But when you fall in love, you fall in love, and we did. And time was short, and soon I'd be on my way somewhere noisy, and God knows what fate would do to any of the three of us. But this I want you to know: we never actually made love. Neither Hughie nor I could do that. Too much of the betrayal of a serving soldier sort of thing we had both seen so much of. So we held hands a lot and necked some (God, how childish *that* sounds) and did funny, foolish things (playing silly buggers, she called it) whenever we could share a leave together. And we wrote to each other a lot during the years between. Before coming on this leave I had heard from her that her husband is expected home from Italy in May, and they will pick up where they left off. Or try, at any rate. But she did say she'd like to say goodbye to me.

She is out of the service and living with her parents in a seaside cottage in Shoreham, so I went down there, took a room in an almost empty little hotel that looked and smelled like a morgue, and called her up. She invited me for tea. All dressed up in my serge, I got myself out there, and she introduced me to her charming parents (who knew all about me) and we four had high tea, like old friends reunited. It was an incredibly civilized scene. After a couple of hours, Hughie and I said goodbye in the driveway, while a covey of destroyers steamed by just offshore, and that was it.

I came back to London on an evening train and went to the Park Lane Hotel, which always used to be the rendezvous for the Hasty Ps on leave. Incredibly it was full of Hasties! They'd booked an entire floor! We damn near had to buy what was left of the hotel before we left, but it was a glorious outbreak and "the hell with the cost" kind of leave. It did cost about seventy quid.*

Not many faces you would have recognized, Pop, but they all knew me and, in fact, I was an "old timer" in the crowd. Mother, you will be of two minds to know, but I cut my costs somewhat by spending two days and nights as a guest of three ladies of somewhat blemished repute who run a key club called The KitKat. You don't know what a key club is? You don't want to know. The ladies called me Junior and mothered me. Actually two of us stayed with them in their luxurious six-room flat in Chelsea and though not a single soul in the entire army would believe it, the only thing of theirs we laid a hand on was their Scotch.

One day I bought a barrel organ sans monkey in an antique shop. Transported by a bunch of Hastings' bucks to the sixth floor of the Park Lane, it proved of much interest to the populace of Greater London, until the rolls finally wore out. I have put the machine in storage as a post-war insurance policy. With Elmer in a pink sweater, carrying a hat, and me with a sign on my chest: "Ex-IO, Brother Can You Spare a Dime," we'll do all right.

The last night we met a bunch of Canadian WRENs who were dancing and singing in a Navy show. They aroused in me a new

* About $350 Canadian.

interest in my native soil. But two of them would insist on pretending they were buzz-bombs, and on trying to collect policemen's helmets. How's that? Well, they would come roaring up behind some poor bobby, making the BUP-BUP-BUP sound of a V-1 and literally knock him off his feet, bent on snatching his helmet. Great chaps, the London bobbies! They would struggle upright, brush off the dust, grin and say: "Now be off with you, young ladies. If 'tis a target you want, try Big Ben."

I mustn't forget a story told to me by an RAF wing commander of Bomber Command who was also a frequenter of the KitKat Club. Seems one of his Lancasters was on a raid over Hamburg when it was hit by flak and its bomb-bay doors jammed open. The pilot turned for home, and somewhere over the Channel the radio operator decided he needed a pee. Being somewhat absent-minded, he didn't disconnect his intercom as he stood up and took a step backward.

"Well!" he was heard to exclaim just before the intercom cord broke and he vanished into space. "Well, I'll be fucked!"

So, back to work. I am becoming quite acclimatized to this high altitude where they don't shoot at you with anything more lethal than typewriters. It's quite a relief to be able to sleep nights without keeping one ear cocked for things that go bump in the night. The only trouble is that while at the unit or brigade I felt fully justified in avoiding loud unpleasantnesses when possible, up here I begin to feel a compulsion in the opposite direction. Now that I don't have to risk my ass (inelegantly put perhaps, but in my case very accurate – I still have a dimple where the MO removed a shell splinter at the Moro), I seem to feel the need to do so. I suspect this results from a desire not to be mistaken for a staff wallah, which produces a kind of compulsive bravado on my part. This does not make me popular around here. People take a very dim but vociferous view of my tinkerings with bombs and shells and mysterious cannisters in my "workshop" in the cellar of the chateau which houses part of Main HQ. Yesterday, having returned from a three-day scrounge into "liberated" Germany collecting Heinie stuff from abandoned ammo dumps, I made a slight miscalculation while disassembling a small rocket with which I was unfamiliar. The damn thing let loose and went zooming around the joint like a mad king cobra, spitting flame from one end and a stinking yellow smoke from the other. I left in a hurry, as did a lot of the high-priced help upstairs. Cottam has since suggested I transfer my "bomb de-bolloxing" activities elsewhere. I am happy to oblige.

[Eindhoven]

April 20

Have made two long trips in the past fortnight to widely separated parts of the front and am much impressed by those parts of Germany I saw. They've had the Supreme Piss kicked out of them! Which is as it should be. But one must not become complacent. There is a hell of a lot more kicking to be done before we even begin to even up the score. I only hope we don't go soft on the job.

Most touching are the little bands of ex-slave labourers trying to wend their weary ways home – to the south, east, north and westward. They are not in good physical shape or in a good frame of mind. While I was passing through a German village recently, one of the *Herrenvolk* came belting out into the street in front of my jeep, demanding help in stopping some of the ex-slaves from ransacking his kitchen. My driver/interpreter (yes, I have one of those now but still miss Benny) gave him this response: "My officer says he would be happy to inter-vene, to make sure the poor devils get everything of yours worth taking." And would you believe it, the Heinie glowered at me, spat on the street, and acted as if I had betrayed the Honest and the Good.

I used to write off a lot of the German atrocity stuff as propaganda by our side, but not any more. One of Ken's jobs is co-ordinating investigations of reputed atrocities committed against foreigners in Germany, and I've seen some of the reports. Everything you've read about how Heinie treated the POWs and civvy labour conscripts from all over Europe is only too bloody true, and then some. The Russkies got it the worst. One SS document concerning their handling reads: "These sub-human elements are not to receive medical treatment unless their survival is imperative for the success of the project employ-ing them and unless replacements are absolutely not available." A stray dog in Germany had a better life and a better chance of surviving than those poor Russian bastards, men and women both. There were no children. Any that were born died within hours or days. And we are not talking about *just* the SS and the Gestapo and that lot of true-blue Nazis. Much of the misery and death was inflicted by good, solid, decent German civilians from factory managers on down. It was no big deal for a Jerry machinist training slavies how to work a machine to belt them with a steel bar if they made mistakes. So what if he broke a few arms and skulls? The cripples could be easily replaced. But enough is enough, and I get sick at my stomach easily these days.

I figure the grain-fed civvies in Canada and the U.S.A. have about as much hope of ever understanding what your "average" German can be like as of grasping the concept of infinity. Ten years from now, they'll be the "poor, misunderstood people who were misled by their leaders." You wanna bet? But it is no skin off my fundament. If they have to be driven back into their pens again at some time in the future, I won't be there. I have fought my last war. Incidentally, I was given the "opportunity" to volunteer for the Far East to take a crack at the Nips. Had to turn it down . . . religious scruples.

[Toronto]

May 2

Dear Friend Squibie. –

Just back from a trip to Ottawa on library work. But I had dinner there with the Howard Grahams. Howard and I pored over his photos and memorabilia of the Regiment and the First Brigade for hours, me drinking beer and Howard drinking nothing on account of he is now second to the chief of the general staff and his ulcers have come back for another visit. It was a good evening, but I only hope that the next time you get the sole of your boot blown off and shrapnel in your bum, you'll tell Poppa about it. Howard said that was the last time he saw you, and he didn't wake you to say goodbye because you were completely dead to the world with a mixture of rum and codeine.

I can plainly see you are having a lovely time at Army – and I'm glad I'm not there. I might have stood up under one of your patrols with Kennedy, or maybe even two, but when you start gelding those damned explosive things, as you used to do even in Canada, I wish to be elsewhere.

Your Moma's dear head did jolt back when she heard how much you had spent in London. Which gave me a fine opportunity to dilate on what a good boy I was on leave. Never spent more than ten pounds. I never had more because we had to spend so much of our pay on dress. Funny, isn't it? Think of going into action in your best serge uniform, brass all shined like a twinkling star, carrying a Webley pistol on your gleaming Sam Browne belt, and a cane. And you know, when I first went out, some of the English officers were still carrying swords.

How very modern we have all become.

I am thinking of taking a month off this summer and go sit on *Scotch Bonnet* in Prinyer's Cove with my typewriter. But I hate to take extra leave lest you by chance might be back in autumn or winter. Now there's something. That just slipped out unbeknownst. I have never before – not once – permitted myself to actually think of you being back. But now I do. And hadn't realized it till this moment. So please do not get too familiar with strange bombs and things.

[Eindhoven]

April 24

Dear Parents:

I am getting tired of being prodded to disclose the intimate details of my work. So here's a detailed account of my last "swan," as expeditions into the blue are called in 8th Army patois. Be it on your own head, and remember, you asked for it.

I was sitting inoffensively in my office doing nothing more exciting than reading *The Yellow Sparrow Murders* when there was a heavy thump on the door, followed by the entrance of a huge chappie with a grim, bewhiskered face, clad in a peculiar uniform and waving a bottle at me. I thought it might be a new kind of bomb and was preparing to duck when he bellowed: "Me Roozian ovvizer! Ev drink?"

Well, you don't catch me that easily, so naturally I told him to get the hell off it, and would he care to see my etchings? But, son of a gun, he *was* a Russian officer, from an intelligence liaison team, and his bottle was full of vodka. But that's another story, and the only reason he gets into this one is that his Roozian greeting set the keynote for my journey.

A couple of weeks ago, British Second Army was striking hard for Osnabrück. We got an intelligence report from one of their forward units to the effect that they had by-passed an immense German ammo dump which lay between them and a Canadian division. It seemed logical that I should go and have a look-see.

We took my scout car, which is a huge steel coffin with rubber half-tracks where its hind legs ought to be. Doc has converted its after deck into a sort of mobile wigwam. Two folding beds, bedrolls and cooking gear, together with a canvas top, make the whole affair quite homey.

My party consisted of Doc, myself, a driver who bears the endearing name of Tink, and a young Dutch officer seconded to Canadian Army from the Dutch Resistance movement named Jan Halverdonk. Jan is officially a liaison officer but he can't stand the atmosphere of Army HQ any more than I can, and so he spends most of his time traipsing about with me.

Anyway we crossed the border from Holland into Germany and took due notice of the large, solemn signs that have recently been erected there, and which read:

YOU ARE NOW ENTERING ENEMY COUNTRY
BE CAUTIOUS

Jan, who is by no means fond of Germans, became almost uncontrollable and insisted on manning the machine gun which is mounted on top of the cab for anti-aircraft protection. During the past several years he has been consistently hounded and hunted all over Holland by the Jerries and Dutch collaborators, without much of a chance to shoot back. Now he never misses an opportunity – in fact, he never misses the chance to invent an opportunity. I could sympathize with his feelings but after he had shot up a German farmhouse because he "didn't like the look of it," I had to place him under restraint.

Inevitably we got off the marked route and became hopelessly lost. It was all rather eerie for, as night came down, distant gunflashes and the flicker of shell-bursts seemed to be visible *all around* the horizon.

Eventually we halted and pulled off the road, and in the process we knocked over some sort of signboard. I climbed down and, with the aid of matches, was able to read it. It said:

ACHTUNG! MINEN!

I climbed hurriedly back into the scout car, and there we all stayed until dawn, shivering a little, even though it wasn't a particularly chilly night.

In the morning, after a hearty breakfast prepared by Doc (you shall have *all* the details) consisting of fried pork liver, fried bully-beef, fried eggs, dutch bread, plum jam, black tea and rum, we held a council. The decision was that it might be well to retrace our tracks – and without any deviations from them, either! This we were doing, very slowly in reverse gear, when a pair of armoured cars belonging to a British reconnaissance regiment approached us from the rear. They were as surprised to see us as we were delighted to see them and, after a few tense moments during which they were trying to decide whether or not to blow us off the road, all was resolved and we were given directions as to how to get back behind the Allied lines again.

The rest of the day was relatively uneventful. Progress along the shattered roads was tedious, for immense convoys were moving up towards what had become a most fluid front, and we had to wiggle our way along as best we could. Every now and again, we would be delighted by the sight of a ragged grey column of German prisoners being marched towards the rear, and at such moments Jan would become quite beside himself and have to be forcibly kept away from the machine gun.

Shortly after lunch, we located the ammo dump. It was an immense place consisting of innumerable concrete igloos stuffed with boxes of shells and high explosives, with the overflow stacked in long rows under the branches of a nearby forest. We spent the afternoon scrounging around and collecting whatever bits of lethal machinery looked particularly interesting. Doc uncovered a vast store of gas-shells loaded with some form of mustard gas, and we took samples of them. Finally, with the scout car loaded to the gunwales, we made our way to the headquarters of Third Brigade which held the right flank position for Canadian Army. The troops were now engaged in a battle of pursuit, and consequently no one really knew where anyone else was or what was going on. We sat around in the mess tent after a good dinner and listened to the BBC, from which source we learned that the Germans had reputedly evacuated Bremen.

We had been welcomed to this HQ by an intelligence officer called Red (because of his political leanings) whom I had known in Italy. Red was much excited to hear that Bremen had been evacuated since, for some days past, he had been sitting on some top-secret information concerning that city. An escaped slave labourer had described to him the location and contents of one of the largest distilleries in western Germany, and Red had been impatiently awaiting the chance to investigate it in person.

He is a most persuasive fellow. By 1900 hrs that evening, the scout car was again lumbering east, with Red serving as our pilot.

Since the area we were travelling through had only just been over-run by our troops, no one was too sure where the enemy was, or even of the location of the "front." It had been reported that one of the three main routes leading to the city had been partly cleared of mines, but we could not discover which one of the three this was. There was also some disagreement amongst the troops from whom we sought directions as to whether or not Jerry had in fact abandoned the city.

I was inclined to proceed cautiously, if at all, but Red was consumed with anxiety to be the first Allied soldier to liberate the distillery and would brook no delays. As it was now dark, he volunteered to ride on the front bumper and, by the light of his flashlight (car lights were, of course, taboo this close to the front), to spot any mine-like disturbances in the tarmac in time for Tink to take evasive action. None of the rest of us put much faith in this procedure. Tink had a method of his own. *His* principle was to open the throttle and drive so fast that, by the time a mine exploded, we would be over it and gone – he hoped. Jan, on the other hand, preferred to man the machine gun and to spray the road ahead with bursts of tracer in the belief that he could explode the mines before we got to them.

We must have presented quite a spectacle, barrelling down that empty road at fifty miles an hour, the machine gun occasionally belching flame and tracer, and only the light of a quarter moon and a single flashlight to show the way. We were to discover subsequently that the culverts under this road harboured five-hundred-kilo aircraft bombs. I think one would say it was fortunate that the retreating Jerries hadn't had time to set the time fuses on them.

We entered the outskirts of the city about 2330 hours with diffuse moonlight throwing the grotesque piles of rubble into vague and ever-changing outlines. The place appeared lifeless. No cat or dog moved in the broken shadows – no doubt they had all been eaten. The crumbling and fragmented ruins presented a vision of all the cities of man long after man has ceased to be. The only sound was the slow-spaced and regular booming of a single German gun firing into the northern outskirts. It might easily have been tolling off the years since life last breathed in Bremen.

It took us an hour to negotiate our way through the outskirts, and still we saw no sign of life. The enemy seemed to have gone, and it was evident that our own troops had not yet arrived. If there were any native inhabitants, they remained invisible.

Eventually we found our way obstructed by the wreckage of several apartment blocks and could proceed no farther with the scout car. Reluctantly we abandoned the vehicle, leaving an even more reluctant Tink on guard, and went forward on foot.

Red had an RAF photo-mosaic plan of the city, but it proved almost useless due to the frightful mangling Bremen had taken. We prowled from rubble heap to rubble heap, halting often, and crowding close together when the thin moon drifted behind the frequent clouds. There was a marked tendency to tread on the other fellow's heels, and I must admit to having had my hand on the butt of my pistol most of the time. I've done infantry patrols in no man's land that were less nerve-racking.

When we had gone about half a mile, we were suddenly and mutually paralyzed by the sound of hobnailed boots on pavement moving purposefully in our direction. Doc flung his arms around me with such passion that I could hardly breathe. Germans could never frighten Doc but ghosts were another matter. The moon came from behind a cloud, and to our unmitigated horror we beheld a strapping big Jerry officer striding towards us. He glanced casually at us, saluted smartly in proper Wehrmacht style and marched briskly on.

When his footsteps had passed out of hearing, there was a whispered but acidulous discussion amongst us.

"Why by hell you not shoot him?" Jan wanted to know.

The question was clearly directed to me, but I was still so breathless that I could not answer.

"Shoot him?" replied Red in a fierce whisper. "Why in the name of God didn't somebody ask him the way to the *distillery?*"

But that opportunity was gone. And it required another hour of wandering through the debris-littered streets before we at last stumbled on our objective.

We found it by its smell or rather, as Samuel Johnson would have insisted, by its stink. The odour of booze hung like a palpable cloud over the shattered ruins of what had once been an immense factory.

We discovered a well-used track leading through the ruins and, having followed it for a few hundred feet, came to an inclined tunnel which descended towards the bowels of the earth. Not without some trepidation, we too descended and found ourselves in a maze of subterranean caverns whose massive concrete walls and passages seemed to have more in common with a military bunker than with a liquor palace. Red led the way, but the batteries of his flashlight were now so weak that the bulb provided only a feeble glow.

Doc, who dislikes enclosed spaces, breathed heavily on my neck as we descended a flight of cement stairs, encountered a sharp turn and found ourselves at the top of a ramp whose surface glittered with shards of shattered bottles.

We had by now become aware of sound, something rather felt than heard. It was a kind of rising buzz and mumble, occasionally punctuated by hollow, staccato reports. My hackles were standing stiffly erect, and my pistol was half out of its holster – but all the same I was by no means prepared for the moment when we rounded a last corner and came face to face with the object of our search.

We had reached the vat room – a naked statement if ever I wrote one, but only Dante could have done justice to that scene.

You must imagine a gargantuan underground cavern whose unseen roof was supported by rows of massive arches sweeping up from a gleaming and wavering floor to vanish into darkness overhead. Between each pair of arches an immense grey vat squatted obesely. Over and between the vats, and coiling on the arches, serpentine pipes squirmed dimly in complex confusion.

All this was revealed to us, not by Red's feeble flashlight but in the weird flickering of scores of makeshift torches that flared like a horde of hellish fireflies.

The floor seemed to be animate, pulsing gently back and forth with a singularly queasy motion. The floor? We never *saw* the floor, for what we looked upon was a sea of alcohol! From bullet holes in a score of vats, streams of booze curved, hissing, to increase the tide. Cherry brandy, kirsch, synthetic whisky, grain alcohol and God only knows what else, blended in this, the most gigantic cocktail of all time.

The fumes were so heavy that a match did not burst into yellow flame but only seemed to glow with a bloody crimson glare. There was no need to drink. As Red said later, "You just had to breathe normal, but check your valuables at the door."

And the noise! Pistol and rifle shots, enormously magnified by the domed vault, echoed and re-echoed. Through this barrage came a welter of voices, screams, wild laughter, curses in unknown tongues. Behind this, again, was the steady rush and hiss of a myriad angry streams, and the gurgling and plashing of the alcoholic sea.

Doc was so unnerved that he began to moan, and his moan is like the bellow of a wounded bull. The rest of us were stricken dumb. As we stood petrified on the edge of the flood, one of the denizens of this inferno manifested himself close before our eyes. A match flared in the murk and a face appeared not a yard away from mine. It was a horrible, bearded face. Blurred eyeballs stared at us and then a hand came into the dim circle of light – a hand clutching a revolver. There was a shot, and a stream of schnapps came gushing from the nearest vat and soaked us all. The face loomed large again, and the stream abruptly ceased to flow as a pair of prehensile lips were glued over the hole.

The face finally came unstuck from the vat, spread its lips in a maniacal grin and croaked: "Me Roozian zoldier! Hev a drunk!"

There must have been five or six hundred Russians, Poles, Czechs, Rumanians, Hungarians, Dutchmen, Frenchmen and many other nationalities in the vat room. Slave labourers and prisoners of war, they were free at last and they were making up for much lost time.

There were also four Canadians on the fringe of this saturated assemblage. But we were made of weaker clay and did not linger. Doc did not entirely stop moaning until we were back in the scout car.

We returned the following day – in the full light of the sun. This time we carried power lanterns and Sten guns, and we took with us a section of infantry. And then we explored a portion of the incredible den under the ruins of the distillery.

All the passageways and tunnels were carpeted with drenched fragments of humanity whose tattered rags were still wet with booze. They would have gone up like signal flares if a flame had been applied to any of them. Surely theirs must have been the most monumental drunk in all recorded history.

We re-entered the vat room but our examination of that haunted place was rather perfunctory. Red was reconnoitring the way in rubber boots, and he had taken only a dozen swooshing steps when his foot hit a floating something. He swung his light downward to reveal the drowned and staring eyes of one who had drunk not wisely but too well.

In one of the upper levels of the factory, we came upon thousands of cases of booze that had been packed for shipment to Wehrmacht units all over central Europe. Of these we took enough to make the scout car sag heavily upon her springs.

So now I am home again, and everyone is my friend. I seem to have thousands of friends who queue up to visit my office and my digs. Ah, what it is to be beloved!

Now, if you value your peace of mind, I suggest you cease and desist from asking for "details" of my daily life.

[Richmond Hill]

May 6

Dearest Urchin.

On behalf of your father, Elmer and myself, I extend to you an invitation to come and visit us — when will it be? We are so thrilled that we can hardly take in the fact that the Canadians are no longer fighting and that there is a good chance of your coming home this very summer.* Angus keeps saying, "Be calm . . . don't count on it . . ." etc. but he is very busy burning the paint off the dining room doors, taking the old paper off the hall and generally redding up the Old Homestead for The Return.

You never mention your malaria. Benny, your driver, is still taking pills against it and says to tell you that you should, too. An extra careful lad, that.

The garden is coming along, and the cherry and apple trees are out. I *do* hope you'll like gardening and tinkering around the place. After all, it will be yours one of these days. Anyway, quite a strain has now been lifted off our shoulders. I hope off yours, too.

[Toronto]

May 7

Dear Boy. –

On Saturday I picked up two very wet soldiers who had been standing in the rain for ever so long while the civvies whizzed past them. They had got off the leave train from Halifax, where they had landed the day before, and were met at Toronto by nobody, so they started out hitch-hiking home to Thornbury, which is away and hell and gone up in Simcoe County. They were feeling a little low and unwanted. So, having a small bit of rye in the house, I took them home and poured it down their throats. When, eventually, they went out of the house into the wet again, they were at least singing.

---

* On April 29 the German 25th Army established a truce in Holland between itself and First Canadian Corps. All German forces engaging units of the Canadian Army surrendered on May 5.

There is much to be disillusioned about in a soldier's return. The civvy population is poised on tiptoe for word that the war in Europe is over and can think only in terms of vast festivities and huge parades in which the individual soldier goes unremarked. I suppose they'll be mobbing around, and hollering like the devil, and raising hell generally when VE day is announced, and the less they have done to bring that day about, the more hell they'll be raising.

By the by, your mom blanched a little when we came to the story of the RAF radio operator falling from the Lancaster. But she quickly rallied and said sweetly, "I do hope his parachute opened."

[Toronto]

May 9

Everybody has been wildly excited about VE day. There has been a tremendous amount of talk over the radio and Mum has sat glued to the machine, lapping up every word. On Monday, when the news broke, the government offices closed at one o'clock, and I headed for Christie Street through a mob scene even noisier than I had anticipated. But you will have heard all about that, so I won't describe it.

Things were considerably quieter in the wards. Bill Graydon had just had another operation and was comatose. Chubby Smith was in a new body cast and will stay in it for some months. Dude Dafoe was waiting for them to make another cut at him. There was also Bill Petit and his charming wife, who had nothing wrong with them but were there, like me, because it seemed like the right place to be. There was a lot of talk, all of it cheerful, and then I went on up to Al Park's ward. Things were running pretty high there. Someone had produced a bottle of whisky and even Al had taken a little one, which was causing him to talk very fast and remember better than usual.

Then I went out into a corridor and saw a peculiar thing. A nursing sister was standing by a window looking out at the crowds in the street, and she was crying. Quietly, but passionately. I did not, of course, ask her why. Was she crying for someone in particular – or for those who fill the white-painted wards of Christie Street and other military hospitals the world over? She didn't see me so I sneaked quietly away, thinking my own thoughts.

I wonder if you people have been advised of the VE day celebrations in Halifax on Monday and Tuesday. The whole damn city bust wide open, apparently, and not a window left intact in the whole downtown section. Stores all looted; liquor stores and beer warehouses stripped to the last drop; fires all over the place; and at least two sailors killed. The only bright spot in the whole picture was the saving of a child from a burning building by a *soldier* just back from overseas. The news accounts are pretty guarded, but it is stated that the show started when five hundred navy ratings broke barracks and marched into town, breaking things up as they went. I must admit there is cause for the navy to resent the Halifax merchants, just as there is for the army against the Kingston or Ottawa profiteers. Undoubtedly, a great many of these have taken advantage of the opportunity to stick the troops three or four prices for everything they bought, but riots play right into the hands of our political and financial masters who now have a fine excuse to tighten their grip. Already they are blaming the "commies" for the trouble.

What did the fighting soldiers do on VE day?

[Amsterdam]

May 13

Dear Parents Mine:

It would seem that I have had another birthday. It had escaped me completely until I asked someone the date so I could head this epistle. But the last ten days have been a pretty continuous celebration anyhow, and any special burst of speed would probably have finished me off.

I don't know what's come over me, but I've got an itch to scribble so I'll let it all pour out on your unfortunate heads.

I've done it in the form of a diary, the keeping of which by members of the armed forces is, of course, sternly proscribed by King's Regulations and Orders. But this will be an *official unit* diary, so that's all right.

War Diary
1st Cdn Independent Liberation Bde
C.A.O.S.

April 25, 1945 – HQ 1 Cdn Army

1630 hours: Ken Cottam, that bumptious carry-over from the days of Drake, has spent the last ten days developing one of his nefarious plots. This one is designed to get him deep into enemy-occupied Holland several days ahead of other Allied troops so that he can have first pickings. He went about it with his usual Machiavellian cunning, persuading the senior staff here that it was imperative to have a "liaison group" join the NBS* – the Dutch underground forces – and also establish a conduit for direct talks between HQ 1 Cdn Army and the HQ of General Johannes von Blaskowitz, commander of the German forces in Holland, who is thought to be interested in a separate armistice with the Allies.

I have become more or less involuntarily a party to these shenanigans. We have established contact with the head of the NBS in Amsterdam, a physics professor who uses the nom de plume of Colonel Oranje, and Cottam has received a signal which, he says, is as good as a safe conduct, from Blaskowitz's headquarters. We are to cross the German lines at noon tomorrow.

April 26, 1945 – HQ 25 German Army

1900 hours: My admiration for Cottam would now be incalculable if I wasn't so darn scared of him. Today, at ten past noon, he drove our jeep through the outposts of the Princess Louise Dragoon Guards and, with a white truce flag as big as a bedsheet waving from the wire cutter on our bumper, proceeded smartly across no man's land. I crouched beside him with the safe-conduct flimsy in my hand while Doc sat stolidly in the rear, being very disapproving of the whole business. However, nobody shot at us and I must admit it was quite an

---

* Nederlandse Binnenlandse Strijdkrachten (Dutch Internal Fighting Forces).

exhilarating experience until we reached the Jerry outposts where levelled Schmeissers and assault rifles made it painfully clear that not only were we not expected, but our claim to a safe conduct was highly suspect by the Luftwaffe troops manning this section of the line.

Ken was magnificent. He speaks German like a Junker and is such a hulking monster of a man that in a couple of minutes he had cowed the Unteroffizier whose section had detained us into taking us (in point of fact *we* took *him* in *our* jeep) to his battalion HQ. It took Cottam a little longer to browbeat that lot into acquiescence, but they finally gave in and allowed us to proceed, with an escort of four armed guards in two m/c combinations, to Hilversum.

My recollections of the thirty-mile drive that followed are somewhat blurred, even though I was now at the wheel. I have a shivery memory of crawling through a column of fully armed SS troops marching towards the front, and of Cottam standing up in the jeep to bellow insults at those of the Skull and Crossbones boys who didn't get out of our way fast enough. The looks they gave us were not kindly, although I don't suppose they realized who or what we were.

Apart from marching troops and horse-drawn transport, there was no wheeled traffic since 25th Army has been cut off from Germany for weeks and must be just about out of petrol. So we sailed merrily along, mostly in solitude, through a spring countryside untouched, apparently, by war, until we reached Hilversum.

Twenty-fifth Army HQ is in a series of deep bunkers on the outskirts of the town, surrounded by barbed wire, dug-in tanks and machine-gun emplacements to protect it from an air drop. *Très formidable*, but we roared bravely up to a main gate, were halted by an impeccable sentry who glanced at our safe conduct without a flicker of expression and called his guard commander. Things seemed a bit tense for a minute or two until a lanky Hauptmann appeared and somewhat curtly ordered us to leave the jeep and follow him. This time, it appeared, we *were* expected.

I am now in the main bunker, where I have just eaten a huge plate of German army stew, and am trying to get used to being surrounded by numbers of Hitler's finest, including Generalmajor Reichelt, who is chief-of-staff. He apologized for the grub which was mainly horse. Things are tough all over! Perhaps in recompense he has been plying me with Slivowitz (I think that's how it's spelled). The place is buzzing with high-ranking officers, all very polite, bowing smartly and heel-clicking. They obviously know the game is up but I find the strain of all this fraternizing, in the heart of the enemy camp, a bit trying. Ken is closeted with Blaskowitz and it will not surprise me in the least if he emerges wearing the Generaloberst's epaulets, having assumed command of 25th Army.

At 2215 hours, Cottam reappeared with a Cheshire-cat smile on his roast-beef face and announced that provisions for a nominal truce along the present line separating 25th Army from First Canadian Army had been provisionally accepted by Blaskowitz! I had had no idea that Ken would so blithely intrude himself (*and* me) into a highly political situation and trembled for the possible consequences to both of us since I knew negotiations were already underway between Seyss-Inquart, Reichskommissar for the Netherlands, and Supreme Allied Headquarters for a truce in Holland. Beaming with satisfaction, Ken explained himself thusly: "Would have taken those silly SHAEF effers in Paris *days* to get it all laid on. You and I mightn't have got to Amsterdam till God knows when! All tickety-boo now, though. And Crerar* will doubtless promote me to full colonel."

"If he doesn't court-martial you . . . and me, too," I interjected somewhat morosely.

"Absolute nonsense, chummie. He'll be tickled pink. Now shift your ass! We're off!"

April 27, 1945 – HQ NBS

This cloak-and-dagger game is far too unsettling. Unlikely as it may seem, I am presently sitting in a very large greenhouse (I seem to have this peculiar affinity for greenhouses) in the middle of a large park in the middle of Amsterdam. A blonde and bosomy wench with a

---

* General H.D.G. Crerar, Commander of First Canadian Army.

revolver strapped to her ample hips is pouring dollops of Bols Geneva into a cup of imitation coffee standing at my elbow. The acres of glass overhead are being rattled in an unsettling manner by the thump of grenades exploding at no great distance. I begin to wish I was back in Blaskowitz's bunker.

As usual I misjudged Cottam. The plot was that after leaving 25th Army HQ, we would high-tail it back to our own lines with the details of the truce proposal. Instead of which Cottam elected to make an end run for Amsterdam where, he said, we would contact the NBS and use their clandestine radio to get the gen back to 1 Cdn Army.

The trip itself was relatively uneventful. Darkness shrouded our identity so well that our first contact with anybody turned out to be a confrontation with an NBS roadblock whose owners *almost* mistook the jeep for a German staff car. Thank God they were not trigger happy. We were then escorted to this, their HQ, by a circuitous route since much of the city is rumbling with warfare between the NBS and the home-grown Dutch National Socialist "Green Police."

Col. Oranje was delighted to see us, and we are being treated as guests of honour. He is a character. Who else would have conceived the idea of putting his HQ in a greenhouse for tropical plants? Surely the last place the Germans would ever have looked for it. He assures us we are safe here from any premeditated attack, but it is the prospect of the arrival of an unpremeditated mortar bomb or two which makes me gulp my Bols and ask for more. I would have already crawled under one of the plant benches if I could have thought of any plausible way to explain such an action to the big blonde.

Oranje and Ken are poring over a large-scale plan of the city, doubtless planning more hellery. This time I shall firmly refuse to become involved.

(Later)

Yes. Well, my intentions were of the best. Maybe it was the Bols that undid me. At dinner, word arrived that a battle was developing between the Grun Polizie and the NBS in the Dam Square at the heart of the city. Everyone grabbed their weapons, and when Cottam volunteered "his force" in a reinforcement role I got carried away.

We crammed into the jeep along with Doc and about a dozen of Oranje's people and went roaring off behind a couple of Mercedes that had once belonged to the Gestapo. The Dam Square was a lively sight. The Green Police were holed up in buildings on the east side of the square and the NBS people were trying to winkle them out with small arms and grenades. The noise was impressive but the damage being done by either side was insignificant.

Cottam roared something about "providing covering fire" and dashed off, waving a Sten at the head of a motley collection of ex-university students and militant females in civvy clothing, sporting berets, orange-coloured brassards and weapons ranging from an old shotgun to a Jerry MG 42. Doc and I, however, withdrew to the doorway of a small café in whose shelter we sipped ersatz coffee in company with some interested civilian customers and watched the show.

Shortly thereafter came a horrendous engine roar and a grinding of gears and a clattering of steel tracks on cobblestones, and a big SS armoured troop carrier careened into the square. About a dozen Death's Head veterans spilled out and began setting up a heavy MG, presumably to support their *confrères* of the Green Police. However, they instantly came under fire from an NBS detachment in the doorway of another café, whereupon they leapt smartly back aboard their vehicle, the engine roared and the tracks clattered and they were gone.

Their departure was loudly cheered from *all* sides of the square (from which I concluded that the Green Police didn't much like the SS either), following which the police came straggling out of their pock-marked fortress and delivered themselves into the hands of the NBS. That ended the Battle of Dam Square which will not, I think, achieve immortal fame in the annals of military history.

We were then taken to the colonel's home to celebrate the victory with something called *Maiwine* (May Wine). Oranje, or Michels, which is his real name, turns out to be a world-famous physicist with nine children and an impressive wine cellar which he miraculously kept concealed from the Germans.

April 28, 1945

Sanity has vanished from Amsterdam today. The entire populace seems to be roaming the streets celebrating the coming liberation from a diet of potatoes and tulip bulbs. Mad things are being done under the noonday sun. A ravening multitude has just passed by harrying a bevy of once-pretty girls who may or may not have slept with German soldiers. Not even a German would want to sleep with them now. They have been stripped to the hide, shaved all over and liberally daubed with vari-coloured paint.

Colonel Michels – Tyce – explains to us that the occasional popping of small-arms fire is not a last-ditch resistance to the new regime, but represents the summary liquidations of quislings. He is forthright about this.

"If we wait until duly constituted authority again controls the Nederlands, most of the traitors will escape punishment. Some may even finish up in government. So we do not wait."

One of his lieutenants told me of his own experiences under the occupation. He spent some time in a concentration camp – not a German one but a *Dutch* one here in Holland, run by his own compatriots. If that's the word. They broke his fingers, one by one, to make him talk (he didn't), then they castrated him and dumped him on the streets of Utrecht as a warning to others in the underground. He told me that at least half the population was at least passively on the side of the Germans until Hitler got tough with Holland during the last two years of the occupation. I guess now that the NBS is in control, they would be more than human if they did not seek revenge.

During the day, the NBS received a radio message that the truce would be in full effect from tomorrow, and Cottam immediately began to fume that a formal surrender would soon follow with the result that Allied troops might get to Rotterdam before he does. This is not to be tolerated. Wearily I prepare myself for further ordeals.

May 3, 1945

There is a hiatus in this diary because there are several in my memory, which may be just as well. Nevertheless I will do my best to reconstruct some of the events of the last few days.

We got away from Amsterdam on the twenty-ninth with extreme difficulty. Mobs literally engulfed the jeep, weeping, laughing and screaming with delight. Eventually we wormed our way clear of the worst of the crowds and found ourselves on the highway running past Schiphol airport. We were then in territory still very much under German control and, instead of mobs of jubilant Dutchmen, had to contend with masses of disciplined German *soldati*. Some of them seemed pretty uncertain about our status and not at all sure how they were going to react to the news that a truce was in effect.

This attitude did not sit well with Ken, about whose background I am beginning to have serious doubts. Lecturer in Exegesis at Oxford, indeed. I think it far more likely that he is the illegitimate offspring of an Amazon warrior and a Prussian count. At any rate, his furious tongue-lashings certainly *did* cut a swath through every clot of Germans we encountered. Once, we were brought to a halt by the lowered muzzle of a 5 cm anti-tank gun sited right down the middle of the road. Doc and I both cringed in our seats but Cottam unleashed such a tirade that I thought the crew was going to give us the damn gun as a peace offering.

Once clear of the Jerry concentrations, we drove pretty rapidly towards Den Haag. Civilians were no problem. If the people en route had heard of a truce, they evidently didn't believe it so everyone was staying indoors out of harm's way.

The night of April 29-30 we spent, I think, in a luxurious roadhouse (until *very* recently a German officers' club) just outside The Hague. I don't know how we got there. I recall an enormous party and have a dim recollection of seeing Cottam driving the jeep through French windows into a ballroom, while Doc fired bursts from his tommy-gun at ornate plaster peacocks on the ceiling. Great hunter, Doc. I suspect we must have fallen into a den of rich collaborators who, like the wealthy nobles in Boccaccio's tale, believed that the end was nigh and were determined to go out with all senses satiated.

It must have been the next day that we liberated Den Haag but of that I can tell little. I spent most of the day asleep, or in a state that passed for sleep, while Ken roistered around doing God knows what.

The following day, or maybe it was the day after that, Cottam decided we should bestow our blessings on Utrecht. I was in no condition to argue.

We had reached the outskirts of Utrecht when we ran into the first of the official liberation forces – a squadron of Canadian armoured cars cautiously advancing towards Amsterdam. Their commander, a Lt. Colonel, was *not* pleased to see us. He ordered us to "fall to the rear" with such vehemence that even Cottam was impressed. Or seemed to be. But once we had passed the little column, he told me to haul off on a side road, glanced at his map and in short order we were heading for Amsterdam – by a shorter, faster route.

"Silly prick," was Ken's contemptuous summation. "Can't even read his map. It's chaps like him that made us take so long to win the bloody war."

Well, now it's won.

[Amsterdam]

May 19

Dear Folks:

I am not yet used to the idea that the war is over. Strange phrase. And one that most of us did not expect ever to hear, and perhaps never really wished to. How could we envisage an end to an existence which spanned so many years of our lives? We have survived the war all right. Can we survive the peace?

From what I can understand of the demobilization point system, married men will go back first and the single man will again get his nose rubbed in it. Furthermore, there are no extra points for combat – a clerk in London for the past few years gets as many demob points as a guy who was in action for the same length of time. There is only one deduction to be drawn from all of this, and from much else. It is clearly our bounden duty to fuck the system whenever and however we can. This is Cottam's credo and by God he's right.

I've been down to the regiment and am told there was little celebrating there on VE day. No whoop-dee-do. If there was any overriding emotion, it seems to have been one of befuddlement. "What happens now?" was the question on every man's mind; there was a chill wind blowing, too, for now the future, which was the dream, becomes the present, which is the reality, and we are not very used to that kind of reality.

Canadian forces here are to be given three choices. We can sign up for the Japanese war, for the occupation of Germany, or we can elect to be demobbed and in due course sent home to Canada. Home? Not for most of us. The only home we've known these years past has been that amorphous entity we called "the unit." Herein lay our trust when we had learned to distrust that other home across the western ocean. I don't know who I'm the most sorry for – the fellows who will go rushing back to smash their own patiently nurtured dreams, or Canada, which will have to receive them and ingest them. Someone is due for the hell of a big bellyache.

It is revealing to see that it is the old sweats who are signing up for the Far East Force, while it is the recent arrivals who are opting for demobilization. Personally, I don't want to go back to Canada. Not yet, anyway. The prospect of trying to live amongst people with whom I no longer have much in common, and for whom I have too little regard, is an unappealing one. On the other hand, I have had quite enough of killing. I had enough of that the first day in Sicily. It seems to me that limbo is the place to be right now, and I seem to be in a kind of special one.

Theoretically, ever since the surrender of Holland, I've been on "detached" duty under command of 1 Cdn Corps HQ which is now in Hilversum. In point of fact, brother Cottam has created a sort of independent command consisting of himself and myself and our respective batmen, working in cahoots with the Dutch underground people in Amsterdam who are very busy rounding up collaborators, National Socialists, black marketeers and other vermin.

I get in an occasional lick as a Technical IO. A certain Nazi, much wanted by Allied intelligence for his knowledge of V-weapons, was thought to be holed up in Amsterdam. I put the NBS onto him, and Col. Michels' guys ran him to earth. Trouble was that Michels *also* wanted this character's scientific gen, so we compromised. They kept him and pumped him for a week then turned him over to me. I have to say that the bod I passed on up the line was considerably the worse for wear but could still talk and, indeed, was so anxious to do so we could hardly shut him up.

I suspect that the good colonel is using us as bait. A number of sleek civvies have crossed our trail and have offered to cross our palms with everything from gold to old masters in exchange for some sort (*any* sort) of association with our forces. What they are looking for, of course, is protection. We report them to Michels, and it is not usually very long thereafter before they just seem to disappear. M. assures me that they are just going into the clink. I'm not entirely sure I can believe him but I guess I will.

I am most comfortably ensconced in a swanky flat once owned by a now-absent collaborator, made available to us by Col. Michels. Doc bustles about as cook, butler, body guard and general factotum. He is having the hell of a time, being much fêted by the NBS "other ranks" of both sexes. I'm not doing badly either. The nights tend to be lively, so I sleep much of the long days away. My God, the stories I've heard from the underground and some well-placed civvies. No use trying to write them now – far too incredible. But I'll tell you about them some day. Meantime I enclose a few pages of vignettes.

Funny thing. This life has become the "real" world for the time being. I went up to Corps HQ last week to do some biz and felt like an alien. All those poor joes fussing about with piles of paper. Nobody knowing quite what to do with themselves. The war is over but a lot of them don't want to let go of it. Most of the HQ types never had it so soft in all their lives, and now the chill winds of having to make a living in peacetime are making them shiver.

As for me . . . damnfino! I'm in no hurry to get adjusted to "normalcy." And I wish you guys wouldn't steep yourselves in visions of me spending the rest of my days in RichHill. If I stay put there I will have to, perforce, harness myself to a wheel, and any wheel will be more or less unbearable for the foreseeable future, or unforeseeable, if you prefer. So I have no coherent plan. I am against plans now, having watched so many of them turn into bloody busts during the late, unlamented hostilities. It is better you should face the likelihood that I'm going to be off again soon. Don't know where or for how long. I hate to say this, seeing as how we are so close and knowing how much you want me underfoot, but that looks like how it is, at least for now.

A Cigarette in Amsterdam

"It is so bad here!" said the concièrge of the apartment building where I was staying. "It is so bad here! Ach, it is so bad! We suffer so much so many years. So bad for us! You have cigarettes for me?"

I gave her one and tried to change the subject, but it was no use.

"Last week I give two hundred guilders for one pound of butter! Ah, it is bad – we suffer so. We are glad for you be here – but we suffer so. It is incredible to you – the suffering. Now we have nothing. For bread we give fifty, sixty guilders. It is very bad here . . ."

I had spent a week in Amsterdam listening to stories of how the people here had suffered. It was getting on my nerves. And I found myself thinking about a little hill town in northern Italy. Carchio had been a stumbling block to our army during an entire winter, and by spring, when we finally captured it, there was nothing left that could have been properly called a town. Not a single undamaged house. But the people were still there – some of them – the unlucky living. They had had no fire to warm them during the long, cold winter, little shelter, and less food. The cattle had died under our artillery fire and the small fields that had once grown grain and vegetables were now lifeless mud wallows. And there I met a woman. She might have been thirty – twenty – forty. She told me without tears, without pathos, that she alone was left. Her three children were dead, also her father. Her husband had never come back from the war. Now that it had got warm again, she would dig a grave for the dead and they would then be able to leave the hovel in which all – the living, the dying and the dead – had gone through the winter.

I had watched her patiently making her way down the war-torn hill as she moved away from me, prodding the wet ground with a piece of bed railing to see if it was soft enough.

"Ah, how much we have suffered here in Amsterdam, when there are no coals for the heating. But you cannot imagine how terrible it has been. Maybe you have another cigarette?"

I felt just slightly sick at my stomach. I knew it was foolish and unfair of me. They *had* suffered in Amsterdam. But . . . there was Carchio.

* * * * * * *

When I went outside and climbed into my jeep this kid materialized beside the little vehicle and thrust his hand at me like it was a gun.

"*Eine Zigarette, herr Kapitän!*" he demanded.

He was an ordinary kid, not ill-dressed nor showing any signs of privation or distress, and he was insistent.

"You give *eine Zigarette* for me!"

I had been pulling out my pack to have a smoke myself, but now I thrust it back into my pocket and fumbled with the gearshift.

"*Nein!*" I said. "I don't smoke. Buzz off, kid. Buzz off!"

He gave me an angry look and walked away. Then I got out my pack, trying to hide my action from the passers-by. But lighting up without being spotted was too difficult. From both sides of the street, men and women began to converge on the jeep. As I pulled out from the curb, an unlit cigarette cupped in one hand, their voices followed in a longing chorus.

"Canada! You give a cigarette? . . . Give for me? . . . *Eine Zigarette?*"

Cursing under my breath, I gunned the engine, shot noisily across a main intersection, turned right along one of the canals and when I came to a stretch of street with nobody in sight, pulled over to the canal bank and lit up. I'd smoked about half of it when I saw a barge approaching. The young fellow at the tiller swung the rudder hard over and headed straight towards me. I couldn't believe it! I thought he was going to run the barge right into the stone rip-rap wall. He had a big smile on his face and was holding his left hand to his lips and sucking in like someone drawing on a smoke.

"'Allo Joe!" he yelled. "You got cigarette for me?"

* * * * * * *

Like most of the bars around the Dam Square, the Monopole had a small orchestra: a pianist, trombonist, violinist and the inevitable accordionist. When they saw me come in, they immediately switched from some Dutch tune to "Tipperary." I knew the routine. Now they would play just for me (or for anyone else in battledress) until I could no longer resist the nicotine habit and had to light up. Then they would get theirs. I sat down and ordered a beer.

As I sipped my drink among all those hungry looks, I became aware of an NBS man in the blue overalls and orange brassard of the underground coming through the door. He was tall, thin and good-looking but with a hard cast to his eyes. He eyed the musicians bleakly and muttered something I could not hear, at which "Tipperary" came to a ragged end and they began another Dutch piece.

The NBS man limped to my table and sat down. He glared at the band for a moment, then turned and looked at me as impersonally as if I was no more to him than a symbolic figure representing John Bull, or Uncle Sam, or Joe Stalin.

"Bastards!" he said bitterly, and in English.

My glass was empty so, rather than ask him to amplify that statement, I asked him to "have one." He nodded abruptly, without any manners at all, and when the beer came, I asked him how it had been going.

"It has been bad," he said. "It has been bad for a man. Now it is worse – for a Hollander."

There was a long pause, and I must have looked as if I didn't understand because he went on. "I say it is worse now. For me. I am a Hollander, you see, and I have pride in my country. That cost me a year in a concentration camp. It cost me my wife. It cost me many things – and these I paid – not gladly, but I paid with the many others, from pride in my country. You understand that? From pride!

And now I see there is no pride, so for me it is worse now."

He finished his beer at a gulp then, to my amazement, pulled out a Dutch cigarette and *offered it to me. He* offered *me* a cigarette! He smiled thinly at my surprise.

"That is what I mean," he said. "I mean that you are here now, not as friends, not as allies, not even as liberators. You are to us merely a source of things my people want and they have no pride to conceal it."

I was embarrassed. It wasn't all true. I have seen the results of privation and I think I know what it can do to men's souls – and after it is over, they seem to be little the worse for it. What we had encountered in Holland was just about what we had expected. We did not really mind being badgered for things. And we had no right to feel disgust with the cadgers.

I tried to tell him all this but it was no use. The man who had spent a year in a concentration camp lit his cigarette and got up and walked out. And the bandsmen, watching, struck up "Tipperary."

[Amsterdam]

May 30

Dear People:

I guess I ought to explain the recent scarcity of letters. After four long years of army life – of being bitched at, bitched about and of doing my own bitching – I just decided to take some time off and work out my kinks and psychoses by setting myself a fast pace.

Well, that is what I did. But now the race is done. You'll be relieved to know I have dumped most of my repressions, suicidal inclinations, homicidal same, inhibitions and rage. Most of them, I say. And I'm sure of one thing: it was a damned sight better that I did it here than back in old RichHill.

You will also be relieved to hear that the reincarnated Elizabethan, Ken Cottam, has gone out of my life. When last seen, he was departing for Berlin in a Mercedes, accompanied by a statuesque German wench who looked like Marlene Dietrich, claimed to have been an Allied agent (ha!), and wrote in lipstick on the mirror in Ken's

bedroom in large letters HERE WE USE ONLY BALL AMMUNI-
TION. Ken said he was bored with Holland. I wouldn't be surprised
if he turns up in Moscow and gives Uncle Joe a hard time.

There may be a few memories worth salvaging from the soon-to-
be-forgotten events of the past weeks. One was a voyage from Den
Helder to Amsterdam in a German E-boat. Poppa would have loved
it. The Jerries had handed over three of the boats to the local NBS
detachment (under duress, I suspect) instead of waiting to give them
to the Royal Navy. Tyce Michels was advised and decided he wanted
one since he had been a bigwig in Dutch naval design before the war.
His lads were perfectly capable of bringing the boat around but he was
afeard they might run foul of Allied forces and get themselves sunk.

So, would I care to go along "in command" of this captured vessel?
What could I say? The voyage was almost uneventful. Petrol was in
short supply, so we had to rein in the beast to a mere crawl of twenty
knots. Wishing shyly to stay out of the way of Allied vessels, we
hugged the coast most of the way and grounded her once on a mud
bar. Only major excitement was being buzzed by a couple of Spits, but
when they saw the red ensign which I was waving like my life
depended on it, they just twitched their wings and went their ways.
What the hell – the war is over, ain't it?

This Michels guy is something. I'll tell you more about him later
since I expect to be working with him for some time. I might even tell
you a little something about Rita, too. Who she? Was the light of my
life for a few weeks, but it is all over now, and Maman would not have
approved so on second thoughts I guess I'll just let Rita lie.

❖   ❖   ❖

A FEW DAYS AFTER OUR RETURN TO AMSTERDAM, COTTAM AND I SET
out to test-drive an Opal sports car Colonel Michels had turned
over to us. We drove the sleek little machine out of town on a road
paralleling a broad canal. Barge traffic had not yet revived, and the
canal seemed empty of boats. Eventually we encountered a single
vessel – a varnished mahogany racing sloop, idling along in a light

air. A man and two young women in swimsuits were taking their ease on her deck in the warm sunshine.

It made an idyllic picture. One which, with our Opal included, could have come from the last summer before the war in Europe began. We were charmed. I pulled over and we waved to the mariners. They waved back and let the little vessel drift up to us.

The man was middle-aged and with such a well-fed look that we took him to be a collaborator, at the least someone associated with dubious enterprises. One of the women was dark and a trifle plump, but comely enough. The other, about my own age, was a true platinum blonde – and utterly lovely.

We were invited aboard and lavishly treated to iced white wine by the boat's effusively friendly owner who seemed perfectly content to have Cottam and me fawn, if not drool, over his passengers. To my inexpressible delight (and incredulity), the blonde – whose name was Rita – attached herself to me, leaving Cottam no option but to take second best, a position which had usually been my lot when similar occasions had arisen in the past.

I may have sensed that Rita was not what she claimed to be – the patriotic daughter of a well-to-do and high-ranking Dutch officer imprisoned by the Germans – but it didn't matter. Had I known that she was actually a café artist whose relationships with Germans had been, at the least, amicable, I wouldn't have cared less. This spectacular young woman was making it clear that she was enamoured of *me*; and I would have reciprocated if she had been cloven-hooved and perfumed with sulphur.

Two days later, Rita moved into our apartment. As a lover, she was passionate and skilled to a degree I had not believed possible outside of fantasy. She bemused, befuddled and bewildered me so thoroughly that I wilfully rejected even the broadest of hints from my NBS friends that I exercise caution. So, of course, I got my just deserts. A dose of the clap.

I took that very hard. Despite Rita's pleas for forgiveness, understanding and, yes, for help, I resolutely cut her out of my life. And I spent ten days incommunicado on a regimen of sulpha drugs procured for me from some medical friend by Cottam. I was not only filled with sulpha but with self-loathing.

Although nobody but Cottam ever knew about this incident, I was for a time so shamed that I would not associate with any local girl. Fortunately, this jejune attitude did not long persist. My psychic recovery was almost as swift as my physical one and within a month I was comporting myself as a veteran, not only of war but now of love as well.

And Rita? She found another protector – a Canadian major who, more mature and more practical than I, got *her* some sulpha. She resumed her former profession and was dancing and singing in a café when I ran into her just before I left Holland. Without rancour she bought me a drink and wished me well.

M o w a t ' s   P r i v a t e   A r m y

❖ ❖ ❖

THE WAR WAS OVER. I WAS TWENTY-FOUR YEARS OLD AND HAD SPENT
the last five in uniform within a system I had come to distrust and
was learning to detest.

I had had quite enough of the soldier's life but, as yet, had no clear
idea of what I might do next. My growing contempt for duly constituted authority had become so pervasive that I could not stomach the
prospect of giving myself into the hands of some new hierarchy of
ambitious buffoons of the business, political, professional or academic
persuasion. The desire to betake myself to some remote and thinly
populated corner of the earth was strong, but I could not hope to extricate myself physically from the military quagmire for some time to come.

In this extremity, I may have subconsciously remembered something Angus had written to me while I was still in England and
feeling frustrated because I did not have enough to do.

"Purpose, my son, is everything. A man must have purpose or
perish. And if you should ever find yourself without a useful enter-
prise or a clear purpose, then you had best contrive one if you are
going to survive."

Angus had made it clear in his recent letters that he understood
my current need for an activity which would preoccupy me until I
was sent home and demobilized. He thought that writing might give
me purpose. I tried to write, but found I was in too great a state of
confusion to be able to do more than dabble at it. Either consciously
or unconsciously, I followed my father's earlier advice.

I created a purpose for myself.

June 2

Mes Amis:

Would you believe it? I've gone back to work. Well, gone to work, if not back, since there is some doubt that I have done any real work for these past several months. And it occurs to me that may have been part of my difficulties of recent times.

Anyhoo, what I've done in effect is make *myself* a job since the army has absolutely nothing interesting to offer. But I owe the idea to Col. Michels. We've had some long sessions discussing the shape of the future and agree there is no way Uncle Joe and Uncle Sam are going to stay pals. Michels believes they will be head-to-toe in short order and is afraid all the little countries will get squeezed to death in between.

I talked to a senior U.S. officer in Antwerp not long ago and he was frank about it. "Sooner or later," he told me, "we are going to have to pulverize Ivan." When I asked him why, he just shrugged and said, "It's in the books. That's why."

So what we've got right now isn't peace, it is a delusion of peace – a breather, as it were. And the big boys are getting ready for the next act as fast as they can. Yankee and Limey boffin teams are already crawling like lice all over the wreckage of the Jerry war machine and the amount of effort going into the evaluation and collection of gen about German rocket developments is fantastic. Presumably the Russkies are just as busy.

And there is another thing. The word is out that Churchill and Truman have made a deal that the rest of the western Allies – all the little brothers – aren't to be allowed access to advanced German military science. I know this is the case because I've seen orders restricting Canadian activity. We are "forthwith" to turn over *all* innovative German weapons or tech gear to our Limey colleagues, and all enemy experimental facilities, rocket or V-1 sites and production centres etc etc are strictly off limits to us now.

They are going to considerable lengths to see that the small- and middle-size Allies don't get to play with the big boys' toys. Antwerp was the recipient of several hundred V-1 bombs and V-2 rockets, and

British Army squads have been·scouring the place, removing every little piece of the bloody things they can find and loading this junk onto barges. This scrap (which is all it is) is then being towed out into the Channel and dumped. On top of all that, we are now "implementing" something called Operation Eclipse. On the face of it, this seems to be a program for disarming the German forces. In fact, it is a subterfuge for ensuring that all German weaponry not in possession of the Russians is collected and concentrated in dumps solely controlled by the U.S. and the Brits.

Michels believes this is all part of a concerted plan to keep the U.S. and Britain predominant amongst the non-commie countries and so deny the rest any power of decision in what, he says, is the build-up to the nearest thing to Armageddon we can imagine, and which he believes (passionately) is on its way. He also says that the Yanks and Brits deliberately intend to keep modern arms' production in their own hands because there is so much dough in it. Would *you* believe that?

So what's to be done? Michels has some definite ideas. He says he won't stand by and see his nation turned into an auxiliary for either of two warring giants. He believes the small nations, such as Holland, must have their *own* arsenals, and *modern* ones. He envisages those smaller nations that haven't become totally dependent on the big boys maybe uniting to form some sort of buffer block between the two Goliaths. He knows as well as I do that German weaponry is infinitely superior to that of the Allies in quality though not, alas for Adolf, in quantity. And he intends that Holland will benefit thereby.

The upshot of all this is that I have returned to being a Tech IO and am again busy as a little beaver collecting Jerry stuff, especially his newest and bestest. Only – and here's the twist – instead of sending it back through "channels," I bring it to a Dutch Army barracks recently abandoned by Jerry at Ouderkerk, not far outside Amsterdam, and now in the hands of the NBS. This is my unofficial base. The underground supplies my every want, technicians, labour, guards, warehouses, even vehicles. And I, in turn, collect *two* of everything that looks interesting . . . and Michels gets one of each.

Officially, I'm still on detached duty under the command of G-Int at 1 Corps HQ in Hilversum, but they only see me when I need some-thing I can't get from the NBS, such as a Mack breakdown truck and 60-cwt lorries – both needed to transport my "finds." Three young lieutenants, just arrived from Canada via London, and stuck in the Int pool, have attached themselves to me and, since nobody at Corps seems to want them, I'm putting them to work on my scheme.

One thing. I ask you to be circumspect in talking about my activ-ities. As you will deduce, it might be taken amiss if it came to the atten-tion of the wrong people.

Whether what I'm doing is good for anybody else is a moot point. I know it is good for me. My eye shineth, and I am filled with piss and vinegar again.

As to coming home. Getting demobbed ain't going to be that easy. A guy with four years in Ottawa piloting a desk, followed by six months in London with the Piccadilly Commandos, will get home before a Joe with three years overseas, two of them spent fighting the Hun. And the 20% point bonus for married men makes it just about impossible for a single character with less than four years overseas even to get as far as England. Well, to hell with that, too. Being in limbo of the kind I've got here for a few months may not be such a bad idea after all.

Will try and write more often, but it appears that everybody's letters now hang around at Base somewhere until there's enough of them to activate the forwarding machine. You surely don't expect the army to get efficient now that it hasn't even got a war to fight.

[Ouderkerk]

June 15

In future you will kindly address me with all due deference as Officer Commanding, First Canadian War Museum Collection Team. A sonorous title, ain't it? Ought to be – I concocted it myself.

How it came to pass is quite a little story. Last week I got back to my NBS base with a load of German naval radios and found a flustered Lt. Mike Donovan (who has become my right-hand man) in receipt of an order from G Int Army instructing him to report with his cohorts, Lts. Jimmy Hood and "Butch" Schoone, to Canadian Army

HQ for re-assignment to the Army of Occupation *and* an order for me to sink back into the Int pool (known unofficially as the cess pool), there to await "other employment."

Panic. Doc suggested we just all cut loose and head for Italy, but wiser heads prevailed. I hastened up to Army and there had a number of conversations with various bods, telling them what I thought they ought to know and finding some sympathetic ears who agreed with the thesis about the future I described in my last letter. The problem was how to "implement such a program." The solution came to me in a brainwave engendered by the morbid horror of having to spend the rest of a fine summer frittering away my hours at some deathly tedious paper job.

I convinced some of those who have the ears of the Powers that I could contribute to the preservation of the memory of the quick and the dead of this war in a concrete way by assembling a collection of the most fearsome weapons in Jerry's armoury. When put on display in Canada, I explained, these monstrosities would engender such a feeling of pride in our brave fighting lads who had had to face these awesome things as would endure for generations, and would also help keep the peacetime army in the public eye and in good with the public treasury.

Please do not burst into hysterics. As I learned from Cottam, you can sell anything to the army if it is fantastic enough. This was. The army bought it. Cottam will be proud of me.

Ergo. Donovan, Hood, Schoone and I have been placed under command of Lt. Col. Harrison, boss of the Historical Section, 1 Cdn Army. He is a good guy and is in accord with our purpose. He has also made it clear that the less he hears from us or about us, the better pleased he will be. "I'm sure you know your job better than I do," he told me very pleasantly. "If you need anything, just let us know." Good guy? This is a *great* guy!

We have taken over a house that once housed the commandant of the Ouderkerk barracks and have made ourselves comfortable for the "duration." Spiffy furniture is courtesy of several collaborators who don't need it any more. The NBS has supplied a first-rate cook, several general-purpose bodies, an honest-to-God Underwood typewriter (the Mayor is close to collapse), three cars (including an Opal sports model) and a liaison officer who knows everybody and can find anything in the Nederlands. Equipped with letters of authorization from Col. Harrison, I can requisition most of what I need from army sources, including transport, rations and bodies, as required. I am also authorized to travel *anywhere*, enter any and all German installations in First Army's zone, and remove whatever I, in my wisdom, deem essential to the War Museum collection. Up until recently I had largely restricted my nefarious activities to Holland, but now the world is my oyster.

And we have been busy, busy, busy! Already we have about two hundred tons of loot (pardon me, *exhibits*), including such items as an eight-inch gun, several tanks and self-propelled guns, masses of radio equipment and no inconsiderable collection of shells, flares and other pyrotechnics with which I entertain myself in my off moments.

I estimate it will take at least three months to complete the collection and get it into shape for shipment home. Already we have a platoon of local labourers hammering and sawing away trying to crate the stuff.

So here I sit, captain of my own ship, eating and drinking (moderately) of the best, with *bon* (and occasionally *bonne*) companions, and enjoying myself. Tonight I go to a *soirée* at Tyce Michels' house in Amsterdam, celebrating the rebirth of the Dutch armed forces and Tyce's appointment as Director General of Ordnance. Ought to be interesting. I think I'll drive the Opal.

[Ouderkerk]

June 23

Well, my collection now totals some three hundred tons and includes some fascinating new items, amongst which is a one-man submarine, a radio-controlled, high-speed motor boat intended to carry a ton of explosives and to be guided from an aircraft against Allied shipping, a Mk.V Panther tank in perfect running order, a factory-fresh rocket engine from an ME 303 (the only such fighter to see action in the late unlamented war), an almost complete set of German artillery pieces, all in working order, ranging from 2 cm aircraft cannon to a 21 cm gun/howitzer and including a whack of anti-tank and anti-aircraft guns and, of course, our old pal, the eighty-eight, together with a bunch of experimental guns from the Jerry test range at Meppen, including smooth-bore, rocket-assisted types . . . and . . . or have you heard enough? Let it suffice to say that almost every portable object of interest owned by the Wehrmacht, Luftwaffe and the Kriegsmarine* is probably represented in our collection. Almost everything. There are some salient items yet to be procured and we are working on that.

What do we do with all this stuff? Using NBS technicians and German specialists illegally sprung from POW camps by the aforesaid mad Irishman, Mike Donovan, who sprechens ze Deutsch, we put everything back into operational order. And on occasion we test the things to make sure they work.

This has led to some incidents. I personally tested the self-destruct motor boat (sans explosives) on the Amstel Canal. Donovan raced me on the highway running alongside the canal, and says I got the boat up to fifty m.p.h. It felt like 150. And she wouldn't answer her helm worth a damn with the result that, on suddenly meeting a pair of Dutch barges (and doubtless scaring the bejesus out of them), I got heavily involved with one of the dykes. We used our Mack breakdown lorry to haul the resultant debris out of the canal, and then Jimmy Hood had to go to Den Helder to "acquire" a replacement boat. *C'est la vie.*

More details? Very well. Had my House papered the other day and all repainted, and yesterday spent thirty guilders on new chintz curtains. The water runneth hot and my cook has finally learned how to make proper oatmeal porridge. In a word, I am become a proud house husband and the pappy of this establishment over which I preside. My "children," alas, are sometimes a bit unruly. But young subalterns at all times have always been so and who am I to discourage their youthful exuberance? Sometimes, however, they do get a little out of hand. During a recent party here, Donovan fired a German signal flare through the roof of our porch, thereby igniting a spirited little blaze

---

* Army, Air Force and Navy.

which Doc and the NBS men just managed to extinguish. Hood, not to be outdone, then began firing parachute flares from a 12 cm naval mortar which brilliantly illuminated the skies over Amsterdam, somewhat to the consternation of the citizens therein who had thought the war was over. I understand that a court of inquiry is investigating but so far we have escaped suspicion.

Still more? A couple of days ago, Donovan and I went to examine the contents of a pre-war, underground Dutch fort which the Germans had converted into a storage dump for ammo. It was full of deep, concrete galleries which, in turn, were full of enormous amounts of crated munitions. We prowled about with flashlights for a time but made a hasty exit when we discovered that what we thought was slime on the floor was really the exudate from a couple of thousand cardboard boxes stacked along the walls. In idle curiosity, Mike read the labels and so we discovered that they were full of dynamite, and we were wading in liquid nitroglycerin which had "bled" out of them. No ballet dancer ever trod as lightly as did we two on our retreat. How the Dutch will ever clean *that* one up I cannot begin to guess!

Oh, so now you've had enough details.

Don't you want to hear about the liberation celebrations in a nearby village which we were invited to attend? I accepted on behalf of the First Canadian War Museum Collection Team, and my jolly juniors thought we ought to contribute to the fun. This we did by dressing a dozen of us in German uniforms and rattling into town in one of our prize pieces, a huge armoured personnel carrier still sporting the insignia of an SS Division, including a large swastika. To add verisimilitude, my happy lads had equipped themselves with a lot of German signal grenades. You tap their bottoms sharply on some hard object, throw them away, and they make a lovely bang and flare without doing any real damage. So the boys tapped them on the back of the carrier and tossed them out behind us on the road through the village.

Alas. The road was paved with wooden blocks liberally soaked in tar . . . No, I suspected you mightn't want to hear all the details of that one.

I hate to tell you, Pop, but the Regiment has effectively ceased to be. It is now no more than a holding unit into which soldiers from all over the army who originally came from the counties are being funnelled for repatriation. All the old sweats have mostly gone to the new units destined for the Pacific. And the young reinforcements of the last months of the war here are so damn young they think a Moaning Minnie (of which we have a complete series in our collection) is either an air raid siren or a worn-out hooker.

Well, Mum, I am eating my greens, drinking my milk (comes from a cow next door), staying clear of bad women* and not drinking much. And where is it getting me? Dysentery. Insomnia. Boredom verging on insanity. So I guess I'll just have to go back to a diet of canned stew, Dutch gin and Jezebels.

[Ouderkerk]

June 24

Your self-reliant offspring who usually scorns advice is in need of some of same.

I am getting scared.

It is now the second month since the war ended, taking with it my excuse for carting around an empty skull. It is time that I snapped out of it. But I can't seem to "snap."

With considerable effort I've established myself in a physical and psychic spot where there should be no obstacles to mental rehabilitation. Yet, damn me, I can't rehabilitate.

I sit down to write. I believe I *can* write. A paragraph or so of reasonably good descriptive material comes out without much trouble. I stare at it. But no more comes. No *story* comes. In fury I rip the paper up and go down to one of our workshops and spend the rest of the afternoon, or evening, stripping down some piece of German military wizardry to see what makes it work. I'd rather dice with a deadly device that might blow up in my face than stare at the hateful machine upon which I cannot write.

But the writing block is not the worst. The worst is that I am

---

* Damned right I was!

turning more and more to total immersion in purely mechanical activities. This seems to be becoming all that I can will myself to do. Now what in the hell does that mean? There is no real satisfaction in it – just a means to pass the time away. Although I suppose it is better than passing time with the bottle, it still leads nowhere. I have to flog my interest even to keep this war museum caper going and perhaps *delude* myself that I am doing something worthwhile. And it all boils down to this: the only certainty I have is that I *can still find ways to pass the time*. A conclusion that cheers me up no end.

Where, for Chrissake, is the *purpose*?

So I ask you, Pop, how did you get into the swing of living once again?

So much for this *cri de cœur*. If I don't cool down I'm going to have liver troubles in my old age. If there is an old age.

[Richmond Hill]

July 3

Dearest Plutocrat.

What *is* all this? A cook, servants, a batman, etc etc to wait on one little man? Well, all you'll get here at home is a mother and a pa. Why I even do my own washing these days, and Angus does all the gardening. Can't get help even if you can afford it.

You are a sinful so-and-so, buying curtains for a house you'll only be in for a few weeks. Bring them home with you for your room here; we can't get any decent materials. And bring some tulip bulbs. So many lads have been arriving home that I can't help hope you'll be with us soon, unless you are getting too much attached to Holland or someone there perhaps?

We've been holding off Angus's holidays until you come, so the ship hasn't seen much of us but we'll go to her at Toronto Island this weekend and make the cabin liveable at least. Although if we take our eyes off the peas and the berries here, the d____ grackles get them. Angus looked all over for some shells for your .22 today, wanting to shoot the nauseous birds but I told him you wouldn't like that, and anyway he couldn't find the shells.

July 4

Dear Bothered and Bewildered. –

I failed to write last week as we were scurrying through Manitoulin Island and points north. On our return there were letters from you describing your ménage and your yip of 24 June about what to do about it all.

I have two thoughts to offer. The first for your comfort and the second for your enlightenment. The one is that you are several jumps ahead of where your old man was twenty-five years ago, because you do realize the trouble, and I didn't. I was just miserable and "lazy" and headed for life in the back alley without the vaguest notion of what was wrong. If I had had the wit to see that, I should have pulled myself out of it a lot sooner. It's a bad sickness. But at least you have diagnosed it, and the fact that you are worried is a most encouraging sign. To be frank, I was preparing myself to go into all this with you on your return. I didn't expect it to happen so soon. But it has. So, good.

Then, for your enlightenment, you've got an inherited characteristic which is going to make it harder for you, and which you will probably never overcome. Not that you ought to. You are sporadic. So's your old man. So was *my* old man. I have never worked steadily, ploddingly at anything in my life and neither will you. We push our efforts at great speed for a time, really concentrating, then we've simply got to drop it for another time and do something else. That may be reprehensible in the eyes of some but it is the way I am, and I've seen it in you, son, so many times I have come to take it for granted.

I hardly think you'd like to settle down and throw yourself with enthusiasm into the business of selling life insurance, for instance. Certainly not. You can't go about half-listening to birds in the woods, or half-dreaming as you dig an acre of spuds, or half-nothing as you splice a lot of rope, or doing other unnecessary things – not and sell insurance.

Now I know I am absolutely right in all the above, so starting from that basis, we have to figure out where you go from here. First, you can't go anywhere until you are out of the army, and out of it long enough to get quit of *that particular* soporific influence. You have to get *cured* of the army, and I use the word advisedly. Like both your parents, you are particularly sensitive to atmosphere and, like them, you absorb and hatch ideas rather than think them out the hard way. Whether you can write now or can't write now, whether you want to write now or want to potter about with bombs, these things don't matter a hoot. There's got to be a transition period of rest and cure.

The second step I am most positive about. Perhaps I oughtn't to mention it until you are cured of the army, but I will anyhow and you can put it out of mind till later if you want to. This is the matter of the new discipline which will have to supplant the army discipline. Face it. Not even people of our temperament can do without discipline. We may even need it more than most. And we've got to impose it on ourselves if we aren't going to spend all our lives digging blindly in the soil, or quite aimlessly whistling in the dark woods. That's what your trouble is right now. You are abandoning the army discipline, and you've never had any other kind inside yourself because when you enlisted you were still too young to have need of it. Also, you still had parental discipline, such as that was.

I am speaking very earnestly from my own experience when I say that the best way I know to encourage and develop this state is through a few years at university. Now don't howl! Forget about it if you want to but I am going to be insistent when the time comes. Speaking from experience? And how! Would I go back to college in 1918? Would I, hell! I used to become profanely contemptuous at the very thought. My mistake, brother. If it hadn't been for the influence of your mother (and the insults of *my* mother), I should never have made the first, tentative steps in that direction.

But it was the best thing I ever did for my mind. Mental discipline made easy. Directed reading. The discipline lay in the direction and in the assignments that came out of it. That's the outside discipline. But the inside discipline, the solid strata upon which I have lived my very happy life ever since, was the reading itself. The exposure of my little mind to the whole mind of the race and all its experiences.

That's the answer, son, for the man of temperament who wants to live fully – not just make a living – and, most emphatically, it is the answer for the man who finds life interesting enough so that he feels the need to write about it himself. Which you have the gift to do, and which I firmly believe you will do, never mind your present illness.

Against my insistence in this matter you will say, as I said, that it's too late, and that you've lost enough time as it is. You will point out that many of your peers have already settled down to sell life insurance while those who thoughtfully stayed home from the war and went to college instead have already graduated. O.K. They'll all be four or five years ahead of you. So what? Everything you were born to do can't be done at its best till maturity, anyway.

You've got everything in hand for the living of a very full (and probably impecunious) life, feller – except the two things I've been talking about. Civilian discipline, and sufficient of the background of your race, or tribe, or species, or whatever you choose to call it. Three or four years of college should suffice to meet this lack whether or not you bother to get a degree. And the new rehabilitation scheme of free tuition and a monthly stipend for veterans attending university announced in Parliament now makes all this possible, which was not the case for my generation.

I trust you won't be hurt but the truth is that you are not one of the ones I am really worried about, although I do ache for you. And I am so deeply gratified that you should write to me as you did.

[Toronto]

July 9

Saturday night I went around and called on the Lawries. Your former feathered friends Doug Millar and Al Helmsley were there visiting Andy, who was home on leave. He gave me two beer bottles full of navy rum, one of which has gone into the squirrel store in the attic and the other into me. Great stuff! Has to be cut four times before you even dare moisten your lips with it.

Al has been home and out of the air force for some time, which is why you couldn't find him in Blighty. He is going to college. Doug, also out of the RCAF, is, at the age of twenty-eight, taking his Senior

Matric so that he can do likewise. Andy will complete his biology degree when he gets out, which will be soon. They all have one message for you. "Tell the little s.o.b. to get out quick, and get back to school. Without a degree, he won't get a job even piling cans of peas in a grocery store."

I looked up your record and find you need several subjects if you are to qualify for university, so why not take steps to clean up your Senior Matric, or at least get a start on it? You'll have to do it sooner or later, both for your material prospects and for your soul.

[Toronto]

July 12

I am to advise you that you are now a contributor to *Saturday Night*. When *Maclean's* admitted that "In Amsterdam There Lived a Man," "Last Days of Bremen" and "Dear Diary" were too good for it, I promptly sent them off to *Sat. Night*, and got only one back. And a personal letter from the editor, B. K. Sandwell, who (as you probably did not know) is one of the literary figures in this country, in which he says: "Your son in Holland certainly wields an extremely dexterous pen. I am delighted to have the two sketches, one about the distillery and the other about Amsterdam. I am returning herewith 'Dear Diary' which is not so effective."

And scribbled in his own handwriting: "They are really awfully good stuff."

So Pop's chirping like the veritable herd of robins and grackles that have descended on the cherry tree and stripped it. I mean to say that, while you are still not a Conrad, or a Hardy, or a Steinbeck, nor even an Alexander Woollcott (although I fear you have some of his personal qualities), there is hope that all may not be lost. And I gather to my breast with even greater assurance the main dream of my life, which is that my son will one day write *the* book (and get $500 for it probably), which I think I shall never accomplish. Not, mind you, that I don't write good books – but not *the* one.

What a pity that you have no academic education. Wot a pity!

[Richmond Hill]

July 17

Bunje Darling.

Angus is at the Island painting the decks of *Scotch Bonnet* and I have been enjoying a perfect summer day stretched out in a deck chair under the apple tree gazing admiringly at A's potatoes, which have grown to look like young trees. Picked a dish of raspberries, too, and were they good!

Myrtle Endean and Mrs. Boyle came over for tea, asking me, as usual, when you were coming home – and wouldn't I like to know!

Isn't it wonderful, *Saturday Night* taking those letters of yours. We can hardly wait to see them in print. What clever men I have. And do you know, I have never seen Angus happier. The war being over, and you coming through it, and this comfy house. And now he really loves gardening.

Don't forget to bring home the curtains.

[Ouderkerk]

July 5

Dear Parents:

Your letters have become more and more irregular, but then I don't feel much like thinking home thoughts anyway these days. It is hard to even hear the name Canada without getting into a boil about the royal screwing the boys of the Grand Army are getting. I presume you've heard about the riots of Canadian troops at the holding units in England? Zombies, my friends, Zombies. The way I hate those bastards shouldn't be permitted. I've got a guy with me here who has two wound stripes, two hundred demob points and eyes that haunt you, and I can't get him accepted for shipment home. But he and his kind aren't rioting. Effing Zombies! Effing country that lets the slackers, the profiteers, the gutless wonders run the show. Imagine expecting the long-service fighting men to go out to the Pacific and fight another war . . . while those bastards riot in Aldershot for quicker passage home to Canada!

Speaking of things that make one mad, did I ever send you the song we composed after the Lamone débâcle in honour of our illustrious brigadier? I can only remember a couple of verses. You sing it to the tune of "Lili Marlene":

We shall debauch into the valley of the Po,
We'll storm across the winter mud and crush the cringing foe,
We'll deal the Hun a mighty blow.
How do we know?
The Brig says so.
 So onward to Bologno,
 Fight onward to the Po.

The Brigadier's desirous to gain a higher rank;
He'll send us o'er the Senio and up the other bank.
And for support he's got one tank
And his ambitions on each flank,
And passports to Bologno,
Safe conducts to the Po.

Them was the days . . . for which I thank my maker that they ain't no more . . . not just right now at any rate. But as you may even have begun to suspect, preparations for the next war are getting along nicely. I have come to agree more and more with friend Tyce Michels and am continuing to do my bit along those lines.

Stop worrying about my return. I'm alive and well, which is more than Alex Campbell and a lot of others can say. Don't delay your holidays. Unless I can arrange to come back riding herd on this collection of mine with some kind of priority, my number on the demob lottery won't come up for several months.

I'm not doing any writing, little thinking and less talking. But I'm happy enough, and I think I shall be able to rehabilitate satisfactorily when I have to – which is not yet.

[Ouderkerk]

July 15

This has been a busy time. During which 1 CWMCT has acquired some fascinating things and has, I fear me, cut something of a swath through various parts of Germany. The account that follows is for your eyes only and is, *on no account*, to be offered to the press. Otherwise your chances of seeing me again before I become an old man will be greatly diminished.

To begin with, Col. Harrison came to see us about ten days ago and we entertained him royally. He was stunned when he saw the size and scope of our collection. His first reaction made grim listening.

"Good God, Mowat! This goes far beyond anything that could be justified as a collection of trophies for the National War Museum! They couldn't begin to even house it! Unless we can come up with something, you are going to have to select about a tenth of it for shipment home, and dump the rest."

Dump the rest? Before the gnashing of teeth, tearing of hair and wild wailing could get out of control, he added: "But let's put our heads together, shall we? And see what can be done."

What we decided to do was raise the ante. When in doubt, go on the offensive. Go for broke. We decided that, far from shrinking our collection, we would make it grow into such a massive situation-in-being that nobody would doubt it had to be of the utmost importance, undoubtedly authorized by the Highest Authority and so not to be trifled with by lesser souls. What the hell, we had nothing to lose by giving it a try. Only the colonel really stood to get clobbered if it all went wrong, and he is not really a military man at all, being a professor of History from your old alma mater, Queen's University. He actually suggested, with a shadow of a smile, that a court-martial might even be a memorable way to bring his temporary military career to its conclusion.

I was instructed to prepare a Bullshit Baffles Brains Brief for Harrison to use as ammo. Thereafter it was "action stations" for my lusty crew. In short order, all of us fanned out on swanning expeditions all over Germany, and not just the sections occupied by the Brits. I did two trips into the Yank occupation zone and one into the Russian zone. The first two were routine (I was after optical stuff, and the Yanks gave me no trouble), but the Russkies were a different matter.

Doc and I went in Lulu Belle. My objective was a small factory that, according to our intelligence, had made the control apparatus for a heat-seeking experimental anti-aircraft rocket the Jerries called "Rhineland," whose spoor I had come across in Amsterdam. But the factory lay in Russian territory several miles the other side of the Elbe River. What to do? Why, bluff, of course.

It almost worked, or should I say it did work but not the way I'd hoped. The bridge over the Elbe we had to use was a pontoon affair built by the Yanks, who manned the checkpoint on our side. They were somewhat hesitant about letting us cross but the fist-full of authorizations I showed them (some of which were actually authentic) finally cleared the way.

Anyhoo, we crossed, very cautiously, and were stopped by a clutch of business-like Red Army guards and escorted to a guard post, thence to another one, and finally to what I think was a regimental HQ. Here a youngish officer who spoke fair English listened to my attempt to bluff our way to the factory in question and burst out laughing. He laughed and laughed, stopping only to share the joke with a growing audience of mostly bearded types, who also grew hysterical. When Doc whispered tensely, "What's up, boss?" I could only reply, "I don't think they buy it."

No more they did. When they got their breath back, out came the vodka, and in came a whole passel of officers, probably from every nearby unit, to join in the fun. Whatever they thought we had really been up to, they evidently didn't hold it against us. Instead of being shot or sent to Siberia, they made us the centre-pieces of a party the like of which I cannot recall. The toasts we drank! I remember toasts to Churchill, Stalin, Truman, mothers, wives, girlfriends and every damned army on the Allied side. I *think* I can. Oh hell, the truth is that I don't remember a damn thing until late next morning when I was awakened by a kindly U.S. sergeant proffering a cup of coffee as I lay in a bunk in the U.S. guard post.

"Goddamn!" he said respectfully when I came to. "Musta been quite a party you guys had with Ivan! Dead to the world when they drove your jeep back. They left a message for you."

He gave me an envelope, which I opened somewhat shakily. The folded paper inside said simply. "You good fellow. Come again!"

Well, I don't know about that.

The other lads have had better luck on their recent sallies into Hun-land. Butch Schoone, who is a German-speaking Dutch Canadian, and Jimmy Hood tracked down an underground factory (in an old salt mine) near Würzburg where V-1 "buzz-bombs" had been manufactured. The entrance was barred up tight and guarded by a detail of snotty Yankee troops who wouldn't even let the boys go inside for a look-see. So Schoone and Hood adjourned to the nearest Jerry village and here is where the luck comes in. They encountered a character who had worked in the factory and who claimed to be anxious to be of service to Canadians because his uncle had homesteaded in Manitoba. Furthermore, he knew about an emergency exit from the factory which was concealed in a storage shed half a mile from the main entrance.

Schoone and Hood are a bit vague about what followed. Suffice it for us to know that they arrived back at Ouderkerk the day after I got back from my Russian venture with not one but *two* V-1s. And, hear this, the second one was a *manned* model, equipped to enable a pilot to fly it on a suicide mission against Allied ships in the Channel. Real kamikaze stuff! It is the only such critter in existence, so far as we can tell, and is now our prize possession. Hood and Schoone have become quite insufferable, and Donovan is darkly swearing to cap their exploit. He won't say how, and I shudder to think.

I myself managed to recover a little lost prestige by a trip to a firing range near Meppen used by Krupp and others of that unsavoury ilk to test not only new guns but every imaginable kind of shell and projectile. I took on that junket because I couldn't interest any of my three subalterns, all of whom have well-developed antipathies to frigging about with high explosives. So Doc and I went off with four other ranks and a couple of 60-cwts.

The "experimental gun establishment" was awesome. It included a bunch of thick-walled concrete structures widely dispersed (in case one blew) over a thousand or so acres of "blasted heath" adjacent to a firing range which must occupy the biggest piece of empty land in all of crowded Germany. At least a hundred huge steel tubes were on the firing line, many mounted on railroad carriages. One utterly unbelievable monster was a 60 cm siege howitzer. I lusted for it, but we estimated it must have weighed a hundred tons. All this gargantuan hardware loomed like devilish sculpture by old Mars himself. *And not a human soul around.*

I tell you, it was spooky and my back hair crawled. When we went through the buildings, we found them mostly filled with shells, fuses and propellant charges, and I insisted that we take samples of everything. "Jeez, boss," said Doc. "What if I drop something?" "Well," I told him soothingly, "then you'll have the honour of having ignited the biggest bang of the war."

It was quite a haul. It will take us weeks to classify all the stuff and ready it for shipment home. But that wasn't what restored, at least partially, my deflated prestige with my peers. I also brought back, on a liberated German flatbed trailer towed behind a 60-cwt, the gun intended for the tank-to-end-all-tanks. We never saw the hull, but the turret was on the firing line, and the gun lay beside it in the mighty wooden cradle in which it had come from the Krupp works. The gun was 12 cm calibre! It would have fired a shell weighing upwards of one hundred pounds, capable of sinking a destroyer let alone blowing any Allied tank into pea-size bits. The turret was built on the same scale and, in fact, at first I thought it was a turret for a naval ship. No so. It was intended for the ultra-secret armoured weapon called, with heavy Germanic humour, the Mouse. We have since learned from captured documents that the Mouse weighed about ninety tons and was intended to be transported to the battlefield on railroad spur lines laid especially for it.

You think Hitler was out of his cotton-picking mind? I'd say that was a reasonable assumption. Meanwhile, I own the biggest goddamn tank gun in the world!

Cdn War Museum Dump
OUDERKERK, HOLLAND
10 July 1945

Lt Col Harrison
OC, 1 Cdn Hist Sec
HQ First Cdn Army

Progress Report
Cdn War Museum Collection

1.   As requested by you, the following is a report on the work of the officers and men employed in the collection of enemy equipment for the Cdn War Museum.

2.   The collection at this date is ranged under the following categories.

Tanks, etc.
14 tks and SP guns have been assembled. Included are a Royal Tiger, Panther, and the original range of tks from Mk II upward. Most of these equipments are "runners."

Transport
23 special purpose vehicles ranging from an amphibious Volkswagen to a 15-ton armoured half-track personnel carrier.

Arty
40 types of arty pieces from 21 cm to 2 cm, embracing airborne recoiless; "squeeze barrel A/Tk"; infantry guns; A/Tk guns up to 8.8; AA guns up to 12.8 cm; field guns; medium guns and heavy guns. All are in firing condition. *Railroad guns up to 32 cm are available but will demand some time to move.*

Small Arms
About 200 kinds of small arms ranging from pistols to 12 cm mortars and including not only German weapons but types of Russian, French, Dutch and Polish manufacture which were in use by the Germans.

Signals Equipment

Specimens of all types of wireless sets in working order. Special equipment such as the modulated light beam transmitter and receiver. Telephone, signal lamps and incidental equipment.

Gas, Anti-gas and Flame

Full range of respirators including horse and dog respirators, anti-gas equipment, five types of flame throwers including "fougasse" and trolley types.

Engineer Equipment

All types of demolition equipment up to and including remote control tankettes. Eleven types of mines. Booby-trap equipment and all types of igniters and switches.

Projectiles and Ammunition

Types from 5.5 mm to 40.5 cm. About 800 examples embracing rocket-assisted shells, sub-calibre skirted ammunition, air-burst mortar bombs and other fearsome curiosities.

Naval Equipment

The more portable types of navy stores including sea mines, a one-man submarine, torpedoes and various ships' weaponry.

Air Force Equipment

Flak equipment, some V weapons equipment (more is in the process of being run down), jet engines.

Optical and Other Instruments

Periscopes, telescopes, sights, control instruments, search lights and AA directors.

Rocket Equipment

Including the "Moaning Minnie" series. Six types of rocket projectors.

3. The equipment now on hand is being "torn down" then reassembled in working order and prepared for shipping. All small articles are being crated in preparation for a long voyage and rough handling. Big items are being prepared against corrosion and damage by a variety of methods.

4.   Future work towards the completion of the collection will largely be concerned with air force and naval stores, since the army side of the collection may now be considered complete to a fairly satisfactory degree. *It is hoped to obtain air-worthy specimens of important aircraft such as the ME109, the FW190, and specimens of V1 and V2.* Additional naval equipment such as one-man torpedoes are also being sought after, and it is fairly certain that they will be obtained.

5.   Throughout the collecting side of the job, it has been appreciated that the museum is not intended to be a "technician's paradise" so much as a place where civilians can see and appreciate the capabilities of the weapons which the enemy pitted against our troops at all stages of the war.

> [signed]
> (F M Mowat) Capt

[Ouderkerk]

July 22

The blitz continues.

Collected and transported by hook and by crook (lots of the latter) to the Ouderkerk Dump during the past two weeks:

1   Jagtiger tank, operational. Weight 63 tons.

4   Acoustic sea mines, each weighing 2 tons.

4   Acoustic, 24-inch torpedoes, heavy bastards!

1   V-2 rocket, 45-feet long, weighing 12 tons.

18   Truckloads of miscellany ranging from toothbrushes, Wehrmacht for the use of, to what Donovan calls a "large, unidentified, ticking object."

It is drawn to your attention that claims for damages from the towns of Zwolle, Enschede, Lingen, Apeldoorn, etc., are probably perfectly valid. They are the results of putting an infantry captain behind the steering bars of a Royal Tiger. But we did NOT repeat NOT cause the collapse of the Bailey bridge at Deventer . . . must have been termites.

I don't know if I should tell you about the V-2 but since I already have and censorship of letters has ceased, I might as well go for broke. But do keep it under your hats. Hmmm, might be hard to do!

The background is that things have really begun to tighten up, and there is a very tough order that nobody but *nobody* without special authorization from SHAEF is to so much as look sideways at a V weapon, especially the rocket kind, let alone lay a paw on one. They are totally *verboten*. Harrison's 2 i/c at Army sent me a special and slightly plaintive message to this effect, concluding with: "It will be much appreciated by the OC of this detachment if this instruction is rigorously adhered to."

Damn. The message came just a split second too late. Mike Donovan had made good on his Irish brag.

He didn't tell me what he intended until afterwards, on the principle that the less one's superiors know about your activities the better for all concerned. Quite right, too. But I suppose I *did* initiate the venture by remarking apropos of nothing at all at dinner one night that anyone who found a stray V-2 was certainly entitled to a leave in England.

Mike went off on recce one day last week. He was gone three days. Somewhere near Hamburg he "happened" on a railroad spur upon which were parked a number of flatcars each burdened with a V-2 rocket. He was not able to get close to them because they were being guarded by a section of London cockneys who would not let him pass. He did, however, spread his Irish around the guard post and left without apparently rousing any suspicions.

Further detailed recce from a distance with binoculars revealed that an access roadway ran alongside the rail spur and that the last V-2 in the train was partly concealed in a pine woods through which the trail meandered to join a secondary road not far beyond.

Mike returned to Ouderkerk where he told me nothing but instead held earnest confab with Jimmy Hood. Next day the two of them took off with our big Mack breakdown and sundry other equipment, including, so Doc told me with some dismay, "Jeez, boss, they took a whole thirty-litre demijohn of DeKuyper's gin!"

I reconstruct. They drove first to Bremerhaven. Here they liberated a one-man submarine trailer (we already had one but it was occupied). The Mack then towed this sixteen-wheel monster to a point in a forest a couple of miles from the V-2 train, where Jimmy concealed the rig and himself.

Donovan drove on in a jeep and presented himself again at the guard post. They already knew him and when he produced a quantity of gin and offered drinks all round, there was little hesitation. You can guess the rest. He got the guard corporal soused first, then the rest of the cockneys, pretending of course to get loaded himself. Just before dusk he excused himself to have a leak, went to his jeep and sent out a call on a little number 38 Set. Hood picked it up clear and loud and sprang into action. Revved right down, the Mack crawled along the access road until the trailer lay close alongside the chosen rocket. The guys then swarmed over it, let go the fastenings (quietly . . . quietly) and then? And then they *rolled* it off the flatcar and down a bunch of timber skids onto the trailer. Gently! . . . gently!

Meantime Donovan was leading a cockney choir in rousing renditions of such famed songs as "She's a *great* big, *black* bitch, twice the size of me . . ."

An appropriate choice, considering that the V-2 was painted an ominous black and she was, as Hood said later, "the very bitch to move onto the trailer."

But move her they did, and the Mack crawled cautiously away as night fell over a scene of revelry at the guard post. When he was sure all was clear, Mike disengaged himself, leaving the still well-filled demijohn with his Limey buddies. "Least I could do for the poor clueless buggers," he told me. "Gawd alone knows what'll happen to them when the truth leaks out."

Once on the main highway, the Mack opened up. Ahead of it sped Donovan in the jeep. At each of the several checkpoints along the way back to Holland, he wheeled in, brakes screeching, and shouted authoritatively at the men at the barrier: "*Bomb Disposal Squad!* Unexploded bomb coming through. Might go off anytime. *So open up!*"

The Mack never even had to slow down and, I believe, did not do so until in the small hours of the morning it turned into our parade ground at Ouderkerk. The lads parked the black monster under my window and went off to a well-earned rest.

When Doc brought me my tea in the morning, he shot up the window blind and . . . I can hear him yet . . .

"Holy shit, boss! They've gone and done it!"

I immediately had the beast pulled into one of our big storage hangars, well out of sight, and cogitated on my next move. I was pretty sure that all hell would soon break loose and by no means reassured by Hood's and Donovan's earnest protestations that nobody would ever connect the theft with us. And then I had what may well have been my most brilliant brainwave of all time.

All that day, and the next, half a dozen of my best men laboured inside the hangar, with the doors tight shut. When I went in to inspect the results, it was to find myself looking at what *seemed* to be a one-man submarine. A wooden conning tower stood amidships. The great rocket fins had been masked by a wooden extension terminating in a blunt (and pretty peculiar-looking) stern . . . and a wooden propeller! And the whole shebang had been painted blue! It was a mighty weird-looking vessel but I concluded that it would fool the army mind, ninety-nine times out of a hundred.

We are now waiting for the stuff to hit the fan. It already has in one sense, because Col. Michels is very mad at me. I didn't get *him* a V-2 and, even worse, won't let him have this one or even let his technical crew go over it. As a result, we are getting a big chill. But it is obvious that this is *the* weapon of mass destruction of the future, and it is an *offensive* weapon, not defensive. In a sense, the Brits and Yanks have it right: the fewer powers who have these monsters, the better for humanity.

But I don't intend to give ours back. And I figure it is time to shift our base of operations. We have become too well known, not to say notorious, in this vicinity, and various branches of the Canadian Army are beginning to look at us askance . . . especially the Provost Corps,* not to mention the adjutant general's boys and various quartermaster

---

* The military police.

blokes who may be having trouble explaining why they supplied us with such inexpensive little items as tank transporters and etc.

Ergo. We will move *out* of Canadian Army territory and out of Holland. Belgium, and 2nd British Army, will become our new hosts. Lucky them! The only person I've consulted is Harrison's 2 i/c. When I phoned him about it, he just sort of gulped and said, "Tell us about it when it's done."

As to me coming home. *I am going to bring this collection home* with me, and I have Harrison's blessing to do it, if we can arrange for shipping. A big "if" maybe, but if you've got enough nerve you can do anything in the current situation where the whole vast military organization is breaking down like a giant cheese rotting away. B.B.B. is more than ever our motto and by the Lord Harry, it sure works.

So don't push me to come home without it. I can't do that, if only because of the lads I've got. Not just Hood and Donovan but about twenty of the best bloody rascals in the world who call themselves Mowat's Private Army and will tackle any damn thing I think needs doing, or getting. If I asked them to get me a German battleship, they'd give it a try. We may be the only unit left that has *esprit de corps*, even if (and maybe because) our "corps" is one we invented for ourselves. What began as a racket to keep me in Amsterdam has become a major commitment, not just to the job but to the people involved. Can't leave the chappies now.

As to this propaganda about going back to college. Barkus is willing but in his own sweet time. And don't be ridiculous about your holidays. You both need time away from Garden, House, Novel and Libraries. Take *Scotch Bonnet* out. Have fun, and tell me about it. Why don't you ever give me any *details* of your daily lives?

[Toronto]

August 6

Dear Squibbie. –

It does seem to me, as an old sweat, that you must have retained more than an atom of your pristine innocence. You say in your last letter that you will stay where you are and bring your collection home

303

when shipping becomes available. What you might as well have said is "I *want to* stay and bring the collection home." Quite. Anybody would want to. But anybody not steeped in innocency would realize that little captains are not permitted to do that kind of thing. They would realize that your collection will eventually be brought home by a lieutenant colonel, or above. Preferably one who never got near a battle zone. All this is just a word of warning so that you will not be too disappointed when a staff colonel drives up to your door in a chauffeured car one of these fine days and says, "Run along now, boy."

I am now proposing to take my holidays in September and lock myself in my study and anguish over the new book, which won't march. I wonder if this goddamned war didn't take a lot out of your old man. I thought it was all good clean fun as far as I was concerned but now I wonder. I'm lazy. As lazy as I was after the last one. Not physically but mentally.

I kept the morning paper from your mum because it is full of the new atom bomb, which would make her upset and worried about what is going to happen in the next war. But here is some good news. Men returning from the recent war are not changed in any significant way by what they have experienced. The *Canadian Forum* says so. The *C.F.* went out on the street and looked at some of them and came back to its office and wrote that it is a lot of hooey about men being changed by war. They look like they always did, except for the odd missing leg, etc. And as the *C.F.* is the chief organ of Canada's intelligentsia, it must be so.

[Richmond Hill]

Aug 12

Dearest Lambkin.

We are having a nasty thunderstorm and Elmer and I are shivering and cowering, and it is making me think of you being shelled day and night in the not-too-distant past. I am cooking a chicken and baking a cake for a two-week library trip to Huron County. We are going to get a housekeeping cabin on the lake and hope for warm weather. Up to now we have had a very wet and cold summer and so haven't missed *Scotch Bonnet* at all.

We note that you are moving to Belgium and are in no hurry to come home, although we hear that the First Division is to come back at the end of August. Your life sounds interesting and withal comfortable, with all those servants. Such is not the case here where Mama and Poppa do all. Elmer never lifts a paw.

Your cousin Larry is back in a civilian job as are many of the lads, but maybe you'd rather stay in the army. Might be a good idea. It would give you time to write. How are the women folk in the various towns you visit? You don't mention them, which gives me pause.

[Oostmalle]

August 2

Mes Enfants:

The cockeyed-est move ever undertaken by a military unit since the days of Genghis Khan has just been completed. The Cdn War Mus Col Tm has now arrived in Belgium, in the village of Oostmalle to be exact. This is where the Shiny First was billeted when we first came to NW Europe. I remembered it as a cosy little place, close enough to Antwerp but not too close, and bossed by a civilian town major with whom I became friendly. Name of Bob Jespers. When the need to find a new roost came along, I hopped in Lulu and went to see said Jespers, and we worked out a deal. In return for certain considerations, Oostmalle will become home to us, and *only* to us. Any other units looking for billets here or in the near vicinity will be given the bum's rush, thus ensuring our privacy, which is now becoming increasingly vital to our peace of mind.

We had another visit from Col. Harrison the day before the move. He was a little grim. Did we, or did we not, have a V-2 on strength? All hell had broken loose at Army HQ as a result of a blast from SHAEF, and the search was on for some irresponsible Canadians who, presumably as a lark, had snatched a V-2 from the Brits. The Brits were not amused. Harrison, naturally, suspected the worst. But what a guy! Without committing myself verbally, I took him over to the hangar and let him look around. He stared at the "one-man sub" for quite a long time, then he turned and smiled at me a little crookedly. "Fine specimen of a submarine," he said. "Looks a bit odd but I suppose it's an experimental model." So nobody told any lies but we will keep a low profile for a while. I have dispatched Hood on leave to Paris and Donovan to London, just in case.

So now the V-sub and the rest of our seven hundred tons (yup, *seven* hundred) skulks in the wooded grounds of a big chateau on the outskirts of Oostmalle, surrounded by a high stone wall and guarded by my own lads, who aren't about to let any strangers in.

We made the move by presenting authorization apparently from 1 Cdn Army HQ to a transport company in Hilversum, which there-upon supplied us with fifty trucks. Another home-made authorization to one of 5th Div's armoured brigades netted us ten tank transporters, and still another got us three heavy wrecking trucks. This lot, with our own vehicles (including four 6 x 6 heavy gun tractors) and a lot of the German "runners," made up a pretty formidable convoy led by yours truly in a German staff car. Very official looking, commanding great respect from provosts and movement control officers along the route. (Have I told you that Donovan is one of the most accomplished forgers still at large?) But no harm done. None of the drivers, etc, or vehicles would otherwise have been doing anything useful. We put purpose in their lives. Although I'm pretty sure the OC of the transport company smelled a rat, he was happy to keep quiet about it. A case of cognac is not to be sneezed at.

What little resemblance this "unit" ever had to the standards laid down for the Canadian Forces has now vanished. In fact, it is difficult to tell the difference between our laddies and the Oostmalle civilians as they wander about the streets. They kind of blend in together, especially since each of our twenty stalwarts is billeted independently with an Oostmalle family. I just hope the Belgian husbands can handle the stress.

Harrison arranged that, "for Admin purposes," we be detached from Cdn Army and placed in dependence on 2nd British so, in effect, the Canadian Military Machine has lost us. We hope to keep it that way. Getting along with the Brits is easy. They ask no questions that can't be answered by a bottle or two of the right stuff.

Jespers has established us three officers in the Hotel De Kempen, a rambling old pub which now belongs solely to us, dining room, billiard room, bars (two of same) and lots of bedrooms, together with a suite suitable to a commanding officer. And the food! I hate to tell you this in your rationed misery, but I have already had to tell the hotel cook that filet mignon twice a day is a bit much. Officially we draw rations from the Brits, but in fact Jespers is our provider of gourmet provender, using ways and means.

The tentative plan now is to move part of our collection to England (for trans-shipment to Canada) some time late in August. It will probably be two to three months before all of it, and all of us, reach home waters. Since it is beyond belief that anybody but us could ever reassemble all our junk and get it into shape for exhibition or whatever, I expect the job to continue for some few months after we get home.

I am far from unhappy at that prospect. Being my own CO has given me a new and fresher outlook on the army. Not as a vocation, of course, but as an entertainment. I find that bamboozling duly constituted authority is the most satisfying sport I've ever engaged in.

I thought you might be entertained by the enclosed correspondence with my nominal superiors at Army HQ.

> 40-3-0/Int
> HQ First Cdn Army
> 12 Jul 45

Capt FM Mowat
1 Cdn War Museum
c/o Cdn Army Leave
Centre – AMSTERDAM

HQ 1 Cdn Corps
IO (Tech) Material

1   A considerable amount of IO (Tech) materials, and other Int files, etc., have just been received at this HQ. Incl are two small

drums, painted grey, about 10" in diameter, one 12" deep and the larger 24" deep. The driver understood they were "mines."

2   NO one at this HQ recognizes these containers or knows anything about them. As this is a particularly unhappy stage of the War at which to have accidents, please advise at once what disposal you recommend.

[signed]

(P E R Wright) Col

GS – Intelligence

Extension Main 22

/rb

Time of signature

1730 B hrs

Copy to: GS Int

        HQ 1 Cdn Corps   RSDS/POST/HAND

---

1 CDN FD HIST SEC (**CDN WAR MUSEUM**)

OOSTMALLE via No 7 BASE SUB AREA

ANTWERP BELGIUM

31 Jul 45

G (INT) (a)

Main HQ First Cdn Army

Ref your 40-3-0/Int dated 12 Jul 45.

1   The Int files which you refer to are presumed to include a certain amount of technical reference data. If this is so we would appreciate having it sent to us.

2   As to the "two small drums, painted grey etc" naturally we don't know what they are, and acting on the assumption that higher formations always know the answer we assume that you will deal with this matter to everyone's satisfaction.

3   I suggest that you get somebody you do not like to bury them.

4   I hope that this letter reaches you in time.

(F M Mowat) Capt
OC 1 Cdn War Museum
Collection Team

[Oostmalle]
Aug 7

The word is out that buccaneers in battledress are on the loose so collectors of German gear are currently being treated with downright suspicion, if not outright hostility. This being the case, we are keeping a low profile and sticking close to home for the moment. Not as bad as it might be since there is a Trappist monastery close by engaged in making a nectar-like brew of truly heavenly quality. It comes in three strengths: single, dopple and dopple dopple. Thank God Mike is a mick in good odour. He arranges things with the Trappists. We have also struck up a friendship with a U.S. military hospital not far away where Hood has endeared us to the nurses with his boogie-woogie skills at the piano. We find we like *them,* too!

There has been difficulty getting pay through for our lads because of the confused administrative trail we've left behind us. We also have "on strength" a number of civilians, four or five (self) attached Cdn soldiers whom I suspect (but do not want to know for sure) are AWL from their own units, and some ex-Wehrmacht technicians whom we can't very well put on the Cdn payroll. So, we have created our very own paymaster. A most trustworthy NCO is responsible for visiting Eclipse dumps *very* far afield in the Yank occupation zone, and liberating truck-loads of tires removed from junked German army vehicles which no longer serve any useful purpose. These tires are disposed of to the needy Belgians so that they can get *their* vehicles, trucks, tractors, etc. back in service. They pay the pre-war price, and the monies received are doled out as "pay and allowances" as required. Close watch is kept to ensure that there will be no personal aggrandizement.

Nobody, in blunter terms, in my outfit is going to get rich off the black market. This may make us seem somewhat puritanical considering the black market deals in which Canadian Army equipment and supplies are traded for jewellery, precious metals, art objects, women, even cars and boats, on a scale you would not believe. The higher the rank, of course, the greater the opportunities. I know of a major general who has arranged the shipment to Canada of not one, but *three* Mercedes-Benz limousines. I don't think they are destined for the War Museum.

We left Holland in good time. The climate there is becoming distinctly chilly. There have been several incidents where girls who consorted with Canadian soldiers have had *their* hair clipped off, and posters are appearing on the walls saying "Liberate Us From The Liberators." Butch Schoone warned us that this was coming. He used to say that at least half the Hollanders were pro-German right to the end. Anyhoo, not so in Belgium. Here we are treated neither as heroes nor as lice, but just good fellows.

This morning I heard humanity's obituary on the BBC. The atomic bomb has come. Not entirely a surprise to us prescient chappies in Intelligence. We've known for a long time that there was a Super Weapon in the wings, and it was just a question of luck who got to fire it first. With Jerry out of the picture, we assumed it would be the Yanks. The V-2 was clearly designed to deliver the atomic bomb. It only carries a one-ton warhead which, considering its weight, size and cost, makes it an ineffective weapon when filled only with chemical explosive. But fill the nose with atomic explosives, and you've got yourself the weapon to end all weapons. I can also tell you that the Hun had a rocket on the boards intended to carry a bomb a distance of four thousand miles or more. It is little wonder that Donovan and Hood's peccadillo raised such a ruckus in high places. The search for our V-2 and its kidnappers still goes on but a friendly source at Army tells me that it is now thought to have been stolen by the French, disguised in Canadian uniforms. Of course! *I* could have told them that.

But there are dark clouds in the offing. A rumour to the effect that our collection is to be broken up. The British seem to be behind this move, supported by Canadian brass. Col. Harrison, bless him, went to

London to see what's what. His 2 i/c has received the following message from CMHQ London which ought to delight Pop's heart if it doesn't give him apoplexy: "RESTRICTED. ref obtaining War Materials for Cdn War Museum. Procedures for meeting requirements for national and dominion museums is laid down in 21 Army Group 38871/G(SDO L) 63 L of 28 Jun – war material inc major items of captured war equipt may be exported out of the theatre only under authority GS HQ 21 Army Gp through channels specified in that order." Harrison's 2 i/c added: "On 19 Jul we sent a message to 21 A Gp asking for authority to cover your trips to Germany to which 21 A Gp replied: 'all items for war museums are being handled by Imperial Gen Staff, and Colonies must present their requests to IGS to be filled'."

"Colonies" by God! Maybe the Limeys will give us a couple of antique Mauser rifles if we sit up and beg!

I gather the big complaint from our own brass is that shipping is expensive and in short supply and also, why bring back German weapons when we could set up Canadian twenty-five-pounders, Sherman tanks, Bren carriers, etc etc in every little park or in front of every Legion branch across Canada as tributes to our heroic fighting men. The stupid farts can't seem to realize that looking into the muzzle of a Tiger tank will do more to bring home the reality of what the war was like for our guys than looking at fifty rusting Shermans all in a line. Of course we can't make a fuss about the other thing we have in mind. What can be learned from these engines of destruction isn't intended to go into the mouldy archives of forgotten wars – it is intended to help keep those same war archives from getting overcrowded in future times.

Maybe it *is* time to let some of the guys back home in on the game. How about briefing Howard Graham? I gather he is now on the councils of the mighty and could probaby swing some weight our way.

[Toronto]

Aug 27

Dear Son. –

Your parents and the much-travelled Elmer are home from two weeks in Huron County, and I have concluded to become a farmer, even if a very little one. After this war, as after the last but with far less cause, Poppa is inwardly much unsettled. He is properly fed up with a world that can't think of anything better to do than make money and invent atom bombs. So he is hoping to find solace, and time to think and regain his poise, in and near the soil and the steady people who work it. Somehow I've got to spend the last fifty years of my life being quiet. Working, of course, but on quiet things like bees and growing lima beans. Hell, whose problem of rehabilitation is this, yours or mine?

Now I fully appreciate your fears that the collection might be broken up. But think! It's all in the nature of things, and you might as well take it that way. All the things you have gathered up are now as obsolete as the crossbow. And even if they were not, what reason have you to suspect that anybody (old soldiers excepted) would be interested in them anyway? Did the population flock to see any collection of javelins after Thermopylae? Or longbows after Hastings? Or culverins after Drake's big scrap in the Channel? Not bloody likely! So you'd better get into line with history and forget about "Their Name Liveth For Evermore" and all that stuff. It doesn't. It liveth just as long as their parents remain alive, or until their wives take a new lot of mates. Bum business? Yep. But that's the way of it, and if you think back over the lessons of nature you've learned, you'll see that it is also the natural course.

[Richmond Hill]

Aug 28

Dearest Bunje.

Get a move on and come home, collection or no collection.

Your story about Bremen came out in *Saturday Night* last week, and I hope you'll soon get into your stride and continue to write as you certainly have the gift, doing it so easily. You were always a reasonable child so you must see it is time you gave up the flesh-pots of Belgium for the writer's proverbial life in a garret in Richmond Hill. Angus's scheme now is to buy four acres in the country and farm and keep bees. But I don't think he would really like to leave Hove To.

Any nice girls around? You don't mention them. Janet Ince is home and out of the air force. We haven't seen her yet but suppose she will be out to visit soon.

[Oostmalle]

Aug 20

Mes Enfants:

"Live, laugh, and be merry, for the age of the atomic bomb has come." My new plan for my future life is simplicity itself. I shall skedaddle to a point some five hundred or so miles north-west of Churchill in the middle of the Barren Grounds and start digging a hole. By the time the Third World War begins (and finishes, all in the space of a couple of heartbeats), I expect to be down deep enough to have some slight chance of emerging alive. But to what???? Oh, the hell with it.

So, still I sit in Belgium with enough German material to outfit a first-rate Wehrmacht division, I calculate – but it appears that nobody loves me and mine. The "authorities" in Ottawa have got cold feet and are now doing their damnedest to reduce the collection to a handful of sabres and flags "with historic connections." We, meaning mainly Harrison and his allies (few in number but apparently with some clout), are fighting them off but we could use some help. I wish you would contact the top brass at the Canadian National Exhibition* and let them know that the biggest and bestest military show in the world is in our possession and if they yell loud enough to Ottawa, demanding it as a loan exhibit, they will most likely be listened to. The Ottawa mandarins may smell money in the making, which has a powerful effect upon politicians. Don't mention the V weapons outright but you can sure and hell hint. Lay it on about everything else: suicide subs, Tiger tanks, glider bombs, flame throwers, monster guns, etc., etc. We either have 'em, or will have before we cross the briny. All this stuff works and we have a bunch of lads who can demonstrate each piece to perfection. You might also tip off the Canadian Legion. If it isn't too ossified, it might see merit in our collection as opposed to the kind of junk that was

---

* Held annually at Toronto.

brought back after your war was over and still defaces the public parks of the nation.

Anyhow, one way or another I'm going to see this thing through, and I'm not coming home without the collection if it takes me another year to swing it, or if I have to end up shipping it at my own expense. Do you, perchance, have any contacts in the research establishment? A discreet leak about the really advanced technologies we've got might do a lot of good. Things like infra-red sensing for weapons, new shell propellants and gun design and, not least, a whisper about long-range, large-capacity rockets, and jet engines. Just a whisper.

[Richmond Hill]

Sept 7

Darling Bunje.

Today Angus went to Oakville to work on *Scotch Bonnet*, while I enjoy the garden and have tea with poor Kay Hawley, who has just lost her husband this week. More people have died from heart recently. So many of our friends. Do you realize, I wonder, how old your parents are getting? I'll be fifty my next birthday, and Angus fifty-three, so you'd better come home soon or you'll find us on our crutches or in wheelchairs.

Sat. Night lies before me with your second story in it and I'd think you'd be thrilled about it. Angus is very disappointed that you don't seem to care, when he is so proud of your writing.

I hear Andy Lawrie is out, and back at school. So please come home soon. We are getting awfully lonely.

[Toronto]

Sept 10

My Dear Son. –

Your stories about the distillery and the Dutchmen look well in print but the telephone hasn't been kept hot with comments from friends or foes. There'll be a cheque a month hence.

I got an "assignment" from the *Picton Gazette* last week. A special welcome edition is to be printed for the arrival home of the Hasties on the twenty-eighth. They wanted me to do an "appreciation" of the regiment. I think it is one of the best short bits I've ever done. It begins with RSM Angus Duffy's famous soliloquy on our cap badge as an icon, develops the theme of regimental spirit, quotes from the war diary you wrote at the crossing of the Moro, and goes into the small matter of "Their Names Liveth For Evermore" and ends with the last verse of Alex Campbell's poem. A damned well-written and moving piece. Says Squib Mk. 1.

I do so wish you were coming home with all the rest.

[Oostmalle]

Sept 8

Dear Parents:

The war is supposed to be over, isn't it? A little while ago I was peacefully having my post-prandial snooze when a platoon of German paratroopers landed in the grounds of the nearby chateau where our collection rests, and the subsequent uproar almost sent me scuttling for the cellar. Well, no, it wasn't paratroopers after all. It was Doc and a couple of buddies armed with a tommy-gun, a Schmeisser and a bunch of concussion grenades . . . hunting peacocks in the park. I don't know what it is about Doc and peacocks, but the very sight of one of the raucous critters seems to send him around the bend. The incident nearly sent *me* around the bend, and I was set to come down on the culprits with both feet until our lady cook (with whom Doc seems to have an understanding) served us a roasted peacock that was so scrumptious it melted my iron determination to dispense discipline.

That was the beginning. Next evening there was a hell of a bang from Donovan's room. Hood and I rushed in to find Mike staring with profound surprise at a hole in his hand from which the blood was flowing copiously. No. Not paratroopers. He had shot himself while cleaning a Luger. And this is the guy who drags loaded V-2s back from Germany. We nipped him smartly to our friendly nearby U.S. hospital where the nurses cooed a lot, and he was equipped with a sling that makes him look every inch the wounded hero of a Hollywood epic.

In threes, you say? Right. And I was the third. I had become just a mite concerned about some of the explosive stores in our collection and concluded that some of the more sensitive stuff should be disposed of before we start for Canada. Good idea, eh? Well, we ended up driving a 30-cwt full of surplus HE in one form or another to an old Belgian Army weapons range about thirty miles from here. We carefully unloaded all the dicey stuff on the greensward – about a ton of it – then several of my lads dispersed to ensure that no curious cows or other civilians were around, while I laid a Jerry two-kilo demolition charge on top of the pile.

These charges are fitted with one of three igniter assemblies coloured respectively red, green and yellow. Green has a five-minute delay fuse. Yellow is two minutes, and red is one. The one I screwed into the charge had a green knob. When Hood signalled, by honking the truck horn, that all was clear, I pulled the little green knob, then sauntered nonchalantly off towards the audience which was waiting happily for the fireworks in a bunker a couple of hundred yards away.

I had got about a hundred feet when something took me by the seat of the pants, lifted me off the ground and turned me into a low-flying bird. Donovan said later that I looked like a grouse flushed out of the bracken, trying to escape the guns behind me. I felt that way. I *think* that's how I felt. It was some hours later, after most of a bottle of White Horse, that my hearing began to return and I could think at all. And then I thought some pretty gruesome thoughts about the Gerald who made that igniter set. A practical joker? Or, possibly, a would-be saboteur of the German war effort?

I was reading Maugham's *The Razor's Edge* the other night when I came across this passage: "The war was over, everyone was sick of it and anxious only to forget about it as quickly as possible." Of course, he was talking about the civilian population in the U.S.A. after your Great War ended. Doubtless the civilians in Canada today feel the same way. But I'm not sure about those who had to do the fighting. Do I *really* want to forget the war? The fear and the suffering, yes. But other aspects – the male world, the freedom from civilian conventions, the kind of friendships that can never come about in peacetime, the sense of absolute, unquestioning community, etc. I'm not sure. Maybe this whole war museum caper has something to do with an unwillingness to forget about it, an attempt to keep the best aspects of it alive and around me. I'll think about that.

And I'll think about it in connection with an event that took place yesterday. Also in the grounds of the chateau is a small cemetery. Eight wooden crosses in a row on one of the big lawns. They are the graves of seven Canadian infantrymen and one English tanker who died in the battle to take Antwerp. Yesterday morning a smartly turned-out Canadian Lieut. showed up at our door. He was from the Graves Registration Commission. He explained that his men were about to exhume the dead soldiers and transport their remains to one of the official war cemeteries. So could I please instruct my sentries to let his detail into the grounds.

We did better than that. Mike fell in every one of our guys and when the two trucks rolled out of the grounds with their cargo, we stood at attention and gave them a last salute. Maybe they are what the civilians really want to forget.

[Oostmalle]

Sept 19

Despite your oft-repeated pessimism re the future of our premier collection of used war goods, it is my pleasure to inform you that we seem to have won our battle and the museum should be coming home, in toto, before the next two months are out.

Donovan and I will accompany same, but my youngest and most amusing subaltern, Jimmy Hood, has too few points. We are moving heaven and high places to get the whole detachment sent home in a single clot so they can be available to put our show on the road. Without them, I fear that our fourteen *Panzerkampfwagens* and associated mechanical ferocities will never roll over the fair hills and dales of Canada. And I want them to roll! I intend that they *shall* roll! No inanimate lumps of rusting iron poised on pedestals if I can help it – but rumbling, snorting, banging reminders of what "A" Company of the Hasty Ps faced on the Senio.

You may note that we are no longer 1 Cdn War Mus Col Team. For a variety of reasons, it seemed that our new beginnings in Oostmalle should see us assume a new name, too. This was easily done. All it required was for Mike to make a trip to Brussels where he found a rubber-stamp firm capable of creating a couple of brand new stamps for us in the army mode. They read: 1 Cdn Tech Equipt Team, and it will be weeks or months before the various provost and military police companies in Europe get a line on who, what and, more important, *where* we are.

It turns out that Squib Mk I and Col. Harrison know each other. He is the W.E.C. Harrison who was editor of the *Queen's Quarterly* before the war and used to solicit articles on library work from Pop. Well met by moonlight! If he gets home before we do, he will give you the inside gen on what we've been up to.

I have just submitted an indent for shipping space to the Embarkation Staff Officer of Antwerp. Turns out we've now got just over nine hundred tons to go. At first the ESO's office pulled long faces and muttered about no space until the new year, but the ESO himself, a Limey Lt/Col, turns out to have a great enthusiasm for American nurses, protracted house parties and White Horse whisky, which the Brits cannot get but which, oddly enough, we can obtain in quantity. Ergo. I have a hunch we won't be lingering in Oostmalle too much longer.

That may be a good thing from the point of view of some of the (male) inhabitants. There have been problems but so far nobody has been shot. The *estaminet* owners love us. A few nights ago, I made a pub crawl of the five alcoholic establishments, and "crawl" it truly was. It was conducted sitting on top of a Jerry mini-tank about four feet long which looks as if it was designed as a child's war toy. In fact, it is a battery-driven remote-controlled crawler tractor intended to make its way across no man's land with its belly filled with HE to blow up enemy strong points. Don't know how well it worked in battle but it is a swell device for pub crawls. If you should fall off, you haven't far to fall. Best of all, you never have to dismount. It goes right through the doorways, clanks loudly across the tile floors and comes to a stop so that the driver is at elbow level to the bar. I figure I'll patent it when we get home. It ought to be a sensation in Toronto or New York.

As to your comments about nobody having much interest in relics of old-fashioned wars now that the atom is here, I agree in principle. But ours has surely been a war worth commemorating since it may well have been the last of its kind. Anyway, I've started this affair, and s'welp me, I'll finish it. It still seems likely that the responsibility for setting up and exhibiting the collection will fall on my shoulders. If so, it will keep me occupied for several months after our return doing something only I know anything about and, therefore, free from interference. May be as good a way of getting "rehabilitated" as any. And it wouldn't preclude me going on to the Ivy-Covered Halls, if I decided to do that.

1 CDN TECH EQUIPMT TEAM
1 CDN FD HIST SEC

12 Sep 45

OC
1 Cdn Corps Tpt Coy
RCASC

B.40720 L/Cpl Stoner, W.P.
Repat Draft

1   We are in receipt of a message dated 111000 from your unit, to the effect that the m/n soldier is to be returned to you immediately for repat.

2   On consulting our files we find the following excerpt on Camp Order, HQ CFN:

TOS 1 Cdn Fd Hist Sec from 1 Cdn Corps Tpt Coy RCASC wef 24 Aug 45.
(Auth – Cdn Sec 2 Ech message EA2/1535 d/ 191200B Aug.)
B-40720 L/Cpl Stoner, W.P.

3   It is understood by us on the basis of the above excerpt that L/Cpl Stoner is on strength 1 Cdn Fd Hist Sec with effect 24 Aug 45, and that he is no longer on strength of your unit.

4   The m/n soldier has signified his desire in writing to remain in this theatre of operation for an additional period of time, and he has requested that his name be deleted from the current repat draft.

5   In any case the m/n soldier is hospitalized with a contagious skin disease and will not be released by the hospital authorities for a considerable length of time.

(F M Mowat) Capt
1 Cdn Tech Equipt Team
1 Cdn Fd Hist Sec

FMM:EM

For your amusement, a typical piece of bumpf in the never-ending war between the bull-heads and the rest of us.

Stony is my best driver and a mechanical genius who is determined to come home with us. By the time his old outfit gets through trying to unravel this gibberish, Stony will be long gone – and so will we!

[Picton]

Oct 1

Dear Mark II. –

Well, it was a great day – and night. We ancients, and the stripling youths of the second battalion, and the wounded and those who had already returned from the first battalion showed up four hundred strong to welcome the Regiment home.

Unfortunately, the Regiment didn't get into Halifax in time to join the fun but will arrive on Wednesday, when we'll stage the second half of the celebrations. A few days' rest between acts will be no bad thing for some of us.

I hope you are right about bringing the collection home within a couple of months. But I don't think so. Neither does Howard Graham, who agrees with me that the army won't let you do that. And he should know, being only one step away from the chief of general staff. Helen and I half wept and half howled at your description of "my youngest and most amusing subaltern," remembering the day before yesterday when Col. Bryson Donnan used to refer to you in those very words. Oh, gosh, it is just too damn bad you are missing these returns and reunions . . .

[Oostmalle]

Sept 23

Dear Folks:

This letter may be premature but I'll take the chance.

What I think is, that after five months of floundering about, the currents have at last carried me far enough inshore so that I can touch bottom and still keep my head above water. I begin to feel *normal*, or at least as normal as I can ever hope to feel.

As an indication of the above, I've finished the first draft of a five-thousand-word short story – a story I've been thinking about for the past couple of years and simply couldn't write. I did it this time in just four days of totally concentrated work.

It isn't much good but that isn't the point. The point being that I did it at all, and that I can again focus my interest on something and keep it focused until the job is done. *C'est bon*, eh?

I may suffer a relapse from this current state of well-being, but it won't be permanent, as I was beginning to feel my lengthy period of mental and spiritual despondency was becoming. So I feel "Ver goot!" as Bob Jespers, our tame town mayor, is fond of saying.

Bob is a hell of a good chap, and long-suffering. Not long ago, he and I were out in Lulu Belle on a scrounging trip for eggs and I drove Lulu across a bridge that wasn't there. Literally wasn't. A canal had been spanned with a Bailey bridge after Jerry blew the original, and some-time recently the blasted engineers had come back and removed their Bailey. I hit the ramp at a sedate thirty m.p.h., and took off from the top. Lulu came down with her front paws *almost* at the other bank. As we

scrambled wetly to the shore, Bob grinned, waved at the blue sky overhead where Heaven is reputed to be and shouted: "Ver goot, tank *you!*"

And that is the way I feel today.

In a way I'm sorry I couldn't be with you to greet the Hasties on
homecoming day. But to be frank, Pop, I don't yearn for bands a-
tootling and crowds of ex-war workers chewing popcorn and cheering the returning heroes-for-a-day. To me that sort of thing is too
much like a funeral without the corpse. The corpse lies scattered all
over Italy and north-west Europe and some day, maybe, I'll write a
requiem for it – for the Regiment that was.

You know, I was getting much afraid that I had been wrong in
deciding to stay on over here. I knew how unfair it was to the pair of
you, and that consideration very nearly weakened my resolve and
made me chuck it. But now I know I done right. I'm so damned glad
I had my worst moments over here, where the sight and sounds of an
inebriated Capitano berserker arouse no excitement and little interest.
Even when he appears to be (and may have been) slightly insane. Lord,
a few of my worst days would have made the inmates of any well-reg-
ulated asylum seem almost normal. 'Nuff said. I know I don't need to
chew over all that old stuff with you two.

I now appear to be the sole surviving wearer of the Red Patch in
Europe. First Div is gone, and orders from on high insist that the few
remaining strays like myself take down the Patch. Eff them! Nobody is
going to *make* me take it down either, not as long as any of my mob is
within call. I actually conked a Limey major in a Brussels bar a little while
back when he publicly referred to the First Canadian Division as a "Division of criminals." Never found out why he thought so at the time, but
I can guess why he does now. Imagine *me* socking someone. Anyone.
Mightn't have done it if long and lanky Donovan hadn't been at my side.

[Toronto]

Oct 9

Dear Old Squib. –

The letter that came yesterday was the one I have been waiting for.
I knew you'd pull out of it some day but I have been unhappy about you

– and with you. I have been trying to put myself in your place, going back to 1917 when all I had to cling to that seemed to make any sense at all was my love for Helen. I have been trying to think what it would have meant if I hadn't got her. But you have no Helen, and that's hard lines. So my hard old heart leapt a bit when you wrote about the short story. It doesn't matter whether it's good or bad. As long as you are doing it, and know in your own mind that your very salvation depends on your power to force yourself to concentrate on the inside things.

All of which is clumsily expressed, since we have ever been in trouble about expressing what we feel to one another. You may remember what one of Richmond Hill's greatest writers had to say about "the remote distance which separates all human beings one from another – even son from father." But just you go on believing that we are not too dumb to understand and are always pulling for you.

So. After the colours had gone by and the salute was finished, Frankie Hammond croaked in my ear, "Why the hell doesn't somebody cheer?" And I croaked back, "Maybe they're like me. Maybe they're afraid to, for fear they'll cry."

And that's how the Regiment came home. I can't give you a catalogue of the friends of yours I hobnobbed with and had a drink with. George Baldwin came home as adjutant. Paul O'Gorman was with them, and Bill Seaton. Oh hell, I can't remember. Everybody was talking all at once and everybody hugging everybody else. And there were a lot of lumpy throats when Colonel Ross at last gave the "dismiss" order, and we all knew it was for the last time.

[Oostmalle]

Oct 2

Dear Folks:

A quickie letter because I am off to Paris tomorrow and will be gone about a week. Just to see the joint. On the way back, I plan to spend a couple of days in and around Ypres and Vimy. I can't recall the exact localities with which Pop became so abominably familiar, but I'll keep notes and write a screed about it later.

We are getting doused in propaganda about the Glory that is

Canada Today. The old Jelly Fish himself, Mack the King, is actually planning a visit to this theatre. Wonder where he gets his steely nerves. Doesn't he realize that there is still the odd Schu mine or Teller mine that hasn't been de-boloxed? I think he will be wise to avoid direct contact with any Canadian troops still here. He can't win. The volunteers hate him for a variety of excellent reasons, and the Zombies because he permitted some of them to be sent overseas.

The editor of the *Maple Leaf*,* our only source of truth, has just been fired for writing a piece in which he deplored the fact that Zombies are being returned to Canada on a high-priority basis ahead of troops who have been overseas and in action for years. Having been told by Gen. Simmonds, the current army commander, to retract, the editor (a captain) replied in effect: "You go to hell, you old bastard — what I print stands!"

It's a healthy sign. More and more *soldati* are taking less and less BS from the powers that be. Bluff and blunder from on high is seen now for what it is.

The short story has not marched any farther. Still, I don't worry. Let it rest for a few weeks, or months. Doc wants the Mayor to pack away in the jeep now, so gotta go. We'll be seeing you before too long.

[Oostmalle]

Oct 6

Methinks I spoke too soon. Didn't get away to Paris as planned because of the unexpected arrival of Col. Harrison. He was full of despondency about our future since it appears that nobody in Ottawa will give the necessary authorizations to get us on the move. Also, he wants to take his own people and himself to England but can't since he still has us on his hands. We settled *that* one quick. From now on, *I* am acting OC 1 Cdn Fld Hist Sec. The good colonel sure and hell is a risk-taker.

So Doc again began packing my gear for the French jaunt, and then I got a phone call from Army HQ. The gist of it is — now *wait* for it . . . the gist of it is that *the Department of National Defence has cabled*

---

* The official newspaper of the First Canadian Army.

full authority to move the collection to Canada, soonest, and authorized the
immediate return with it of Lt M Donovan and Capt FM Mowat.

My only worry now is about my men. Naturally I will not leave this theatre until they, too, are authorized to leave. This little matter is to be taken up by a Col. Stacey, who is flying from Canada to expedite matters.

It is indeed fantastic what *dedicated* bullshit can accomplish. Having recently addressed several of the most preposterous, unmilitary and even alarmist epistles to the highest of the high, I receive in response not a dressing-down for my presumption but a full colonel winging across the Atlantic to ease my path. Is the Lord on my side? Or do I detect the fine Italian hand of someone else? You *did* get to Howard Graham, didn't you? Even if you are not supposed to tell.

Another thing. One of my lads' friends has written from Canada with the following comment:

"We are told in the *Star* that your war collection will be on exhibit at the Canadian National Exhibition next fall, and it sounds like it sure should draw the crowds."

That wouldn't have been Howard. That had to be *you!*

[Hilversum]

Oct 9

This is being written by a disgruntled and grouchy Capitano at the end of a three-day purgatory at Army HQ. I came up here as OC 1 Cdn Hist Sec in order to "confer" with a bevy of Cols. and Brigs. re shipping arrangements and etc. But I am only a captain and it seems they were expecting a Lt. Col. So I have spent three days cooling my heels and "being available." By today I had had enough. I got paraded into the office of the Col. in charge of the conference and told him that they could contact me in Antwerp because that was where I was going. Right then. He didn't like it (surprise, surprise). He buffled and wuffled and attempted to come the old rank act but I was so bloody mad I didn't care. Besides . . . I had in my pocket the DND Defensor message, with which I can defy the old dodos in this theatre with impunity.

So back to Oostmalle tonight to my own cockeyed organization, a fancy meal and a decent sleep. Tomorrow I go to Brussels with Hood and a brace of nurses from the nearby U.S. hospital. I shall be squiring one Helen Miller, of whom I have already written. I *think* I did. I *should* have done. An excellent type, from Montana. She loves horses and Canadians, in that order, and has a great plot in mind for smuggling a Belgian horse aboard our ship when we depart. Why not? We can always claim it is a Prussian Cavalry Charger from World War One.

From here on it is just a matter of finding a suitable ship. My guess now is that I should come driving up Elizabeth Street to Hove To in a Panther tank by mid December.

By the by, a brig ticked me off in the mess here at Army last night for "failure to adhere to dress regulations." Can you imagine? I was wearing German jack boots (they are the most comfortable foot gear in the world), serge trousers, an 8th Army sweater with epaulets sewn onto it, my go-to-hell hat and a crimson scarf in lieu of a tie. I wasn't even *wearing* my silk cummerbund. I told the somewhat steamy brig. that my dress was officially approved for members of the Cdn Tech Equipt Team in order to facilitate liaison with our Russian opposite numbers. *And he swallowed that!* It's the only way to deal with the doughballs who think they run this world. Make mock of the poor silly buggers.

[Oostmalle]

Oct 18

Latest communiqué. Hot off the wires!

I've won the final disputed point with the powers that be over here. Today a message received from NDHQ authorizing the movement of all my men who have point scores over one hundred back to Canada SAP. Don't know if we'll all sail together, but this doesn't look so likely since the Antwerp ESO tells me the only freighters he has available have no passenger accommodation.* He also, with an enormous wink,

---

* Things had not gone quite as smoothly as this letter indicated. Although we did have official sanction for an *eventual* move of our collection to Canada, we had not as yet received specific authorization. Assuming that this would soon be forthcoming, I had gone ahead with arrangements to charter a vessel, with the good-natured connivance of the ESO and the help of a few documents whose signatures may not have been fully authentic.

assures me that my Montana lass won't be allowed to pine when I am gone. Little does *he* know what *she* thinks of *him* — something to do with the wrong end of a horse.

To celebrate, we are all starting out on one last, glorious scrounging trip through as much of Germany as we can cover. Everyone has his own chosen target. Mine is a JU–87 Stuka dive bomber — one of the abominable black bastards that came screaming out of the skies over southern Sicily to lay their eggs close enough to my slit trench to deafen me for several days and to give me nightmares to the present day.

By the by, I am now, officially, a War Artist — that is how I appear on the Historical Section's establishment. Can't paint for beans, but am having a hell of a time as OC 1 Cdn Fd Hist Sec, responsible direct to CMHQ, and only dealing with heads of departments. Col. Harrison wrangled a promotion for me, too, if I'd wanted it. But all promotions in Europe are frozen unless the candidate signs an agreement to serve in the European theatre until no longer needed. That means Army of Occupation. And who, begging your pardon, would want to be a major, anyhoo?

The story I told you about has now gone into the stove. Not surprising, since it was really pretty bad. But not to worry: I was and am pleased that I wrote it at all, even though both plot and treatment weren't worth keeping. I am, in fact, much strengthened in the resolve to write for a living. It occurs to me that at some safely distant date I might even make a yarn out of this War Museum romp — a cautionary tale, perhaps.

Meantime the chateau grounds and outbuildings echo and shake to the sounds of hammers, saws and exhortations as my crew and our hired help frantically finish off the preparations for the voyage. *Every*-thing has to be boxed except the tanks and big guns, and some of the resultant "packages" would do justice to the creations of Heath Robinson. One final task that I had to supervise myself was the removal and disposal of the V-2 warhead. I had hoped to bring it home intact but even our friendly ESO wouldn't go for that. So one morning we backed the Mack breakdown up to the nose of our funny blue sub, unbolted the warhead and swung it clear with the Mack's derrick. It was filled with some two thousand pounds of a *poured* explosive. I thought briefly of trying to wash the stuff out of the casing with a high-pressure hose, and then I thought: the hell with it; I'm going home. In the end, we called in a British bomb disposal unit, who gingerly took it away on a bed of inflated inner tubes on the back of a truck.

[Toronto]

Oct 31

Dear Almost Major Mk II. –

Yours of the eighteenth is just at hand and so interesting I have to reply at once. Mum says she told me so and you'll be home for Christmas but I still remain sceptical. Also steel yourself against the disappointment of being suddenly superceded at the last moment by a colonel or something of that sort. I can picture you and "Old Doc" standing on the wharf hurling curses and cobblestones at the stern of the departing ship.

Do you think the Montana nurse might give over raising horses and begin raising families? I'd sooner see you married to a gal from Montana than a lot of others I can think of.

You are a damned young fool to write a story and then burn it. I never burned a story that I had finished. I might lay it away in lavender with the tear stains as memories, but burn it? Never! It is improvident. You never know when you might pick it out of the files and re-write it in satisfactory form. And anyway, everything you write is a product of the subconscious and is going to crop up again, as sure as hell.

Are you going to keep "Old Doc" with you for life? If he's half as handy as Benny Bennett, we could use him. But who will pay?

Xmas you say. Ha! Are you coming by the Hudson Bay route to Churchill and Winnipeg? Or overland from San Francisco via Montana?

[Antwerp]

Oct 26

Dear Parents:

This may or may not arrive before I do. If it does, then you can expect your wandering son to follow closely on its heels.

The entire museum collection is, as of this afternoon, safely

loaded aboard the SS *Blommersdyk* lying in Antwerp harbour. The
Mayor and I are in our stateroom – actually a cabin built on the stern
to accommodate a naval crew for the four-inch gun that is mounted
on the roof, right overhead. Seems fittingly symbolic. The quarters
are spacious but spartan, and I share them with L/Cpl Roy Weatherdon, who is my chief engineer and *constructeur*. He is the only one
of my crew travelling with me because there ain't no more accommodation on this here Liberty ship. The rest of the crowd, including Doc, are to sail from Liverpool in a few days aboard a normal
troop ship and will likely be in Canada some days before we arrive.

We expect to sail on Monday, the twenty-eighth, and will dock at
Montreal if the St. Lawrence remains ice free; otherwise Quebec. The
crossing should take about fourteen days in this low-powered ten-
thousand tonner. I'm in the very best graces with her captain (that's
what we call each other), first because I don't call him "Skipper" and
secondly because I provided him with a jeep and driver to take him to
Amsterdam for a weekend with his family. He's going to teach me
deep-sea navigation during the voyage.

Too bad you couldn't have seen the embarkation. 'Twas a spectacle
to remember. It began two days ago when our convoy formed up on the
streets of Oostmalle for the thirty-mile journey to the docks. At the head
of the column was Lulu Belle flying an enormous Canadian flag just in
case those who would see us en route might think the Germans were
coming back. It sure and hell looked as if they were. Swastikas were very
much in evidence. Lulu was followed by a fifteen-ton armoured half-
track towing an eight-inch siege gun which, in turn, was towing the
trailer bearing our one-man sub. The *real* sub. The rest of the column
(and it was over a mile long) consisted of more of the same, with every
Jerry vehicle and tank towing some sort of trailer loaded sky-high with
crates, or guns, or both. As a matter of pride, and for the hell of it, we
used as few Allied prime movers as we could. *This*, my friends, was
1 Cdn War Mus Col Team on the move as a unit . . . for the first and,
I suppose, for the last time. Mowat's Private Army on parade!

I watched it go by with Bob Jespers and most of the populace of
Oostmalle, some of the females of which were in tears. I didn't see any

Belgian men in tears but then men usually manage to suppress their emotions better. Mike had the place of honour in Lulu, while Jimmy rode herd in an amphibious Volkswagen with a couple of Jerry mechanics to look after breakdowns, of which there were hardly any. Almost seemed as if the German vehicles themselves knew that this was the last time. Me? I went on ahead and watched the column creep, clank and grunt past a second time (top speed was about four miles an hour) in the outskirts of Antwerp. Lord, if only we'd thought to have the press guys come and film it! Traffic was tied up in that part of the city for most of the day. People, civvies and military, couldn't quite believe their eyes. The Limey provost corps went quite insane. Nobody had bothered to warn them what was coming and they were gibbering. Much good did it do them. Implacable as fate, the column wobbled on until it reached the dockside loading area. And then Mike gave the signal, and from every vehicle came some sort of noise – horns, gas-warning sirens, drums made of Jerrycans, signal crackers and a rather ragged cheer from the drivers, and from our guys, and from the various odds and sods we had employed – German, Belgian and even a few Dutchmen.

Quite a moment. Not to be forgotten. So was the party afterwards.

I'll probably have to be a week or two in Ottawa after our arrival arranging things, then I'll have a couple of weeks' leave which will be spent, all of it, in Richmond Hill. I'll wire or phone as soon as we dock, so you'll have fair warning.

No, we did not take Montana's horse aboard. But we do have Corporal Roy Weatherdon's dog, Spike. He's going to be an illegal immigrant into Canada. Crossing the Atlantic in winter, in a tramp steamer, with a V-2 and a Nazi sub lashed on deck ought to be interesting. I like the symbolism. Ah yes, the port authorities wouldn't let us stow the explosives in the holds, so they are lashed in wooden cases on the afterdeck alongside and behind my cabin. Nobody but me knows it but these boxes also contain the Jerry gas shells we collected. I do hope they don't leak . . .

So I guess that's it.

God bless.

Squib Mk. II.

Epilogue

❖   ❖   ❖

THE NORTH ATLANTIC WAS IN NO AMIABLE MOOD THAT AUTUMN
as the *Blommersdyk* made her slow and painful passage westward. A
full gale in mid-ocean forced the ship to heave-to. Towering grey-
beards burst clean over her bluff bows and water ran so deep on her
decks that Roy Weatherdon, Spike and I were marooned in our
cabin for a day and a night. I was convinced we would lose both the
V-2 and the submarine overboard but they were still with us,
though white-streaked with salt, when we steamed into Montreal
on November 15, eighteen days after leaving Antwerp.

We had brought our collection home . . . but to a country
which was reluctant to receive it. I had not expected a hero's
welcome; however, I was surprised to find that nobody in Montreal, not even the harbour authorities, seemed to be expecting us.
There was, however, an urgent message from Major General
Howard Graham. I was to telephone him "IMMEDIATELY repeat
IMMEDIATELY" upon arrival.

In some trepidation, I put a call through from dockside to the
office of the deputy chief of the general staff. He did not sound
pleased to hear my voice.

"Damn it, Mowat, where the hell have you been? Catch tonight's
train to Ottawa. I want you in my office at 0900 hours tomorrow."

Next morning he kept me standing at attention before his desk
until the red-tabbed colonel who had escorted me in withdrew
from the office. Then Graham gave me his always somewhat
sardonic smile.

"All right, Squib. Sit down. You were so long overdue we

thought you and your load of nuts and bolts must have sunk.
Might have been no bad thing at that. Do you realize that *somebody*
has incurred a shipping bill against the Canadian government
for $76,000? And, as far as I can find out, there's no authorization
for it.

"To be frank, you and your collection are about as popular
around here as the proverbial skunk at a garden party.

"The war's over, you know. And this government doesn't want
to spend another dollar on it. Even the War Museum wants no part
of your collection – afraid it might have to pay the shipping bill.
Nobody else seems to want what you've got except some of the
boffins at Defence Research. They say they'll take your rocket stuff.
What's to be done with the rest I really don't know.

"Now, suppose you tell me all about it."

So I told him all about the Canadian War Museum Collection
Team – or as much as I thought he ought to know. He chuckled
when I finished.

"Where's that shiny-faced kid that came to us in England in
'42, eh? Turned into a pirate by the looks of it. Well, my lad, since
you're a Hasty P, we'll have to try and save your neck. And never
fear, the Treasury Board *will* hang you if they ever twig to what I
think you've done.

"Go along home now and have your leave. And tell Angus I'm
sorry for him."

When I returned to Ottawa from two weeks spent as promised
in Richmond Hill with my parents and Elmer, Graham assigned me
to an obscure department of National Defence Headquarters. The
rest of my crowd arrived home shortly thereafter and were discharged back to Civvy Street, except for Mike Donovan, who was
retained to keep me company writing interminable reports and
explanations, some of which taxed even our imaginative skills. So
we two were kept "on strength" (but under a cloud) for almost five
months while various authorities, civil and military, tried to unravel
the tangled skein of our activities. General Graham (once a lawyer)
argued our case . . . and won.

"It wasn't so difficult," he told me some years later. "Nobody amongst the high-priced help in Ottawa could bring himself to believe that a mere captain could have been responsible for such a shambles."

In April, Mike and I took our long-delayed departure from the Canadian Armed Forces, Honourably Discharged at last.

HOWARD GRAHAM WAS NOT AS SUCCESSFUL IN HIS ADVOCACY OF our collection. It was dismembered and dispersed. The tanks and other armoured vehicles were sent to Camp Borden, where they sat abandoned in a vast wooden hangar for several years. Then the hangar burned to the ground and they became scrap metal. At that they outlasted the rest of the vehicles, the guns and most of the other large items. These were sold for a "nominal" sum directly from the docks to a Montreal junk dealer. Most of the smaller items were stored in deep basements in Hull where, in the spring of 1946, they were inundated by flood waters and subsequently carted away to be dumped into a land-fill site.

A few items did eventually end up in the War Museum. And I personally persuaded the Royal Canadian Navy to take the one-man submarine which, I believe, is still on display at HMCS *Stadacona*, the Ottawa naval station.

The V-2 had a more satisfying history. Loaded on a flatcar the day after the ship made port, it was spirited off to the Defence Research establishment at Val Cartier, Quebec. There it was quickly disassembled and all its internal components were blue-printed and photographed . . . and then they vanished. Some years afterwards, I was told by one of the civilian scientists that they had been afraid the government would turn the rocket over to the United States had it realized that Canada was the possessor of such forbidden fruit.

Not long after the war, Canada undertook its own modest rocket program designing rockets for the peaceable purpose of exploring the nature of the stratosphere. Two models were pro-duced, the Velvet Glove and the Black Brant. Both owed their genesis to our V-2. Well into the 1960s they were still carrying scientific instruments aloft from a base at Churchill, Manitoba, where, in 1957, I watched one of them swoosh gracefully skyward.

Painted black again but badly battered and completely gutted, the shell of our V-2 did eventually go on display at the Canadian National Exhibition in Toronto – for a single season. Overshadowed by the glittering products of the burgeoning rocket rivalry between the U.S.A. and the U.S.S.R., it drew little public interest, so it, too, was dispatched to limbo.

Angus and Helen remained in Richmond Hill until his retirement in 1956, by which time he had completely reshaped the Ontario library system, together with the lives of two of my closest wartime friends, Doug Reid and Mike Donovan. He persuaded both to go into library work.

Angus was a very persuasive man. After I was discharged, he persuaded me to enrol at the University of Toronto, but the academic scene was unable to hold me long and by 1947 I had been seduced by the Arctic and was beginning the writer's life which I have followed ever since.

Angus never published another book. Despite his extra-curricular activities, he and Helen remained together until, at the age of seventy-two, he abandoned my mother for a lady librarian thirty-three years his junior. Although he never returned to Helen, she bore him no grudge. Whether he ever forgave himself is another matter.

During his final years, relations between him and me grew strained, partly because of my feelings about his treatment of my mother, and partly because he began to disapprove of my work on the stated grounds that I had betrayed my talent by writing non-fiction instead of novels. Since he had heretofore expressed much pride in my work, I was hurt and resentful and, consequently, did less than I might have done to heal the differences which were dividing us one from the other.

When he died in 1977 at the age of eighty-four years, I

mourned his passing as a son mourns a father, and perhaps that is how things would have remained had I not found myself (or been led?) back into another time by re-reading and re-living the letters he wrote to me during the war.

Now I mourn him in a different way: as a loving friend whose steadfastness and infinite understanding helped me to endure and to survive the roughest years of my life.

Abbreviations and Military Glossary

❖ ❖ ❖

AA/Ack-ack	Anti-aircraft artillery
ADC	Aide-de-camp
AFHQ	Allied Forces Headquarters in the Mediterranean theatre
ALO	Air Liaison Officer
AMGOT	Allied Military Government
Anzac	Serviceman from Australia or New Zealand
AP	Armour-piercing
AWL	Absent without leave
BHQ	Battalion headquarters
BM	Brigade major. The brigade commander's operations staff officer
Bailey bridge	Easily assembled sectional bridge used by our engineers
Blighty	First World War slang for England; in occasional use in World War II
Boche	First World War slang for German; in occasional use in World War II
Boffin	Civilian scientist involved in the development of military technology
Bofors	40 mm rapid-fire anti-aircraft gun
Bren	The Canadian and British standard light machine gun
C.M.H.Q.	Canadian Military Headquarters in England
C.N.R.	Canadian National Railway

CP	Canadian Press
C.P.R.	Canadian Pacific Railway
CSM	Company sergeant-major
C.W.A.C.	Canadian Women's Army Corps
D.R.	Dispatch rider, usually a motorcyclist
DSO	Distinguished Service Order
Div	Division
E-boat	German motor torpedo boat
ENSA	Entertainments National Services Association provided entertainment for British and Commonwealth troops
Eighty-eight	8.8 cm calibre German anti-tank, anti-aircraft and general-purpose gun
F-echelon	That part of a battalion which engaged in combat
FOO	Forward observation officer, an artillery officer who directs the fire of his guns from an OP (observation post)
Feldwebel	A sergeant-major in the German Army
G-1 Air	The General Staff officer at Corps or Army Headquarters in charge of air/ground co-ordination
G.O.C.	General Officer Commanding; in this book usually refers to the officer commanding a division
HE	High explosive
Hauptmann	A captain in the German Army
Hun	First World War slang for a German; in occasional use in World War II
i/c	In charge; in command
IO	Intelligence Officer
Jerry	A German (also Gerald or Gerry)
Jerrycan	Five-gallon German army fuel container, copied by both the British and U.S. armies and used for a multitude of purposes
LO	Liaison Officer
LSI	Landing Ship Infantry. A medium-sized vessel used for landing troops during a combined operation assault
MC	Military Cross. Awarded to officers for valour

MG 42/34	MG 42 was the latest model of German light machine gun. MG 34 was a pre-war model
MM	Military Medal. Awarded to other ranks for valour
MMG	Medium machine gun
MO	Medical Officer
Moaning Minnie	Large-calibre rocket generally fired in salvos from multi-barrelled launchers
Mufti	Civilian clothes
N.A.A.F.I.	Navy Army and Air Force Institute. British organization supplying "soldier's comforts" and other services to the troops
N.C.O.	Non-commissioned officer
NDHQ	Canada's National Defence Headquarters, in Ottawa
OC	Officer Commanding
O-group	Orders group. A gathering of subordinates to receive orders from a commander
OP	Observation post
OR	Other Rank. A designation usually encompassing all below the rank of officer
One-oh-Five (105)	The standard German field gun, of 10.5 cm calibre
PBI	Poor Bloody Infantry
Piat	Projector Infantry Anti-tank. A hand-held anti-tank weapon
Pip	Insignia of rank worn on the shoulder epaulets by junior officers. 1 pip = 2nd Lieutenant; 2 pips = Lieutenant; 3 pips = Captain
Plow Jocks/ Plow Jockeys	Hastings and Prince Edward Regiment
RCA	Royal Canadian Artillery
RCAF	Royal Canadian Air Force
R.C.E.	Royal Canadian Engineers
RCR	Royal Canadian Regiment
RSM	Regimental Sergeant Major

R.T.U.	Returned to unit
"S" mine	German anti-personnel mine
SHAEF	Supreme Headquarters Allied Expeditionary Force
SOS	Struck Off Strength. Also "shoot on sight" when applied to a defensive artillery barrage
SP	Self-propelled gun. An artillery piece mounted on a tank chassis
SS	Schutzstaffel. The armed force of the Nazi party
Sally Ann	The Salvation Army
Sapper	An engineer
Schmeisser	German sub-machine gun
Schu mine	German non-magnetic anti-personnel mine
Spandau	Allied slang for a German light machine gun
Staff Captain	The staff officer at brigade headquarters responsible for administration
Sten	British sub-machine gun
Stonk	A sharp but usually short concentration of artillery fire on a limited target
Stuka	Junkers 87; German dive bomber
Subaltern	An officer below the rank of captain
Tac HQ	Tactical Headquarters
TOS	Taken on Strength
Tedeschi	A name by which Germans, and especially German soldiers, were known in Italy. It also means "barbarians."
Teller mine	German anti-vehicle mine
Unteroffizier	German noncommissioned officer
WAAF	Women's Auxiliary Air Force
W.E.	War Establishment
Wren/ W.R.N.S.	Women's Royal Naval Service
2 i/c	Second-in-command
48th	48th Highlanders of Canada